ISBN 978-1-332-10662-2
PIBN 10285510

1 MONTH OF
FREE
READING

at

www.ForgottenBooks.com

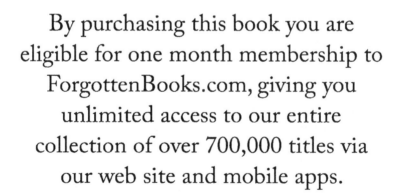

By purchasing this book you are eligible for one month membership to ForgottenBooks.com, giving you unlimited access to our entire collection of over 700,000 titles via our web site and mobile apps.

To claim your free month visit:

www.forgottenbooks.com/free285510

Similar Books Are Available from
www.forgottenbooks.com

THE BRERETONS

OF CHESHIRE

1100 to 1904 A. D.

Sons of the Northmen, so fair, and so free!
Norman cum Saxon cum Celt pedigree!
Our Father is God; our blood is the blue;
Let Love be our Guide; our lives good and true.
"OPITULANTE DEO."

BY
ROBERT MAITLAND BRERETON, M. I. C. E.
WOODSTOCK, OREGON

———

1904
THE IRWIN-HODSON COMPANY
PORTLAND, OREGON

My object in writing the following history of this very ancient family, and in showing its pedigree from the time of the Norman conquest down to the present year of 1904, is that my children and grandchildren may, when I have passed over to the spirit life, keep in memory some interesting facts concerning their paternal ancestry, and also retain a kindly interest in their kinsfolk in the old country and in the old homes of their fore-fathers. I feel that it is good to take a wholesome pride in being able to trace, without any doubt, our genealogy for a period extending over seven hundred years of English history, and that, too, from father to son consecutively. During this period history records many notable events; the mingling of the old Celtic, Saxon, and Norman blood in families; the evolution of the Anglo-Saxon race from barbarism into chivalry adapted to turbulent times, and from thence into the present age of a far nobler civilization, with a truer perception of the brotherhood and the fatherhood of man.

In this new country the rising generation is apt to forget and to overlook the value and importance of Home with its useful associations. The nearest family ties are too often lost sight of, and the old Christmas and New Year family greetings grow less frequent. There is less excuse for this unmindfulness in these days of rapid world intercourse than there was thirty years back. The upholding of family interests, sympathies and wholesome pride, tends to make the best citizen, and the neglect of them has a tendency to a life of selfishness, to a lack of honorable conduct in life, and to the unwholesome struggle to get rich as quickly as possible, without any regard to divine conscience. It may seem incredible to many in this country that it can be possible to trace from father to son through twenty-six generations, any individual family. In England during the feudal period and down to the seventeenth century there were royal herald's visitations and postmortem inquisitions made to each county, for the special purpose of recording the genealogies of the living and deceased of all the families of barons, knights, and gentlemen with estates. From these existing official documents, from the old charter deeds and grants of land which are found treasured in the Bodleian Library at Oxford, and in the Harleian Library at the British Museum, and from the old parish church registers of baptisms and burials, and, also, from the old tombs and monuments still existing in the old churches, which date back to the fourteenth fifteenth and sixteenth centuries, we are able, at the present time, to trace the lineage.

The Brereton family, being one of these ancient and noble ones, and having, also (according to Ormerod's pedigree of the family) royal blood descent from the maternal side, which carries it back to Kenneth, first Celtic King of Scotland, A. D. 850; and to Egbert, first Saxon King of all England; and to William the Conqueror's sister, Margaret, 1066; have have had their pedigree especially recorded throughout the above mentioned ancient documents. Some of the leading members are mentioned in history as holding high offices in the courts of Henry VII., Henry VIII., Queen Elizabeth, James I., Charles I., and Charles II. This is all very interesting and much for us to be proud of as a family. At the same time I would wish my children to keep well in mind that we can claim a far higher genealogy from our immortal origin. As a *true man* I view my descent from the Father of Spirits. I am in full sympathy with our old English poet Cowper, in those beautiful lines which he wrote on viewing his mother's picture:

> "My boast is not that I deduce my birth
> From loins enthroned and rulers of the earth;
> But higher far my proud pretensions rise
> The son of parents passed into the skies."

No man can deny this assumption to himself if he follows the teachings of the Bible, wherein is stated that Adam was the son of God, the Great Spirit of the universe. In St. Luke's statement of the genealogy of Christ he could get no farther back than Adam, the son of God. The descendants of Seth, the son of Adam,

4

called themselves the sons of God. Well did the American poet express this view of human origin in his "Psalm of Life:"

"Life is real! Life is earnest!
And the grave is not its goal.
'Dust thou art, to dust returnest,'
Was not spoken of the soul."

Thus we can better understand and appreciate what Christ taught: "Call no man your father on earth, for One is your Father. He is God. And when ye pray, say, 'Our Father in Heaven'". St. Paul, also, taught: "There is a natural (flesh) body, and there *is* a spirit body." He further illustrates this important fact in his description of the origin of Melchisedec, King of Salem: "Without father, without mother, having neither beginning of days, nor end of life; but made like unto the Son of God."·

I believe this to be the true genesis of immortal man, and from this view we can derive nobler thoughts and a better perception of the true meaning of fatherhood and of brotherhood, and thus be able to lead a nobler, and more useful life on earth. I would wish you to believe that as there is evolutionary progress from lower to higher forms in earth life, there is the same going on in spirit life throughout eternity. Without this continuity of evolutionary progress upward, and forever upward, we cannot comprehend the true meaning of eternity, or of the one everlasting Supreme Father Spirit. From the same logical inference we can understand there can be no perception of moral good without evil. All of animal creation, save man, we may term *unmoral*, but never immoral. So, also, in the spirit world there must be evil, and low as well as higher forms of life. Man endowed with conscience is a god, knowing good and evil. Having conscience, and in obeying it, he can choose the good, and so more quickly evolve to a nobler stage in life, and through remorse likewise; else, what is the object of conscience and remorse from which bird, brute and fish are exempt? Thus spirits of man of a low type are born into our world today, and we wrongly term them "degenerates." They are simply behind our age of higher progress and civilization, and so are out of place. Their place is with the lower orders of the human race on earth. I believe that the remarkable attribute of spirit man is the undoubted individualism observable. For a physical instance of this, amongst the hundreds of millions of the human race on earth no two of them have exactly the same identical scent to their foot; the owner's dog can distinguish this. This individualism can be observed in every large family, and in the case of twin children; in physical features they may be very much alike, but never exactly alike in their intellectual or psychical makeup. Hence we reason that it must be spirit which imparts this individualism. *We can view ourselves as the parents of our children's bodies only.* Adam's body was made out of the substances of the earth; it was the spirit only which animated his body and made him a living soul. This spiritual inference need not appear opposed to the present stage of scientific thought, or to Darwinism, which deals only with material forms. The outward and physical forms evolve from age to age conformably with the surrounding conditions of earth life, and as these assume a higher grade for material existence, so do higher spiritual forms quicken. Science has, hitherto, been mainly confined to the study of material forms and matters, the psychological being too intangible for mere material thought and appliances. The same spiritual life influences and forces create individualism throughout the kingdom of nature, whether animate or inanimate. On a small garden plot we see the violet, the primrose, and the lily of the valley growing side by side, under identical conditions, and in the same constituents of soil, yet each have their own individual perfume. Such, also, is the wonderful marked individualism in the varied forms of crystalization in the mineral world. This forming *will force,* underlying the seeable in all natural objects,. is eternal and all pervading and unchangeable in its laws, and matter seems to be only its mould. Spirit man can only be made manifest in earth life through the natural process of generation, but in the true spirit world the spirit man is the offshoot or emanation from the great spirit of life. Christ truly taught that in heaven they neither marry nor are given in marriage. After this earthly life is ended our spirits return to God who gave them an earth life for an allwise purpose.

6

I have enlarged upon this view of man's life that my children may be led to think more seriously of the duties and responsibilities of an earthly existence, and so endeavor to lead an honorable, an honored, and useful life on earth, and ever conscious that those who love them and who have passed over to the higher life, are still with them, though unseen. We may well be proud of our ancestors, who were knights of war and chivalry suited to their age, and who displayed a lion heartedness and valiantry that won for them in war and tournament not only the smiles and ribbons of fair ladies, but the hearts and estates of the best heiresses in the proud Norman Palatinate of Cheshire. In this present age, we, their descendents, need the display of a higher type of courage than that of the mere physical, which is common to the barbarian and the brute. Moral courage should be the blazon of our shield, and with which we can more appropriately associate our old family motto, "Opitulante Deo," which signifies "God Assisting Us." In this age of progress and spiritual enlightenment, the display of moral courage forms a far nobler type of chivalry. Our soldiers and sailors, no longer clad in steel armor, now face the millions of bullets which hurtle through their ranks from unseen directions. Our business men have to face, with the shield of innate honor and high moral perception, the darts and temptations of mere selfish greed and filthy lucre, which prevail through the neglect of conscience, if they would invite the confidence of the public, and leave behind them an honored name and be able to re-enter the spirit world without a feeling of shame and remorse.

Your affectionate father,

ROBERT MAITLAND BRERETON.

Woodstock, Oregon, 1904.

LIST. OF AUTHORITIES QUOTED 'FROM.

Archæologia (Library, British Museum) Vol. XXXIII., p. 72.
Ballads and Legends of Cheshire, by Egerton Leigh, 1867.
Blomefield's History of Norfolk.
Brooke's (Richard) "Visits to Battle Fields," 1850.
Burke's Dictionary of the Landed Gentry, 1846 and 1868.
Burke's Extinct Baronetcies, Supplement, 1878.
Burke's Peerage, 1886.
Burke's General Armory of England, 1878.
Camden's (William) "Magna Britannica," Gibson's Edition, Vol.
    II., 1772.
Cheshire "Gleanings," by William E. A. Axon.
"Cheshire," by T. Worthington Barlow, 1855.
Cheshire Historical Antiquities, by Sir Peter Leycester, 1673.
Cheshire Church Notes, Astbury Church, by Thomas Cooper, 1888.
Cheshire Church Notes, The Chetham Societies' Papers.
Cheshire Church Notes, Harleian Mss. 2151, pp. 4 and 35.
"Cheshire Sheaf," Historical and Antiquarian Gleanings.
Dictionary of National Biography, Vol. VI.
Drayton's (Michael) "English Heroical Epistles," 1597.
Drayton's (Michael) "Poly-Olbion, Song XXII.," 1613-1622.
Domesday Survey of Cheshire, 1086.
Dwarris's (Sir Fortunatus) Memoir of Brereton Family, Arch-
    æologia, Vol. XXXIII.
Earwaker's History of East Cheshire, Vol. I, p. 260.
Erdeswick's Survey of Staffordshire, by Harwood, p. 231, 1844.
Froude's (James Anthony) History of the Fall of Wolsey, 1856-
    1870.
Harleian Society's Papers, Vol. XI., p. 14; Vol. XVIII., pp. 41-46.
Harleian Mss. 2119, fol. 85.
History of Queens of England, by Agnes Strickland, Vols. III.
    · and IV.

History of Slanguris, by Hamer and Lloyd, p. 359.

Holmes's (Randall) "Heraldic Collections for Cheshire."

Index to Pedigrees of English Families, by Charles Bridges, 1867.

Ormerod's History of Cheshire, by Helsby, Vols. II. and III.

Pedigrees of Families in the County of Hants, by Wm. Berry, 1833.

Staffordshire, Collections of History of, by Wm. Salt Society Vol. I

Surrey Archæological Society, Vol. II.

Visitation of Somerset, by Sir T. Phillipps.

Visitation of Staffordshire, by same, 1663-4.

History of Wiltshire, by Sir R. C. Hoare, Vol. II., fol 49.

Page 11.   Chester Cathedral, in Which Some of the Ancient Breretons Were Buried.

THE BRERETON FAMILY HISTORY AND PEDIGREE.

The basis of the following history is to be found in ancient charter deeds and historical references preserved in many thousands of volumes and manuscripts of the Bodleian Library at Oxford, and in the Harleian Library in the British Museum, in London, and in Randall Holmes' Heraldic Collections for Cheshire. The most complete record of the genealogies of this old family is to be found in George Ormerod's and Earwaker's histories of the Cheshire families; also, in Burke's "Landed Gentry and Extinct Families;" also, in Sir Fortunatus Dwarris's "Memoirs of the Brereton Family." The churches and church yards of Brereton, Astbury, Malpas, Bowden and Cheadle, all in Cheshire, contain, at the present date, monuments, tombs and inscriptions of several ancient members of the family, some of them as far back as the fourteenth century. The church records of births and burials, on parchment and pigskins of the sixteenth, seventeenth and eighteenth centuries, furnish proofs of many members. The earliest records of the names of the family occur in the end of the eleventh century, and in the beginning of the twelfth. These are in connection with the Venables family of Norman origin. Rafe de Brereton, Grosvenor and Davenport are found mentioned as three grantees of lands from Venables, the Baron of Kinderton, Cheshire, as shown by ancient deeds to have existed at or near the conquest, though not mentioned in Domesday (1086). The founder of the family was probably a Venables and a relative of the Baron of Kinderton, in whose baronry of six dependencies was included the demesnes of Brereton, within the then large parish of Astbury. At that period Brereton was called Bretune, and is found so named in Domesday. The fact that the coat of arms assumed by the Brereton family is the same as the Venables, differing only in tincture, goes far to prove the family connection. Furthermore, a decisive test of consanguinity is that upon any

11

intermarriage of the Venables with the Breretons (of which the pedigree furnishes evidence) a dispensation from the pope was required. As was the custom in those feudal times, the Norman knights and esquires assumed the name of the manors or demesnes which they received by grants from their lords the barons within the Palatinate. Thus Rafe de Venables would become Rafe de (or of) Brereton. The Venables are clearly traced back to the time of the conquest (1066). Stephen, Earl of Blois, living 1086, married Adela, daughter of William the Conqueror. He was father of Stephen, King of England, 1135. Gilbert de Venables was the younger brother of the Earl of Blois. He is mentioned in Domesday as the venator, or hunter. His son, Gilbert de Venables, was the first recorded Baron of Kinderton in the reign of Henry I. (1100-1134). Rafe de Brereton is found mentioned in old deeds as witness to two grants of lands in Marston, which were made by the grandson of the second mentioned Venables: (1) to his sister Amabilia, in 1156; (2) to his brother Hugh, Rector of Astbury, in 1188. This Hugh was also Rector of Eccleston, near Chester, which, in the sixteenth century, belonged to Randle Brereton, son of Sir Randle de Brereton II., of Ipstone, also Rector of Rostherne, Cheshire. Rafe de Brereton was prob ably esquire to the Baron of Kinderton, and the younger brother of Sir William de Brereton I., of Brereton, with whom the pedigree of the family commences about 1175.

ROYAL DESCENT.

In regard to this old claim of the family to royal descent on the maternal side, I would have my children understand that I am not so fully satisfied with the evidence furnished as to accept it with implicit faith. This claim has been based solely upon an ancient tomb found in Astbury church yard, with an old inscription in Latin attached to it bearing the Brereton coat of arms, and upon an old monument and inscription in Brereton church, erected by Sir William Brereton XI., of Brereton, in 1608, who was raised to the peerage; also, upon the authority of Sir For-

Brereton Church, Interior.

tunatus Dwarris, who was Recorder of Newcastle-under-Lyme, and one of the masters of the Queen's Bench Offices, which appears to have been based upon the wording of the patent granted on the creation of the above mentioned Sir William Brereton as Lord Brereton in 1624, which reads as follows: "This patent, after the manner of these instruments in the sixteenth and seventeenth centuries, declares Sir William Brereton to be sprung from an ancient, noble, and most renowned family; inasmuch as he is descended through many illustrious ancestors from Ada, sister of John, surnamed Scot, seventh Earl of Chester, and daughter of David, Earl of Angus (and Huntingdon)." There has prevailed much controversy about this canopied tomb and the other two ancient tombs existing in Astbury church yard, and it appears strange that the tomb in the Brereton church, together with the inscription connected with it, has never been brought forward in support of the older inscription in the canopied tomb at Astbury. There are three tombs in Astbury church yard, all closely adjacent; one is the canopied tomb in which are the effigies of a knight in armor with a lady by his side, and with the following inscription in Latin: "Hic jacent Radulphus Brereton, Miles, et Domina Ada, uxor sua, una filiarum Davidis Comitis, Huntingdonis." Over this is a shield with two bars. The other two tombs, one is that of a knight, the other of an ecclesiastic. William Camden, the noted historian and antiquary of the sixteenth and seventeenth centuries (1551-1623), in his "Magna Britannica," in 1609, when describing these Astbury tombs, mentions only two, which he terms "grave stones" in the church yard, having the portraiture of knights upon them, and in shields having two bars; but these, being without their colors, it is not easy to determine whether they belong to the Breretons, the Mainwarings, or the Venables, which are the best families hereabout and bear such bars in their arms, but with different colors. It seems very strange that he makes no mention of the canopied tomb with its inscription, or of the tomb with the effigy of a priest on it. The Brereton family tradition has it that this canopied tomb was originally within the church, but was removed to the church yard when the church was rebuilt during 1300-1310. The Church Notes of Astbury, which

13

are found in the Harleian Mss. 2151, page 4, contain notices of the monuments and coats of arms taken A. D. 1576; also of this ancient monument in the church yard. Among other arms men tioned in these notes is one, No. 5 Brereton, in the church window, and underneath, the following inscription: "Orate p, a, i, abus Wil. Brereton, Milites, et D'ne Elene uxoris sue." As no date is attached it is a question as to which this refers. There were, according to the pedigree, two Breretons whose wives were Ellen: (1) Sir William de Brerton VI., of Brereton, whose wife was Ellen, daughter of Philip de Egerton, A. D. 1300; (2) Sir William de Brerton VII., of Brereton, whose second wife was Ellen, daughter of Sir William Masey, of Tatton; he died 1426. If the canopied tomb did not rightly belong to the Brereton family, of Brereton, Sir William Brereton XI., of Brereton, could not have claimed it in the way he did; for if the Venables or the Mainwarings of that period had felt they had any right to it, they would most assuredly have prevented him from making such a bold assumption, and in such a notable fashion. In the appendix I give some further notes regarding this doubtful royal descent claim, and proceed to give an account of this Lady Ada's parentage and descent, which is interesting, even if there be no truth in her connection with our family history. The old family from the paternal side alone is good enough for me, and was purely of noble Norman origin, the line of pedigree from which is without controversy.

LADY. ADA.

Lady Ada, the alleged wife of Sir Ranulphus, or Radulphus de Brerton, of Brereton, was the third married daughter of David, Earl of Huntingdon, third son of Henry, Prince of Scotland, only son of King David I., of Scotland. Lady Ada's mother was Maud, daughter of Hugh de Keveilioc, Count Palatine, and fifth Earl Royal of Chester, and sister and heiress of Randulph de Blundevill, sixth Earl Royal of Chester, who was fifth in descent from

Margaret, sister to the Conqueror, and mother of Hugh Lupus, the first Earl Royal of Chester, or Count Palatine, of Cheshire. Her only brother was John the Scot, seventh and last Earl Royal of Chester, who died without issue, said to have been murdered by his wife. Her paternal uncles were Malcolm IV., and William II. (the lion), kings of Scotland. Her eldest sister was Izabel, mother of Robert Bruce, of Annandale, the great grandfather of Robert Bruce, King of Scotland. Her second sister, Margaret, was mother of John Baliol, the founder of Baliol College, Oxford, and the grandmother of John de Baliol, King of Scotland. Her great grandmother Maud, wife of David I., was the daughter and heiress of Waltheof, Earl of Huntingdon by his wife Judith, niece of the Conqueror; and her great great grandfather was Malcolm III. (Cænmore), who married Margaret, daughter of the Saxon King Edmund Ironsides. Thus she inherited the Norman, Saxon and Celtic royal blood mixture, and hence descent from Egbert the first Saxon King of all England, who died A. D. 837, and from Kenneth, the first Celtic King of Scotland, who died A. D. 850. Her first husband was Sir Henry de Hastings, afterwards Baron Hastings, by whom she had issue, one of which, John Hastings, was among the claimants for the crown of Scotland on the death of Margaret, the maid of Norway, in 1291. She is said, according to the pedigree of the Brereton family as given by Ormerod (the greatest authority on the Cheshire families of renown), to have afterwards married Sir Ranulphus, or Radulphus Brereton, of Brereton, who, according to family tradition, was one of the knights of the Crusades with King Richard I., and was the Sir Kenneth of the Leopard, in Sir Walter Scott's "Talisman." Lady Ada's father died A. D. 1219' and as her first husband, the first Baron Hastings, died in 1268, she must have been nearly fifty years old when she married Sir Radulphus Brereton, who, according to the Brereton pedigree, was living in 1275, time of Edward I. The canopied tomb, above mentioned as disputed, of Sir Ranulphus and his wife Ada, is still existing in the church yard of Astbury. I have seen it. This was the burial spot of the family at that period of the thirteenth century.

INTERMARRIAGES WITH THE NOBLE FAMILIES OF CHESHIRE.

The Breretons, during the thirteenth, fourteenth, fifteenth and sixteenth centuries, were among the most distinguished families of England, They intermarried with other ancient and noble families of Cheshire, the Venables, the Caringtons, the Cholmondeleys, the Davenports, the Hanmers, the Traffords, the Radclyffs, the Egertons, the Mainwarings, the Corbets, the Vernons, the Booths, the Duttons and the Stanleys. From the daughters of the family are descended some of the present peers of England, who have inherited some of the old estates of the Brereton family.

NAME OF BRERETON AS SPELLED IN EARLY TIMES.

The early ancestors of the family spelled their name Brerton, Bretone, Breerton, Brierton. The present spelling, Brereton, seems to have been adopted by Sir William Brereton IX., of Brereton, in 1516. The Norman prefix "de" was dropped at the same time. His uncle, Sir John de Brereton, also added the second "e." Some of the Irish family spelled their name Brierton. I find a John Brereton, possibly the son of John Brereton, of Leek, the fourth grandson of Sir William Brereton IX., of Brereton, spelled his name Brierton in a book he wrote in 1602 describing his voyage of discovery to North America in company with Captain Bartholomew Gosnold. This old book, written in black letter type, is in the library of the British Museum. I have a copy of it. To his kinsmen of the present day, especially to those who are settled in the United States and Canada, this first discovery of the New England coast of Massachusetts is most interesting. John Brereton and Gosnold, with two other English gentlemen, were the first Englishmen who had ever trod the "white sands" of Massachusetts bay. They gave the name of Cape Cod to the headland; they gave the name "Martha's Vineyard" to the island in Nantucket sound; they called Buzzard bay "Gosnold's Hope;" they landed on Cuttyhunk island, which they named "Elizabeth Isle."

Brereton Hall, Entrance Lodge.

There they built the first English fort and storehouse and planted the first English seed of wheat, barley and oats in New England. This John Brereton was a B. A. of Caius (Keys) College, Cambridge, in 1592-3. I do not know to which branch of the family he belonged. His history is addressed to Sir Walter Raleigh, the colonizer of Virginia. A few years later, another kinsman, Sir William Brereton Bart. IV., of Handford, and known as the "Warrior" during the Civil war, obtained large grants of land in the northeastern portion of Massachusetts, from Sir Fortunatus Gorges, the father of the old Plymouth colony, in 1620. He was, also, interested with Sir Walter Raleigh in the colonization of Virginia. The name Breerton is also found so spelled in many of the old church registers.

Sir Urian's family, at Handford, seem clearly to have formed the idea that the name was derived from "Brier" and "Tun," a cask or barrel. At the entrance to the old mansion is found a large oak beam, supported at each end by an oak post. On the cross beam or arch is an inscription carved in old English characters; underneath this, and on each post, are carved letters and figures. On one post is the letter "U," and on the other post the letter "B," the first being for Urian, the second for Brereton; and between them, in the center of the arch, is carved a tun or cask, and also a brier, the stem and foliage of which extend on each side from the tun to the letters U and B, indicating a rebus or puzzle punning upon the name Brereton (or Brier-tun). Again, in the Handford or Brereton chapel, in Cheadle church, where members of the family were buried, is found a carved wood cornice containing this same rebus of a brier and a tun, for Brereton, repeated thirteen times with the initial letters U and B between them alternately, for Urian and Brereton. (Richard Brooke's "Visits to the Fields of Battles"). I have been told that in some book about the Norman people, mention is made of the Brereton family having come from Breary, near Vesoul, now the capital of Haute Saone, in France; in this book the name is given "De Brereto," without the final "n."

BRERETON DEMESNES OR MANOR.

At the period of the Norman conquest, the spoil of lands taken from the old Saxon holders was divided among the companions in arms of the Conqueror. These lands were then known as baronies, which comprised separate manors, some of which the barons granted to their knight followers and esquires. Thus, Gilbert de Venables, styled Venator, or Hunter, possessed the Barony of Kinderton, consisting of six dependencies, of which Brereton and Smethwicke formed a part in the then large parish of Astbury. The knights who held these manors by grant deeds from their lord baron, usually assumed the name thereof. At the time when the Conqueror caused a survey to be made of the lands in the several counties, and recorded in Domesday Book in 1086, we find Brereton described therein as follows: "Gilbert (Venables) Venator holds of the Earl Neubold. Ulviet (Saxon) held it, and was a free man. The same Gilbert holds Bretune; Ulviet held it. There are two hides (hide represents 100 or more acres, as will support a family) rateable to the Gelt (gelt or geld means a tax or tribute due to the lord of the manor). The land is four carucates (a carucate meant as much land as could be cultivated by one caruca or plough team, usually four oxen yoked abreast). One is in the demesne (manor); and there are two Neatheads (cowkeepers), and two villeins (tenants of land who are servants of their lord) and three bordars (smaller tenants or laborers, or serfs). There is an acre of meadow, a wood one league long, and half as broad, and a mill of the value of twelve pence. Of this land two of his men hold one hide, and have one carucate with two serfs, and two villeins and four bordars. In King Edward's time (the Confessor, 1070) the whole was worth twenty shillings, and the same now. The Earl Neubold found it waste. The same Gilbert holds Cin-Bretune (Kinderton), Godfrie (Saxon) held it, and was a free man. There are three hides, rateable to the gelt. The land is five carucates, one is in the demesne, and there are two serfs, and three bordars. There is one acre of meadow. There is a wood half a league long, and the same broad, and a Hay (means an inclosure or small field); it is worth ten shillings. It was waste and so found."

Brereton Hall and Lake.

Page 19.

It must be remembered that the value of money in those times was vastly different from that of the present age. In those days a penny was sometimes known as an easterling, equivalent to a Roman denarius, a silver coin; it was, also, called Solidus, and sterling. A very much later description of Brereton is given in George Ormerod's history of the families of Cheshire, as follows:

"Breerton standeth upon the London Way, two miles north from Sandbach, and hath yearly a Fair, which is held on Breerton-Green on Lammasday, being the first day of August, (when the lambs are taken away from the ewes). Not far off is the Parish Church of Breerton, and near unto the church the goodly Manor-Place, newly builded (1586), all of brick; the like whereof is not in all the country again. Therefore, it is not to be omitted, and not so much for the buildings, as for the number of ancient and valiant knights and gentlemen who had, and have, their origin from thence."

Brereton Hall is situated on a gentle slope on the bank of the stream Croco, which was formerly collected into a lake, known as Blackmere, or Brereton's lake. There is a very old legend attached to the lake, which is, that on the eve of the death of the Lord of Brereton the lake threw up black logs from its bottom which floated for a while. In Sir Philip Sydney's "Seven Wonders of England," are the following lines·

"The Breretons have a lake, which, when the sun
Approaching warms (not else), dead logs up sends
From hideous depth, which tribute when it ends,
Sore sign it is the Lord's last thread is spun."

Over the doorway is the date, 1586. Queen Elizabeth is said to have laid the foundation stone. Her arms are over and under, the arch above the door. She was interested in this family, as her mother, Anne Boleyn, was beheaded by that capricious and licentious King Henry VIII., together with Sir William Brereton and three other men of the court, upon what seems to have been a trumped-up charge of adultery, in order that he might marry her lady-in-waiting, Jane Seymour, which he did with indecent haste after Anne's death. Henry VIII. committed nothing short of murder in beheading William Brereton, who was only twenty-eight, and a young husband, having not long before been married to the daughter of the first Earl of Worcester. Miss Strickland, in her history of Queen Anne Boleyn, gives strong evidence of his being innocent of such a charge, and the fact that Henry VIII., soon after appointed his younger brother, Sir Urian Brereton, of Handford, to fill the same positions at his court, shows that he wished to make amendment to the family. This hall was erected by Sir William Brereton XI., fourteenth Lord of Brereton, who was raised to the peerage as first Baron Brereton, of Leighlin, Ireland. He was the one who erected the inscriptions in Brereton church in 1618.

DESCRIPTION OF MALPAS AND SHOCKLACH.

Ormerod describes Malpas as follows: "Malpas, called in Latin, Malus Passus, is a proper town, standing on a hill in the southeast corner of Cheshire, within three miles of Shropshire, Denbighshire, and Flintshire, and eight miles from Nantwich. It hath five streets paved, a grammar school, and a hospital, both erected by Sir Ranulph Brereton (IV. of Malpas) whose house is at the end of South street."

BRERETON HALL LAKE OF OLD TIME.

"Of neighbours Black-Mere named, of Strangers Brereton's Lake."
"That Black ominous Mere accounted one of those that England's
     wonders make."—Michael Drayton.

Mrs. Hemans, the English poetess, wrote the following lines on the above quotation from Dryden

"Yet: I have seen the ancient oak;
On the dark green water cast;
It was not felled by the woodman's stroke;
Or the rush of the sweeping blast;

Page 20.   *Brereton Hall, Entrance Door.*

For the axe might never touch that tree,
And the air was still as a summer sea.
I saw it fall, as falls a chief
By an arrow in the fight;
And the old woods shook to their loftiest leaf
At the crashing of its might;
And the startled deer to their coverts drew;
And the spray of the lake as a fountain flew.
'Tis fallen! but think thou not I weep
For the forest's pride o'erthrown;
An old man's tears lie far too deep,
To be poured for this alone;
But by that sign too well I know
That a youthful head must soon lie low.
A youthful head with its shining hair;
And its bright quick flashing eye;
Well may I weep! for the boy is fair,
Too fair a one to die·
But on his brow the mark is set;
Oh! could my life redeem him yet.
He bounded by me as I gazed
Alone on the fatal sign
And it seemed like sunshine when he raised
His joyous glance to mine.
With a stag's fleet step he bounded by
So full of life—but he must die.
He must, he must, in that deep dell,
By that dark water's side;
'Tis known that ne'er a proud tree fell,
But an heir of his father's died;
And he—there's laughter in his eye,
Joy in his voice—yet he must die.
The noble boy! how proudly sprung
The falcon from his hand;
It seemed like youth to see him young;
A flower in his father's land;
But the hour of the knell and the dirge is nigh,
For the tree hath fallen—and the flower must die.
Say not 'tis vain! I tell thee some
Are warned by a meteor's light;
Or a pale bird flitting calls them home,
Or a voice on the winds by night;
And they must go! and he too! he!
Doom'd by the fall of the glorious tree."

Sir Randle IV., of Malpas, also, built the Brereton chapel, or chantry, at the south side of Malpas church, in 1522. He and his wife Eleanor were buried in this chapel, and their tomb still exists. The Shocklach manor lies west of Malpas. It was purchased by Sir Randle Brereton V., of Malpas, in 1572, from Sir Richard Corbet. Malpas and Shocklach, at the time of the conquest, formed portions of the Barony of Malpas, of which Robert Fitz-Hugh was baron. He received it from Hugh Lupus, first, Earl Royal of Chester. According to the record given in Domesday he had dispossessed the former Saxon holder named Dot. The elder line, the Breretons of Brereton, were the barons of Malpas Castle. Between this period, 1572 and 1600, the Brereton family of Malpas had acquired very large estates in this corner of Cheshire, extending for eighteen miles between Malpas and Chester, and between Malpas and Middlewich, extending over forty parishes. At the death of the last direct male line in Sir Randle Brereton VII., of Malpas, all these estates passed to Sir Richard Egerton, of Ridley, by his marriage with Mary, the sole child and heiress. Their son squandered nearly the whole of this immense property.

DESCRIPTION OF THE HANDFORD PROPERTY.

Handford hall was situated about ten miles south of Manchester, in a low situation, on the bank of a small brook. Only one side of the quadrangle is standing, built of timber and plaster. The porch has sides of carved oak, and the following inscription is cut in black letters over the entrance ·

"This handle was buylded in the yeare of our Lord God MCCCCCLXII (1562) by Uryan Brereton, Knyght, whom maryed Margaret, daughter and heyre of Wyllyam Handforthe of Handforthe, Esquyre, and had issue III sonnes and II daughters."

At one end of the inscription is the coat of arms of Brereton, quartering Ipstone and impaling Handford. Brereton has for difference a cross crosslet between the bars, and a crescent on the first bar; the crest is on the other end.

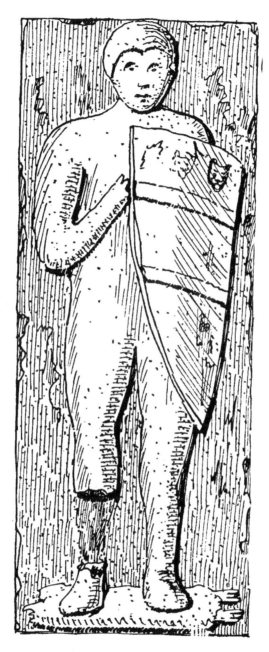

Page 23.   *Altar—Tomb of Knight.*

OLD GRAVES AND MONUMENTS.

The existing ancient tombs, monuments and inscriptions of the family, which are to be seen, are as follows:

(1) That which is alleged by the old time folk to be of Sir Ranulphus de Brereton, with his wife, Lady Ada, who died about the end of the thirteenth century or the beginning of the four-teenth. This is a canopied tomb of coarse red sandstone, located in the Astbury church yard, on the northwest side of the church. The tomb is of the altar shape, on which are two recumbent figures side by side, and of life size, a knight in armor and a female, their heads resting upon stone cushions; inside the canopy or arch there is inscribed in Latin capitals the following:

"HIC. JACENT. RADULPHUS. BRERETON. MILES.
ET. DOMINA. UXOR. SUA. UNA. FILIARUM.
DAVIDIS. HUNTINGDONIS."

Over this inscription is also inscribed a shield or escutcheon with two bars, which is the Brereton coat of arms. This inscription and shield are on the west side of the tomb. There can be no claim for this tomb on the part of either the Venables or of the Mainwarings, as there are no leopards' heads. The shield and the inscription are clearly cotemporaneous; the only question is as to when this canopy was fixed over the tomb. On the north side of this canopied tomb, and close to it, there is another altar tomb, with the figure of a monk or priest recumbent upon it in an attitude of devotion, with the hands closed across the chest, and something, not defined, in them, pointing to the chin; there is also a ruff or frill round the neck, and a skull cap on the head, but no mitre to indicate either abbot or bishop. Immediately on the south side of the canopied tomb is yet another altar tomb; upon it is the figure of a knight in armor, of life size and recumbent, his feet resting on some animal's body which is not distinguishable. The knight has a skull cap, and on the left side a shield on which is the heraldic coat, viz: two bars in chief, three leopards' heads, of which only two are now to be seen. The impression of the antiquity of these tombs is conveyed by there being no plate armor on the knights, as it was not until the time of Henry IV. (1399-1413) that the knights wore complete suits of plate armor. The first recorded mention of these ancient tombs is found in the Church Notes of A. D. 1576, which are found in the Harleian Mss., 2151, p. 4. As the inscription inside the canopied tomb existed, according to these Church Notes, in 1576, it seems clear that Sir William Brereton XI., of Brereton, who erected the inscription in Brereton church in 1618, could not have erected this canopied tomb in Astbury church yard. The tomb of the ecclesiastic probably may represent the remains of Gilbert de Brereton, second son of Sir Ranulphus de Brereton, who was Rector of Astbury about A. D. 1300. The other knight's tomb, on the south side of the canopied tomb, may be that of a Venables, as it bears the leopards' heads on the shield, which the Breretons' shield never did. However, so far as is recorded, the Venables never claimed these tombs, and the Egerton family, who claim them as representing the old Brereton and Venables, has enclosed them to protect them from further injury.

(2) In the Brereton chapel within Malpas church is the tomb of Sir Randle Brereton IV., of Malpas, and his wife Eleanor, who died 1532. This is a handsome tomb in the south aisle of the church, enclosed with a well carved oak screen. This chapel now belongs by marriage and inheritance to the Egerton family.

(3) In the Church of Cheadle, the burying spot of the Handford family, there is to be seen a monument to the last of the male line of that family, Sir Thomas Brereton V., of Handford. His father, Sir William Brereton IV., of Handford, known as the "Warrior," was one of the first baronets of England.

In "Visits to Fields of Battle," by Richard Brooke, 1850, is found the following description of the Brereton family tombs in Cheadle church: A chapel, called the Handford chapel, is on the south side of the church. In this is a large altar tomb, on which are recumbent marble figures of two knights in complete plate armor of a very richly ornamented style, and each with his hands conjoined; one is bareheaded, but with the head resting on a helmet; the other figure has a helmet which is orna-

Malpas Church.

mented with a wreath and a fillet, and has a crest seemingly the head of some animal, said to have been that of a deer. Each of the figures is decorated with a collar of SS, and the feet of each rest upon a lion. Another altar tomb is placed close up to, and on the north side of, the above mentioned tomb, but on a lower elevation; on it is a third figure in stone; it is the effigy of another personage in plate armor, but instead of greaves it has rather small jack boots, and is bareheaded, with long flowing hair; and what seems very remarkable in such an effigy, instead of a gorget it has a neckcloth or cravat, tied with the ends of it falling down over the upper part of the cuirasse. The head rests upon a helmet with a plume of feathers, colored blue, white and red; the feet do not rest upon any animal. On the north side of the tomb is the following inscription: "Here lyeth the body of Sir Thomas Brereton, of Handford, Barronett, who married Theodosia, daughter to the Right Honorable Humble Lord Ward and the Lady Frances Barronesse Dudley; he departed this life the 7th of January, A. D. 1673, Aetatis suae 43." All the three effigies are said to be those of Brereton, and there does not seem to be any doubt of the fact. The chapel has a carved oak screen or frame work enclosing it on the west and north sides, with some carving like lace work, but much injured; with a cornice containing the rebus (riddle) of a brier and a tun (barrel) for "Brereton" repeated thirteen times, with the initial letters "U" and "B" between each alternately, for "Urian" and "Brereton," on the north side, but the rebus has been destroyed on the west side. In the east window of the chapel is a mutilated shield of arms, in stained glass; on the dexter (right) side on a chief azure, three bucks' heads caboshed (means, where the head of the buck only is seen, and no part of the neck) OR, for Stanley; impaling the arms of a female, evidently one of the Handfords, of which only the following quarterings remain distinguishable, viz: second, gules a saythe argent, for Praers; fourth, sable, a star, with six or eight rays argent for Handford; the crest seems to be an eagle's head erased, holding in its beak an eagle's leg and claws erased.

(4) In the Carington chapel of Bowden church, Cheshire, is to be seen an ancient tomb representing whole length figures of William Brereton, of Ashley, and his wife Jane, daughter of Sir Peter Warburton of Arley. He was the grandson of Sir Richard Brereton, of Lea Hall, the third son of Sir William Brereton IX., of Brereton, and the founder of the family branch of Ashley. He was High Sheriff of Cheshire in 1609. He died in 1630, and his wife in 1627. On this monument the husband is habited in a gown and ruff and lies under a circular arch; the lady is placed on a lower slab, and over her is a marble ceiling ornamented with cherubs and supported by Corinthian pillars. Each are shown resting on pillows, with closed hands. Beneath the fifth and sixth is an infant in swaddling clothes. Under the arch are the Brereton arms with eighteen quarterings, impaling the arms of Warburton of Arley, with nine quarterings. Under the tomb is the following Latin inscription:

"Sub hoc marmore humata requiescunt corpora Gulielmi Brereton de Ashley, in comitatu cestriae, armigeri, et Janae uxoris ejus, quorum alteram genus, et originem duxit ab antiqua et illustri familia et progenie Brereton de Brereton, in praedicto comitatu, altera ex clara, retusque orta fuit Warburtorum pro-sappia, et ex fileabus erat una et cohearedibus Petri Warburton de Arley, in praedicto, comitatu, armigeri, nupperine defuncti. Lineros susceperunt mares, Richardum, Thomam, Gulielmum, Franciscum, Mariam, corperis etiam vinculis solitam, Annam, et Catherinam. Casto ac conjugali amore se invicem fonebantur; pauperes advenasque liberali, benignog hospitio excipiebant; vin culum amicitiaem cum familiaribus initae sercabunt intemeratum; purae et orthodoxae religioni constanter adhaerebunt, et quum hujus vitae stadium (ut Christianos decint), pie religioseque pere-gissent, vitam cum morte commutabant, laetam nunc et glorissam in Christo, corporum resurrectionem expectantes, ambo e vivis ex excedentes, quietis portum, quietis quidem, die scilicet dom-inico, appelerunt; Jana cilicet: Marti 2nd Anno Domini 1627, aetatis suae 63, Gulielmus autem Augusti 29, A. D. 1630, aetatis etiam sua 63."

Tomb of Sir Randle Brereton IV.

Page 24.

Translation: "Under this marble lie buried, rest the human bodies, of William Brereton, of a large number of attendants, (the owner) of a castle, an armor bearer, and of Jane, his wife; the former of whom sprang from the ancient and illustrious family and progenitor Brereton, of Brereton, of an especially large number of attendants; the latter (Jane) was of (sprang from) the celebrated family of Warburton, and was one of the daughters and coheirs of Sir Peter Warburton of Arley, recently dead, an armor bearer of renown, and of a large number of attendants. They bore the children, Richard, Thomas, William, Frances, Mary, also, Anne, separated from the chains of the body (dead), and Catharine, whom they married to Ashton. They treated paupers and strangers with liberality, and with kind hospitality, they kept from the first undefiled the bond of friendship with families; constantly they adhered to the pure and orthodox religion; and when they had completed the journey of this life, as becomes Christians, they exchanged life with (for) death. Now joyful and glorious life in Christ, awaiting the resurrection of the body; both departed from life went to their rest in peace, indeed in peace, on Sunday; Jane, in truth, died on the 2nd of March, 1637 A. D., at the age of 63; however, William died on August 29, A. D. 1630, also at the age of 63."

Richard, their eldest son, was born in 1590; Thomas, second son, in 1594; William, third son, in 1596; he was unmarried, and died in 1632; Peter, the fourth son, not mentioned in the monument, was born in 1601; he also died unmarried, at Gray's Inn, London, in 1659. Frances was born in 1592, married Alexander Barlow, of Barlow, Lancashire; Mary, second daughter, born 1595, died unmarried; Anne, third daughter, born 1597, married Robert Tatton in 1628; Catherine, fourth daughter, born 1598, married Raufe Ashton, of Kirkleigh, Yorkshire. William, the father, was High Sheriff of Cheshire in 1609, and died in 1630. Jane, his wife, died in 1627. Richard, the eldest son, never married, but had an illegitimate son by his servant, Ellen Higginson, called William Brereton, living in Chester in 1653. (See notes in Ashley Pedigree).

MEMORIAL WINDOWS, GRAVES AND MONUMENTS.

In Brereton church·are to be seen legends on the painted window in the form of scrolls between the legs of knights. Beginning on the left hand side of the spectator these appear to read as follows: (Some portions are obliterated by age).

1. Willms. Traci.
2. Reginald Fitzarci.
3. Martorm Thoma (in the center).
4. Necnon Martelis Hugo.
5. Richardus Breto.

Legend beneath—Ricardus Breto, Necnon Martelis Hugo, Willms, Traci, Reginald Fitzurci, Martorum Thoma, fieri facere, beatum anno nullens contens, Septuagenonen.

Referring to the names given in this very old legend, I should mention that they are those of the four knights of the bed chamber of Henry II., who murdered Thomas a'Becket, or Thomas of London, the Archbishop of Canterbury, in 1170. Henry II. was a man subject to violent outbursts of passion. Becket was an overbearing, haughty priest, and was hated by the king. On one occasion Henry demanded of these knights, "Whether no man loved him enough to revenge the affronts he perpetually received from an insolent priest?" Upon this hint, Sir Reginald Fitzurse, Sir William de Tracy, Sir Hugh de Morville, and Sir Richard de Breto (Brereton) went and murdered Becket before the altar of St. Benedict in the north transept of Canterbury Cathedral, on the twenty-ninth of December, 1170. After the murder they fled to Scotland, and finally went to the Crusades on a penance of service (with the Knights Templar in Jerusalem) given them by the pope. This Sir Richard de Breto was probably a near relative and contemporary of Sir William de Brerton I., of Brereton, with whom the pedigree starts.

The inscription on the painted window runs thus:

"Lest this monument in glasse being on ye upper window of the north syde of the Chauncell of Brereton church should be broken, I, S. Willm. Brereton, Knight, to the end hyt may remayne in memorie to ye posteritie, have caused the same to be here pictured the xxvth of March, 1608, W. Brert."

Page 26.

Tomb of Sir William Brereton, of Ashley, in Bowden Church, Cheshire.

From the above date this must have been made by Sir William Brereton XI., of Brereton. The half legible lines on each side the signature of Richardus Breto are from an old chronicle written at St. Albans (Herts) in 1483, describing the death of the archbishop in 1172. Lord Lyttleton gives the year 1170, quoting from Gainie Gervaise, an English monk, and Chronicler of the Archbishops of Canterbury of that period (born 1150).

He gives the names, Reginald Fitzurse, William de Tracy, Hugh de Morville, and Richard Breto. There is another memorial inscription in Brereton church in Latin, date 1618, over which still hang the surcoat, helmet, spurs, and gauntlets of a knight. It runs thus

"Antiquis temporibus guando haec ecclesia de Brereton fuit capella, donativa inter parochiam de Astburie antecessores Gulielmi Berreton militis, baronis de Malpas, et hujus monumenti fundatorus, Anno Domini 1618; Sepulti erant in cemeterio de Astburie, ubi antiqua quorundum eorum monumenta adhuc extant Anglice onita Knightes burialls, sed postquam dicta capella ecclesia parochialis, facta fuit, antecessores dicti Gulielmi Brereton, militis, hujus ecclesiae de Brereton patroni; in hac cancella sepulti fuerunt, praecter eos qui in externis regnis et comitatibus moriebantur."

Translation: "Once in ancient times this chapel (Brereton) was given as a benefice to the members of the church of Brereton, within the parish of Astbury; the ancestors of the soldier (knight) William Brereton, Baron of Malpas, and of the founder of the monument were buried in 1618 A. D. in the cemetery of Astbury, where, up to this time, are extant, written in English, the monuments of buried knights; but after the said chapel was made (into) a parochial church, the ancestors of the said William Brereton, the soldier (knight), the patron of this church of Brereton, except those who died in foreign lands, and with a retinue, were buried here in this enclosed space."

In the northeast angle of the chancel, within the communion rails, is a marble monument with fanciful ornaments in a style of mixed Italian and Gothic, over which are the arms of Brereton with twelve quarterings, which are as follows:

1st. Argent, two barrs sable. Brereton.

2d. Within double tressure flory (fluery) on an inescutcheon, A. Huntingdon.

3d. Or., three piles gules, Scot, Earl of Chester.

4th. Kevelioc and Lupus, Earls of Chester, quarterly.

5th. Gules, three pheons (arrow heads); argent, Belward.

6th. Azure, three garbs (sheafs of wheat); Or., Kevelioc.

7th. Azure, a wolf's head erazed; argent, Lupus.

8th. Argent, a cross patonce azure, Malpas.

9th. Argent, a lion rampant, gules, with an orle of pheons, sable, Egerton.

10th. Or., two ravens proper, Corbet.

11th, Argent, five chevrons, gules; on a canton of the second, a lion passant. Or. Orreby.

12th. Gules, two lions passant, and a label in chief (colors gone). Orreby, ancient crest, a bear's head sable issuing from a ducal coronet; muzzled Or.; dexter supporter, a bear, sable (effaced); sinister supporter, a wolf rampant, argent, collared, azure. Motto, "Opitulante Deo."

The proper names shown on this monument belong to the families from which descent is claimed. I assume the key to this to be as follows:

No. 1 represents the Brereton family. No. 2 indicates the Lady Ada Huntingdon. No. 3, John, the Scot, Earl of Chester, brother of Lady Ada. No. 4, Kevelioc and Lupus, Earls Royal of Chester; the latter was Hugh of Avranches, called Lupus or Wolf, because of his savage ferocity in his wars with the Welsh. He was nephew of the Conqueror, and died 1101. He succeeded the Saxon Thane or Earl Gerbod; he was the first Earl Royal of Chester in 1071. His son Richard, afterwards second Earl Royal of Chester, married Matilda, daughter of Stephen, Earl of Blois. Hugh Lupus was ancestor of Lady Ada's mother; Hugh Kevelioc was her maternal grandfather; he was the fifth Earl Royal. Belward is Richard de Belward, who married Lettice, only daughter and heiress of Robert Fitz Hugh, son of Hugh, Baron of Malpas; from them are descended the Cholmondeleys and the Egertons. By the marriage of Sir William Brereton VI., of Brereton, with Ellen, daughter of Philip, sister and heiress of David de Egerton, about 1350 A. D., the Breretons, of Brereton, became joint barons with the Cholmondeleys of Malpas. Nos. 6 and 7 are No. 4 repeated. No. 8 is 5 repeated. No. 9 is the Egerton family, of Egerton, with which there were intermarriages with the Breretons, of Brereton. No. 10 is the very ancient family of Corbet, who were descended from Sir Robert de Corbet, one of the companions in arms of the Conqueror. His great grandson, Sir Robert de Corbet, of Caus Castle, Shropshire, attended King Richard I., at the siege of Acre, and there bore for arms the two ravens, as now borne by his descendants, the Corbet family of Moreton, Shropshire. William de Brereton, Esq., heir of Sir William de Brereton VI., of Brereton, married Alice, sister and heiress of Sir Richard de Corbet, of Leghton, in the barony of Caius. Their daughter Alice married her cousin, Peter de Corbet, of Leghton. Nos. 11 and 12, Orreby stands for a family of that name, with which the Brereton family were indirectly connected through the Corbet family. Sir Philip de Orreby purchased the manor of Alvanley, near Warringtui, Cheshire, in 1209; his son and heir, Fulc de Orreby, of Stapleford, was Chief Justice in 1261, and Constable of the Chester, Beeston, Shutwick and Dysert Castles in 1256. His daughter, Alice, married Peter Corbet, of Leghton; it was their great granddaughter Alice who married the above mentioned William de Brereton, Esq. The present family of Corbet, of Moreton, Shropshire, are the descendants. The Fitton family, of Gawsworth, was also allied by marriage with the Orreby family, and also with the Brereton family. I am surprised to find that Sir William Brereton should have given the name of the Orreby family in this inscription, as they had no near connection with his family, and should have omitted the Venables, the Dutton, the Warburton, the Vernon, the Masey, and the Cholmondeley families, who appear in the family pedigree.

As many of the heraldic terms in the inscription are unknown to my children I have given an explanatory glossary of them in an appendix.

The roof of Brereton church is of carved oak; it was erected in 1684 by the architect, Thomas Wittingham. The parish church registers of births and deaths began in 1583. The church was originally a family chapel dependent on Astbury; it was made parochial in 1190. (Sir William Brereton gives 1618?).

ECCLESTON.

The old church at Eccleston, near Chester, no longer exists, but in it were buried the members of the old Eccleston branch of the family in the sixteenth and seventeenth centuries. There was an old chapel attached to the church, known as Eaton chapel, which was set apart for the use of the Grosvenor family, the present owners. In this chapel there were a number of monuments of which records were kept in the church books. Among these was one of "Maud, the wife of Richard Brereton, who died March 17, 1616. She was the daughter of Richard Hurlestone, or Picton, and the mother of eight sons and eight daughters." There was, also, another monument which ran thus: "Here lyeth the body of said Richard Brereton, who died — day of —." No date is given. Probably the writer found the figures illegible. The pedigree, however, gives the date as 1630. The vestry records of that period, being on parchment and pigskin, are much obliterated, but the following are found: "Dorothy Brereton, daughter of John Brereton, baptized April 25, 1613." Another is one of Jane, widow of Henry Brereton, buried on the same date. This Henry Brereton was probably one of the eight sons of Richard Brereton. He had a second consort, Margaret, daughter of Richard Grosvenor, of Eaton. In the lineage of the Brooke family of Norton Priory (formerly Mere hall) at Halton, near Runcorn, Cheshire, mention is made of Thomas Brooke, son of Sir Peter Brooke, who married Margaret, daughter and heiress of Henry (Richard?) Brereton, of Eccleston, about 1650. There is, also, a record of a Joseph Brereton who was Mayor of Chester in 1623. He probably was another of the eight sons.

Monument in Brereton Church.

G
9
B

THE BRERETON FAMILY COAT OF ARMS.

The coat of arms of the elder line, the Breretons, of Brereton, is: Arms, Argent, two bars sable. Crest, a bear's head proper issuing from a ducal coronet; OR, a bear's head couped, muzzled, OR; Supporters, Dexter, a bear proper; Sinister, Argent, a wolf collared, Azure; armed gule.

That of the younger family, the Breretons, of Malpas, is: Arms, Argent, two bars sable; Crest, a bear's head erazed proper, on a wreath, muzzled, OR.

The motto of both families is: "Opitulante Deo," (meaning, by the help of God). The difference consists in the crest; the elder line has the bear's head couped, or cut off straight; the younger line has the head erazed, that means, torn off by violence. The crest of the elder is on a ducal coronet, indicating a royal descent.

On the outside of Malpas church, east side, is to be seen both bears' heads, one muzzled and the other unmuzzled.

Family tradition has preserved the following interesting fact as to the origin of the muzzle upon the bear's head in the Brereton arms: Once upon a time in a battle, of uncertain date, the Brereton of the day, a stalwart knight, was guilty of an excess of ardour, and pushed an advantage too far, in the Prince Rupert style. The king who witnessed the brave fault, and thought it called for a mild rebuke, exclaimed: "I shall put a muzzle upon that bear," and directed it to be notified to the Herald's college.

John Brereton IV., of Brinton, Norfolk, appears to have adopted the muzzled bear proper, that is, the whole of the animal, instead of the erazed head and neck, for his crest, and which forms one of the supporters to the regular family coat of arms.

FAVORITE FIRST NAME OF THE HEAD OF THE FAMILY.

The favorite first name of the elder line was William, of which there are sixteen in the pedigree record; Randle, or Randulph, was the favorite of the Malpas line; John and Cuthbert, of the Norfolk line. During the past two generations, Lloyd and Cloudesley Shovell have prevailed. Admiral Sir Cloudisley Shovell spelt his first name Cloudisley. He was born at Cockthorp, Norfolk, in 1650, and died 1707. He assisted in the taking of Gibraltar from Spain in 1703. He was the grandson of John Shovell, Sheriff of Norwich 1667. His mother was Anne, daughter of Henry Jenkinson, by his wife Lucy, daughter of Thomas Cloudisley, of Cley, Norfolk.

EARLS AND BARONS OF LAND.

In connection with this history we find earls and barons of lands, and it may be useful to describe them. The Earl Royal of Chester, at the period of the Norman Conquest held a far higher position and jurisdiction than did the earl of the same period and afterwards. The former held the entire county as a feudal kingdom, and was known as the Earl Palatine, possessing all the royal services and powers of granting lands, and of escheating them, and for holding courts and offices of justice. Cheshire was, therefore, called at that period a Palatinate instead of County. The simple earl took his title from a county, as the Earl of Huntingdon, Earl of Surrey, but held no territorial possessions or royal powers and privileges like the Palatine. The title of earl was the oldest and the first in rank of nobility before the conquest and afterward until A. D. 1337, when the first duke was created, and it fell to the third rank A. D. 1386, when the first marquis was created. There were Saxon Earls of Chester before the Normans came. Leofric, the Saxon Earl of Cheshire, in A. D. 1056, held large estates in Cheshire; he was the husband of Lady Godiva, of Coventry renown, which was a philanthropic legend, though purely a fictitious one, as, at that period, Coventry did not exist; it was only a "villa," or country residence of her husband. The title of earl was first made hereditary after the conquest, and then the earl for a time was known as count; from him the name of county arose, and ever since the

34

Brereton Coat of Arms.

Page 33.

wife of the earl has been called countess. It will be observed that the feudal system was in vogue in the Saxon time, before the advent of the Normans.

BARONS.

The Norman title of baron was attached to the possessor of certain territory of lands in the county held under the feudal system, directly under the sovereign, and conditionally upon the performance of some honorary services to the king, such as attendance in the battlefield and the council; the furnishing of a stipulated number of knights and men-at-arms. This number was regulated by the extent of the possessions held by the baron, these being divided into allotments, for each of which he had to provide a knight, armed "cap-a-pie;" hence, according to the size of his possessions, he was said to possess so many "knights' fees." This old title of baron by tenure of lands ceased many centuries back, and since then, for a period, the title was created by "royal writ" to attend the sovereign in council or Parliament. The first of these on record was made by Henry III. This mode of creating "earl by writ" ceased about the end of the seventeenth century. Since then a baron is created by the issue and delivery of "Letters Patent." Baron now holds the fifth or lowest step of the peerage. Of the fifteen barons created by "Letters Patent" in Ireland in the seventeenth century, Sir William Brereton XI., of Brereton, held the fifth place in the date of creation.

1208941

BARONETS.

The first creation of this title was made by King James I. for Ireland. His son, Charles I., extended the title in England. Of the 122 baronets created by the Stuart regime in the seventeenth century, Sir William Brereton IV., of Handford, the great general of the Parliamentary forces in Cheshire, known in history as the "Warrior," was ninth in date of creation.

KNIGHTS AS LORDS OF LAND.

In the feudal times in order to become a knight it was prerequisite to be an owner of lands; hence, the evidence we have of our original ancestor being the original Lord of Brereton. In those days there were two degrees of knighthood, one a Knight Bachelor, or lord of a manor; the other a Knight Banneret, a knight who had distinguished himself in battle before his king or his baron; as such was Sir Randle Brereton IV., of Malpas. He was so knighted for brilliant bravery at Terouenne, and at Tourney, in France, by Henry VIII. The knight bachelor always carried a penon or pointed flag; the knight banneret had his penon cut off square by the king.

PEDIGREE AND FAMILY BRANCHES.

From the middle of the eleventh century to the middle of the fourteenth century the parent stem continued without the record of branches from Brereton. About 1550 Sir William de Brereton VI., eighth Lord of Brereton, became the ancestor of the elder line of Brereton, of Brereton, and of the younger line, the Breretons of Ipstone and Malpas. By his first wife, Ellen, daughter of Philip, and sister and heiress of David de Egerton, of Egerton, Baron of Malpas, the elder line proceeded. By his second wife, Margaret, daughter of Henry Done, of Utkington, the widow of Sir John de Davenport, of Henbury, the younger branch descended through Sir Randle Brereton, of Ipstone, and first of Malpas. This Randle's full sister, Elizabeth, married William de Cholmondeley, and his second sister married Randall Spurstow, Lord of Spurstow; his daughter, also, married a Spurstow, of Spurstow.

36

Brereton Inn, Date 1615.

BRANCHES FROM THE ELDER LINE.

The Breretons of Ashley.

Sir Richard Brereton, of Lea Hall, third son of Sir William Brereton IX., of Brereton, by his second wife, Eleanor, daughter of Randulph, or Randle Brereton, son of Sir Randle Brereton II., of Ipstone and Malpas, and who was the widow of Sir Philip Egerton, of Egerton, married, about 1530, Thomasine, daughter and heiress of Sir George Ashley, of Ashley. This family continued for about one hundred and thirty years. The last of the direct male line, Thomas Brereton, died without issue, and left all his estates to his three sisters and their heirs. The elder, Frances, married Alexander Barlow, of Barlow, Lancashire. This Alexander's son married Mary, daughter of Sir Urian Brereton, the founder of the Handford branch. Anne married Robert Tatton, of Withershaw, Cheshire. Baron Egerton, of Tatton Park, is descended from them; as their descendant, William Tatton, of Withershaw, in 1747, married Hester Egerton, sister and heiress of Samuel Egerton, of Tatton Park, who was the grandson of John Egerton, second Earl of Bridgewater, who had inherited the Tatton estates (which originally belonged to the first Brereton branch of Tatton, descended from the elder branch of Brereton), and which were left by the last male owner, Richard Brereton, descended from the younger line of Malpas, who died in 1598, to his kinsman, Sir Thomas Egerton, who became Baron Ellesmere and Viscount Brackley, and whose son, John, was created first Earl of Bridgewater. William Tatton, upon his marriage with Hester Egerton, assumed the name of William Tatton Egerton. It will be observed that this William Tatton was descended from Anne Brereton, who married Robert Tatton, of Withershaw. (See the Tatton Branch).

THE BRERETON BRANCH IN IRELAND.

Andrew Brereton was second son of William Brereton, Esq., of Brereton, and grandson of Sir William Brereton IX., of Brereton, who was Chief Justice of Ireland, also Lord High Marshal, 1546; died at Kilkenny in 1541. His mother was Anne, daughter, of Sir William Booth, of Dunham; he married Catherine, daughter of Sir Andrew Fitz-Simon, of Dublin, Ireland. His residence was Thoyle Abbey, County Kildare. He was uncle to Sir William Brereton XI., of Brereton, who built Brereton Hall and who became first Baron Brereton of Leighlin, County Carlow, Ireland. He founded the Carrigslaney family.

Edward Brereton, sixth son of the above William Brereton, of Brereton, and younger brother of Andrew, married Edith, daughter of William Birche, of Birche, Lancashire. He obtained grants of land in Ireland in 1594, and became Brereton of Shananmullen, Queen's County.

His great grandson, Bowen, of Shananmullen, Raheenduffe, and Loughtiage, in 1688, married his kinswoman, Eleanor Brereton, of Carrigslaney, and the estates at a later date became combined; the present family is known as the Breretons of Carrigslaney. Two of the daughters of the family, in 1785, married their cousins, two descendants of the old Norman family of Perceval, from which family the Earl of Egmont is descended. This Irish family of Brereton still exists. It has figured mainly in the English army and in India with much distinction. The Carrigslaney estate was sold by Arthur Brereton about 1860. He died in Chicago, U. S. A. There are several members of the Irish families settled in the United States.

BRANCHES OF THE YOUNGER LINE OF MALPAS.
Breretons of Wettenhall and Eccleston.

The second of the offshoots from Sir Randle Brereton, of Ipstone, and first of Malpas, begins with Randle de Brereton, eldest son of Sir Randle de Brereton II., of Malpas. He was called the Escheator, and as Ormerod styles him, the base son of Sir Randle Brereton; (yet, in his pedigree of the Malpas family, he gives him as the eldest son by his wife, Joanna Holford). He married Katherine, daughter of Richard Manley, of Pulton; he

MAP OF CHESHIRE

DERBYSHIRE

MANCHESTER
STOCKPORT

LANCASHIRE

Cheadle
Carlaton
Warburton
Ashton

High
Legh
Ashley
Hall
Handford
Hall
Davenport
Hall

MACCLESFIELD
Gawsworth

LEEK

LIVERPOOL

MERSEY RIVER

Runcorn
Halton
Hall

rley
Hall
Dutton
Hall
Marston
Hall
Tabley
Hall
Tatton
Hall

NORTHWICH

KNUTSFORD

Over
Peover

MIDDLEWICH
Leg
Hall
BRERETON

SANDBACH
Astbury

CREWE

STAFFORDSHIRE

CHESTER

Shotwick
Hall

Eccleston
Hall
Eaton
Hall

Ukington
Oulton
Hall

Wettenhall

Spurstow
Hall
Eggton
Hall

NANTWICH
Cholmondeley
Hall

RIVER DEE

Holt

Coddington
Edge
Shocklack
Hall
MALPAS

Ishoya
Hall

SHRO

FLINTSHIRE

DENBIGHSHIRE

died 1537. His second son, John, who succeeded, married Katherine, daughter of Louth Dutton, Alderman of Chester, of the old family of Dutton, of Dutton and Warburton. John died 1568. His son and heir, Richard Brereton, married Maud, daughter of Richard Hurleston, of Picton; he died 1630, and had eight sons and eight daughters. His son and heir, John Brereton, born 1611, married Atlanta, daughter of Thomas Piggot, of Chetwynd, near Newport, Shropshire. He sold the manor of Wettenhall. His son, Richard, succeeded, but there is no record of him. John Brereton's brother Henry had two consorts; one was the daughter of Richard Grosvenor, of Eaton Hall (Duke of Westminster's family). The mother of Randle Brereton, the founder of this branch, it will be noted, was a daughter of the Holford family, of Holford. Sir Hugh Cholmondeley, of Cholmondeley (1553-1596), was the eldest son of Sir Richard Cholmondeley by his wife, Elizabeth, the daughter of Sir Randle Brereton V., of Malpas and Shocklach. Sir Hugh married Mary, daughter and heiress of Christopher Holford, of Holford, by his second wife, Elizabeth, daughter of Sir. Randle Mainwaring, of Over Peevor, Cheshire. This illustrates how intimately the Brereton, Cholmondeley, Mainwaring and Holford families were connected, by marriage and blood in the sixteenth century. This Sir Hugh Cholmondeley was five times High Sheriff for Cheshire, and several times for Flintshire, and also Lord Lieutenant of Ireland. His wife, Mary, for forty years, fought for her right to inherit the Holford estates and finally won. King James I. called her that "bold lady of Cheshire." From this Sir Hugh Cholmondeley are descended the present family of Baron Delamere, of Vale· Royal, Cheshire, with the strain of the Brereton blood through the above mentioned Elizabeth Brereton, of Malpas, daughter of Sir Randle Brereton V., of Malpas.

THE TATTON BRANCH OF BRERETONS.

Sir Richard Brereton, the founder of this family, was the second son of Sir Randle Brereton IV., of Malpas, by his wife,

Eleanor, daughter of Sir Piers Dutton, of Halton. He married Joan, or Jane, daughter and heiress of Sir William Stanley, of Tatton, by his wife Joan, daughter and heiress of Sir William Masey of Tatton. This Joan Masey was the widow of Sir John Brereton, the half brother of Sir Andrew Brereton, of Brereton, (1460-1506). Sir Richard died in 1557, in Islington, London. His son and heir, Geoffrey Brereton, married Alice, daughter of Piers Leycester, of Nether Tabley, Cheshire. He died in 1565 and was succeeded by his son and heir, Richard, who married Dorothy, daughter of Sir Richard Egerton, of Ridley, the great grandson of Sir Philip Egerton, of Egerton, by his wife, Eleanor, daughter and heiress of Sir Randle Brereton III., of Malpas; Richard died in 1598 without issue. He settled all his estates upon his kinsman, Sir Thomas Egerton, who was afterwards Lord Chancellor of England (1603-1607). These Breretons held the Tatton estates from 1543 to 1598. (See the history of the Ashlev Branch).

THE BRERETONS OF HANDFORD.

The founder of this branch was Sir Urian Brereton the ninth son of Sir Randle Brereton IV., of Malpas. He married, first, Margaret, daughter and heiress of William Handford, of Handford, near Cheadle, Cheshire. He was called Escheator, which meant a royal officer appointed to look after the king's escheat estates or lands. He died 1577. He was a favorite in the court of Henry VIII., and Queen Anne Boleyn's favorite lapdog was named "Urian." William Brereton III., Lord of Handford, married Margaret, daughter of Richard Holland, of Denton, Lancashire. He died 1611, and was succeeded by his son and heir, Sir William Brereton IV., Lord of Handford, born 1604; died 1661. He was created a baronet by King Charles I. in 1626. His first wife was Susan, daughter of Sir George Booth, of Dunham, by whom he had one son, Sir Thomas Brereton, and three daughters. His eldest daughter, Frances, married Edward, second Baron Ward, of Birmingham, afterwards Earl of Dudley and second Baron Ward. His second daughter, Susannah, married Edmond Lenthall, grandson of the Speaker of the House of Commons. His third daughter, Catharine, died unmarried. By his second wife, Cicily, daughter of Sir William Sheffington, of Fisherwick, Leicestershire, he had two daughters: (1) Cicily, who married Edward Brabazon, younger son of Edward, second Earl of Meath; (2) Mary, unmarried. He had two brothers, Richard and Urian, both of whom died without issue, and one sister, Margaret, who married Sir Richard Egerton, of Ridley. Sir William died at the Archepiscopal Palace at Croydon, Surrey, of which he had received the grant from Parliament for his brilliant military services. His body was taken to Handford for burial, but was lost in a flood en route. (Earwaker in his History of Cheshire, gives a long description of his brilliant military exploits). In an old pamphlet published in 1663, called "The Mysteries of the Good Old Cause," this Sir William Brereton is described as "a notable man at a thanksgiving dinner, having terrible long teeth and a prodigious stomach, to turn the Archbishop's chapel at Croydon into a kitchen; also to swallow up that palace and lands at a morsel." His only son and heir, Sir Thomas Brereton V., of Handford, married Theodosia, youngest daughter of Humble, first Baron Ward, of Birmingham. She afterwards married Hon. Charles Brereton, youngest son of William, second Baron Brereton, and had issue, Charles Brereton, born 1677, died without issue. Sir Thomas died 1673 without male issue; he was buried in the Handford chapel of Cheadle church. With him ended the direct male line of this family, which had held the Handford estates for nearly one hundred and fifty years.

THE BRERETON FAMILY OF NORFOLK.

The founder of this branch was John de Brereton, third son of Sir Randle de Brereton IV., of Malpas. He was the brother of Sir Urian de Brereton, of Handford; of Sir Richard Brereton, of Tatton; of Sir William Brereton, who was beheaded by Henry

VIII., and of Sir Roger Brereton, of Halton. He married Alicia, daughter of ———— He was Rector of Malpas, also of Astbury, Bebrington, and St. Mary's, Chester. He died in 1542. His eldest son and heir was William Brereton, of Hoxne, near Eye, Suffolk. His grandson, Cuthbert, was Sheriff of Norwich in 1575. John Brereton IV., of Brinton, Norfolk, was eighth in descent from Rev. John de Brereton, of Malpas; ninth from Sir Randle de Brereton IV., of Malpas; twelfth from Sir Randle de Brereton I., of Ipstone and Malpas, the founder of the younger line; seventeenth from Sir Ranulphus de Brereton and Lady Ada, and twenty-first from Sir William de Brereton I., of Brereton (1175), with whom the family pedigree starts, representing a period of about 650 years. This John Brereton IV., of Brinton, was born 1752 and died 1823. The present rising generation of the Norfolk branch of this old family can trace their descent from *father to son consecutively* from 1175 to 1904, which extends over a period of 729 years. My grandchildren, who are the great grandchildren of Charles David Brereton, of Little Massingham, Norfolk, are the twenty-fifth in descent of the family since the twelfth century.

THE BRERETONS OF BURROS, OR BUROSHAM, DENBIGHSHIRE.

The founder of this branch, the first of the Malpas line, was William Brereton, second son of Sir Randle de Brereton, of Ipstone, and first of Malpas, by his wife, Alice, daughter of Sir William Ipstone, of Ipstone, A. D. 1400. He married Katherine, daughter and heiress of Thomas de Weyld, of Burros or Burosham. This earliest branch of the Malpas family became intimately allied through marriage with that very ancient Welsh family of the Lloyds, of Plas Madog, Denbighshire, and also with the ancient family of Hanmer, of Hanmer, Flint; also with the ancient families of Eyton, of Eyton, in Shropshire and Flintshire. Edward Brereton I., only son and heir of William Brereton, of Burosham, had two consorts: (1) Elizabeth, daughter of John Roydon, of Pulford, by his wife, daughter of Thomas Hanmer, of Bettisfield, by whom he had two sons, Randolph, the elder, died without issue, and John Brereton, of Burosham, who married Margaret, daughter and heiress of Richard, ap. Tenan, ap. David, ap. Ithel Fychān, of Llanewgain, descended from Ednowain Ben dew, chief of one of the noble tribes of Wales; (2) Edward's second wife was Dorothy, daughter of Richard Hanmer and sister of Sir Thomas Hanmer, who was knighted at the taking of Ter win and Tourney by King Henry VIII., at Boulogne; he married Jane, third daughter of Sir Randle Brereton IV., of Malpas, the sister of John Brereton, the founder of the Norfolk branch. Sir Randle Brereton, his father-in-law, was the leader of the Cheshire knights selected by King Henry VIII. to conduct the war in France in the place of the knights of Kent, which Wolsey had intended to send. By this second marriage Edward had issue, one son and three daughters, viz.: Thomas Brereton, Rector of Northope in 1539, of Llandrinio in 1557, of Gresford in 1556. He married Margaret, daughter of Ithel, ap. Gruffyd, ap. Belyn; Elizabeth, wife of James Eyton, of Eyton; Joanna, wife of Cyn wig, ap. Richard, of Penlachlech; Catherine, wife of Lancelot Lloyd, of Tref Alun (Allington). Thomas Brereton's eldest son, Peter, married, 1597, Jane, daughter of Owen, ap. Howell Fychan. John Brereton, of Burosham, son of Edward Brereton by his first wife, had one son, Owain Brereton, of Burosham. He was High Sheriff for Denbigh, 1580 and 1588. He had two consorts (1) Elizabeth, daughter of John Salusbury, heir of Lleweny, M. P. for Denbigh, 1554, by his wife, Catherine, daughter and heiress of Tudor, ap. Robert Fychan, of Berain (his mother was one of the Fychan family). By this marriage he had issue, two sons: Edward Brereton, of Burosham, Sheriff for Denbigh, 1598, in which year he died; (2) John Brereton, of Exlusham. The pedigree gives his children, but does not mention his wife. He had two sons and one daughter: (1) John Brereton, of Exlusham, died 1622; married Margaret, daughter of Hugh Wynn, of Wigfair; (2) Edward Brereton, of Burosham, married Anne, daughter of John Lloyd, of Bodidris; (3) Catherine, wife of Wil liam Lloyd, of Plas Madog, by whom he had issue, two sons; (*a*) Edward Lloyd, of Plas Madog; (*b*) Owain Lloyd. John Brereton II., of Exlusham had issue, two daughters, but no son; his eldest daughter, Elizabeth, was wife of Thomas Bulkeley, of Coedan; (2) Jane, who married, first, John Ffachnallt, of Ffach-nallt, Flintshire, by whom she had no issue; second, Owain Lloyd, second son of William Lloyd, by Catherine Brereton, his wife, daughter of first John Brereton, of Exlusham. They had issue, one son, Thomas, a merchant at Hamburgh, who died issue-less, and one daughter and heiress, who married her cousin, Edward Lloyd, of Plas Madog; he died 1692, and she 1676. I find on referring to the early pedigree of the Lloyds, of Plas Madog, that one of their ancestors, John, ap. David Lloyd, of Plas Madog, married Anghared, daughter of Howell, ap. Jeuan, ap. Gruffyd, of Bersham, by his first wife, Philippa, daughter of Sir Randle Brereton, of Malpas. This Philippa Brereton does not occur in Ormerod's pedigree of the Malpas family. Referring back to Edward Brereton, of Burosham, eldest son of Owain Brereton by his wife, Elizabeth, daughter of John Salusbury, heir of Lleweny, and brother of John Brereton, of Exlusham, one of his descendants was Thomas Brereton, of Burosham, who mar-ried Catherine, daughter of Salusbury Lloyd, his second wife, with whom he received Shotwick Hall and estates in Cheshire. By his first wife, one of the three daughters of Sir Jonathan Trelawny, of Trelawne, Cornwall, he had one son, Owen Brere-ton, born 1715; Thomas died 1756 and was succeeded by his son, Owen, who assumed the name of Salusbury; he, Owen Salusbury Brereton, was F. R. S. and R. A. and M. P. for Ilchester, Som-ersetshire, 1775-1780, and Constable of Flint Castle from 1775, and also Recorder of Liverpool. He lived at Windsor, died 1798 and was buried in St. George's chapel. He left no issue and so the estates of Burosham and Shotwick Hall passed to Colonel Charles Trelawny, fifth son of General Harry Trelawny, who

Brereton Crest.

G
9
B

assumed the surname and arms of Brereton. He died 1800, and was succeeded by his grandson, Horace Trelawny Brereton.

THE HALTON BRANCH OF THE MALPAS FAMILY.

There is very little recorded of this branch of the family. The Herald's Visitation Record of 1663-4 gives the pedigree commencing with Sir Roger Brereton, of Halton, the founder of the family, about 1540, and shows four generations of descent. I think this Sir Roger was the sixth son of Sir Randle Brereton IV., of Malpas, and the younger brother of John Brereton, the founder of the Norfolk branch. His mother was Eleanor, daughter of Sir Piers Dutton, the Lord of Halton and Dutton, in 1500. Sir Piers was descended from Odard, one of the companions in arms of the Conqueror. He (Odard) assumed the name of Dutton upon receiving a grant of that town from Hugh Lupus, first Earl Royal of Chester, the ancestor of Lady Ada's mother. Sir Piers was the great grandson of Sir Thomas Dutton, of Dutton, who was the Governor and Receiver of the Castle of Halton in 1330. Sir Piers was the son of Sir Lawrence Dutton, who married Johanna, daughter of Sir Andrew Brereton, of Brereton, and from whom are descended the present family of Baron Sherbourne, of Sherbourne, Gloucestershire. The Warburton family, of Arley, were also descended from the same Odard. Sir Roger Brereton married Katherine, widow of Edward Fulleshurst and daughter of Sir William Brereton IX., of Brereton, by his second wife, Eleanor, daughter of Sir Randle Brereton III., of Ipstone and Malpas, and the widow of Philip Egerton, of Egerton. Hence, she was aunt to Sir Roger, being his father's full sister The pedigree of Sir Roger's descendants does not give the names of their consorts. There were three generations of Rogers, of Halton; the last Roger's son, Ralph, is mentioned as a citizen of London. The last Roger must have sold the Halton estates, as the ancestor of the present owner of Halton, Thomas Brooke, of Norton Priory, bought them in 1652.

THE SOMERSETSHIRE BRANCH OF THE MALPAS FAMILY.

Of this family there is little record. The last Herald's Visitation, in 1640, records a Sir Thomas Brereton, of Yard, near Taunton, who married, A. D. 1600, Jane, daughter of Robert Hill, of Yard. Sir Thomas Brereton was the third son of Sir Randle Brereton VI., of Malpas, and brother of Sir Randle Brereton VII., of Malpas, and of Richard Brereton, second son, of Mitcham, Surrey. Sir Thomas Brereton's issue is given for only one generation. He had one son, Thomas, who married Elizabeth, daughter of Christopher Anketell, of Stower, Dorsetshire, who was descended from a very ancient family, mentioned in the reign of Edward I. Sir Thomas had two daughters, the eldest, Jane, wife of Christopher Anketell, of Stower; Eleanor, wife of Thomas Courtenay, second son of Sir William Courtenay, of Powdenham Castle, Devon (Earl of Devon family), by his wife Elizabeth, daughter of Henry, second earl of Rutland, who rebuilt Belvoir Castle, and whose wife was Lady Margaret Neville, daughter of Vere, fourth Earl of Westmoreland. The Anketell family, of Stower, appears to have become extinct at a little later date in Dorsetshire. A branch of this ancient family is found existing now in the influential family of Anketell Grove, County Monaghan, Ireland, which estates were acquired by Mathew Anketell in 1636.

THE SURREY BRANCH OF THE MALPAS FAMILY.

There is found but little record of this branch of the Malpas line. The following information is gathered from the Reliquary (Jewitt), Vol. XIII., 1872-3, in a letter from Rev. R. G. Rice, Vicar of Mitcham, Surrey. In Vol II. of the Surrey Archaeological Society's Collections, is printed a part of "The Visitation of Surrey, made 1623, by Samuell Thompson, Windsor Herauld, and Augustine Vincent, Rougcroix, Marshalls and Deputies to

Wm. Camden, Esq., Clarenceux King of Arms," edited by Joseph Jackson Howard, L. L. D.

I quote the following from Aubrey's History, 1718·

"On the south wall of the chancel is a fair marble monument bearing the figures of a man with a skull in his hand, and a woman with a book; underneath is a group of smaller figures, viz.: five sons and five daughters, the eldest of each sex before a desk with books lying open before them, the rest behind them; and on a black marble tablet, in capitals, gold letters, is the following inscription: 'Here lyeth ye Body of Theophilus Brereton, Esq., descended from Sir Randall Brereton, of Malpas, Cheshire who had issue by his wife, Mary, daughter of Thomas Roland deceased, eleven children, viz.: five sonnes and six daughters, and ye said Theophilus departed this life ye fifth day of December, A. D. 1638, age 64 years.' "

The church was pulled down and rebuilt in 1820, and all that now remains of the Brereton monument within the present church is the above inscription slab, which is placed on the east wall of the tower; but in a vault underneath the vestry, used as a coal cellar, I found the rest of it in pieces as it was taken down. In 1896 the church was reseated, and myself and a friend, Mr. J. Harwood, had the monument got out, and a stone mason arranged the pieces on the ground. Theophilus and his wife are full sized demi-figures; the children are small, but beautifully carved on a slab of alabaster, the material of which the monument is chiefly composed; it has the arms of Brereton: 'Argent, two barrs, sable, impaling Roland, argent, a pile wavy, sable. The whole composition, which is about ten feet six inches high, is surmounted with a dog's (bear's?) head sable, muzzled OR, "The Brereton Crest."

From the above mentioned Theophilus and Mary, or Maria Brereton, of Mitcham, Surrey, were descended the Breretons of Worcester, Gloucestershire, and Sussex. (See the lists of pedigrees in appendix).

GENERAL REMARKS.

Dates of the Family Branches.

From the elder line:
1—Ashley, Cheshire, founded about...............A. D. 1530
2—Irish, founded about.........................A. D. 1549
3—Helmingham, Suffolk, founded about..........A. D. 1700
4—Bedford, founded about.......................A. D. 1800

From the younger line of Malpas:
1—Burosham, Denbigh, founded about............A. D. 1450
2—Eccleston, Cheshire, founded about...........A. D. 1500
3—Tatton, Cheshire, founded about..............A. D. 1530
4—Norfolk, founded about.......................A. D. 1530
5—Halton, Cheshire, founded about..............A. D. 1540
6—Handford, Cheshire, founded about...........A. D. 1550
7—Somersetshire, founded about.................A. D. 1600
8—Surrey, founded about........................A. D. 1600

From the foregoing history of the Brereton family, of Cheshire, it will be noted that during the sixteenth, seventeenth, and eighteenth centuries there were four branches from the elder line of Brereton, and eight from the younger line of Ipstone and Malpas in the fifteenth and sixteenth centuries. The now living descendants, in name, of the younger line appear to be far more numerous than are those of the older line. At the same time, the only owner of any land in the old country is that of the Irish branch and that of the Briningham family, Norfolk. Owing to the Norman law and custom which prevailed during the middle centuries, the inheritance of estates passed to the eldest son and to his heirs. Where there was no son to inherit and only one daughter and heiress, the estates passed to her husband and their heirs. Thus the younger sons and daughters were left to shift for themselves. Consequently the history of their descendants was not always recorded in the Herald's records, unless these younger sons were found to have married the only daughter and heiress of some other family, as shown in the above history of the several branches.

Astbury Church, Interior.

Page 49.

During the earliest period of the Brereton pedigree history, about 1200, Sir Ralph de Brereton, of Brereton, the father of Sir William de Brereton III., of Brereton, gave to his daughter, Isolda, the lands of Brinley. She married Gilbert de Stoke, and from them were descended the ancient family of Brinley, of Brinley, which is extinct. Sir William de Brereton III., of Brereton, the father of Sir Ranulphus de Brereton, of Brereton, who is said by some pedigrees to have married Lady Ada, gave his daughter, who married Thurston de Smethwicke, the lands of Smethwicke, which formed a portion of the Brereton demesnes, on her marriage. From them descended the Smethwickes, of Smethwicke. This family is also extinct. In the Brereton church is to be seen an ancient monument of this family, which Ormerod has described in his history as follows:

"In the southeast angle of the south aisle, over the Smeth wicke pew, is a large marble monument with half figures of William Smethwicke and his wife, Frances Colclough. Both figures have been painted; both have ruffs. The hands are clasped and a hood is thrown over the lady's head and a book placed on each side of her. Under the male figure on a tablet of black marble is inscribed: 'Here lieth interred the body of William Smethwicke, of Smethwicke, who, mindful of his death, erected this monument for himself and his wife, pious to God, pious in good works. Which William was born October 1st, A. D. 1551., and died June 6, 1643.' On a similar tablet underneath the female: 'Here lieth the body of Frances Smethwicke, daughter of Sir Anthony Colclough, Knight, married to William Smethwicke, aforesaid, and lived in wedlocke with him 58 years, a devoute and hospitall matron, borne A. D. 1557, in the Castle of Kildare, in Ireland, November 6, and died 1st of May, 1632. Mors absorpta est in victoria mortis in hac camera speculare hic mobile compar, par, aetate sua, par pietate sua; una fides vivis, mens una, unita jugumg transit honoratum copula lustra decem vita una juncti, tumulo hic junguntur in uno, uni quis strueret vina sepulcri pari ille inipum; memor ille Dei, memor ille sepulcri; condidit hic; sub quo conditor ipse rogo.' "

Translation: "This one song of death to show this active pair. Alike in their age, alike in their piety. One trust in life, of one mind, the honored yoke and lustrious band of wedlock dragged them united in life; here they are united in this one mound. Whoever would make two graves for this one pair would be foolish. Mindful of God, mindful of the sepulchre, he made this; the builder himself (is) under this funeral pile."

The monument was originally finished with a shield, which is now lying in the chancel, on which were the arms of Smethwicke, OR, (OR means gold color) three crosses patee-fitche, sable. On the friezes below were originally nine shields, as follows: (1) Smethwicke, impaling Brereton; argent, two bars, sable. (2) Smethwicke, impaling Davenport; argent, a chevron on sable, between three cross crosslets fitchee of the second. (3) Smethwicke, impaling Ratclyffe; argent, two bars engrailed, sable, a label of three points, gules. (4) Smethwicke, impaling Kingsley; vert, a cross engrailed, ermine. (5) Smethwicke, impaling Downes; sable, a hart (deer) lodged, argent. (6) Destroyed. (7) Smethwicke, impaling ———; argent, fretty gules, on a canton azure, a cross patee, argent. (8) Dexter coat destroyed, impaling Vernon; OR., on a fesse, azure, three garbs, OR. (9) Destroyed.

For the meaning of the foregoing heraldic terms, see the glossary in the appendix. The term "impaling" signifies the marriage connections with the families of the names mentioned. The name Downes refers to the Knights of Donnybrook Castle, Kildare, with whom the Colclough family were probably connected. Those of the Vernons and Davenports were the same as those with whom the Breretons, of Brereton, also married. For instance, Sir William de Brereton V., of Brereton, married Rose, daughter of Sir Ralph de Vernon, of Shipbrook, and his daughter, Margery Brereton, married Sir John de Davenport, of Davenport, in 1301. Matilda Brereton, fifth daughter of Sir Andrew Brereton, of Brereton, married Sir John Davenport, of Davenport, about 1500. Sir John Brereton, of Lea Hall, Cheshire, son of Sir William de Brereton VIII., of Brereton, by his second wife, Phillippa, daughter of Sir Hugh Hulse, married two only daughters who were heiresses: First, Katherine, daughter of Sir Maurice Berkeley, of Beverton, Gloucestershire, by his wife, Anne, daughter of Reginald West, fifth Baron West and first Baron Delawarr. This Katherine was the sister and heiress of Sir William Berkely, of Stoke Gifford, Gloucester, and also heiress of the manor of Moore, Wiltshire. Sir John Brereton's only child by this consort was Wyburga, who married Sir William Compton, Knight, of Compton Wyniate, Warwickshire; died 1528. From them were descended the Earl of Northampton family. Sir John Brereton's second wife was Jane, or Joan, daughter and heiress of Sir Geoffrey Masey, of Tatton, the widow of Willian Stanley, of Tatton, by whom he had one son, Philip, heir to the Tatton estates, who died without issue. Sir John Brereton's half grandnephew, Sir Richard Brereton, younger son of Sir William Brereton IX., of Brereton, was afterwards his successor at Lea Hall. He obtained the Ashley estates through his wife, Thomasine, daughter and heiress of Sir George Ashley, of Ashley. Also, his kinsman, Sir Richard Brereton, second son of Sir Randle Brereton IV., of Malpas, at a later period, became Lord of Tatton through his marriage with Jane, daughter and heiress of William Stanley (of the Derby family), of Tatton. Thus two of the Brereton family had become Lords of Tatton by marriage with the heiresses of Tatton. Elizabeth, daughter of Sir William Brereton VIII., of Brereton, married John Radclyffe, of the ancient family descended from Richard de Radclyffe, of Radclyffe Tower, from whom the Earls of Sussex and the Radclyffes of Ordshall, Lancashire, descended. Ellen, daughter of Sir Andrew Brereton, of Brereton, married Sir John Fitton, of Gawsworth, another ancient family of Cheshire; also Sir John Brereton, son of William, first Baron Brereton, married Anne, daughter of Sir Edward Fitton, of Gawsworth. Margaret, daughter of Sir William Brereton IX., of Brereton, married William Goodman, of Chester. Henry Brereton, of Eccleston, married Margaret, daughter of Richard Grosvenor, of Eaton, by his wife, Christian, daughter of Sir Richard Brooke, of Norton Priory, Halton, whose father, Thomas Brooke, married Margaret, daughter of Henry (Richard?) Brereton, of Eccleston. Elizabeth, daughter of

Sir William Brereton VII., of Brereton, married Sir John Savage, of Rock Savage, Cheshire, another ancient Cheshire family; also William, first Baron Brereton, married Margaret, daughter of Sir John Savage, of Clifton, Kent; she was the granddaughter of Thomas, first Earl of Rutland, of royal descent from Edward I. William Brereton, eldest son and heir of Sir William Brereton VII., of Brereton, married Alice, daughter and heiress of Sir Richard Corbet, of Legh, of Leghton, in the Barony of Caius, descended from Sir Roger de Corbet, one of the companions in arms of the Conqueror; their daughter, Alice, married her cousin, Peter Corbet, of Leyton. Two of the daughters of the elder line of Brereton, and one of the daughters of the younger line of Malpas, married members of the noble family of Cholmondeley, of Cheshire. From the above history it will be seen that the ancient and noble family of Brereton, during the middle centuries, was allied closely with most of the other ancient and noble families of Cheshire, and held high position at the court of the kings, and were Chamberlains and High Sheriffs and M. P.'s of Cheshire at different periods of the fourteenth, fifteenth, sixteenth and seventeenth centuries. At that time Chamberlain of the county was treasurer of the crown rents and revenues.

The High Sheriff of the counties of England is the highest officer of the county, and as representing the crown, he is superior in official county rank to any prince and nobleman living in the county during his period of office. As an illustration of this, I have a much valued testimonial presented to me by the County of Norfolk, which is signed first by the High Sheriff, secondly by the Lord Lieutenant, and thirdly by the Prince of Wales (now King Edward VII.), according to their relative county official rank.

The Tatton branch of the younger line of Malpas were especially well connected by marriage with the most ancient and noble families of Cheshire. Geoffrey Brereton married Alice, daughter of Piers Leycester, of Nether Tabley. Her father was descended from a common ancestor of the Conqueror, through Gumora, Duchess of Normandy, and Robert de Bellamont, Earl of Leicester, living 1118. Of this family of Tabley was Sir Peter Ley-

We the Principal Landowners and Ratepayers of Norfolk desire to record our hearty appreciation of the useful manner in which, during the past six years, our County Surveyor of Roads and Bridges, Mr. Robert Maitland Brereton C. E. has performed his County duties

We consider that by the Energy ability patience and tact he has displayed during this period he has fairly earned this Testimonial

We are sorry that the County is about to lose his services and we trust that this Testimonial may assist him to obtain an appointment wherever he may go.

[signature]	High Sheriff	March 7th 1885
[signature]	Lord Lieutenant	Jan 1885
Albert Edward P°	Sandringham	January 1885
[signature]	*[...]*	January 1885
[signature]	Bishop of the D.	January 1885
Kimberley	Secretary of S. for India	June 1885
Wodehouse	Witton Park	January 1885
Albemarle	Quidenham Hall	Feb – 1885
Walsingham	Merton Hall	Feby 1885
[signature]	Postwick Hill	Feb. 1885
[signature]	*[...] Park*	Feb – 85

Facsimile of Testimonial Given to R. M. Brereton by the County of Norfolk, bearing Autographs of the Sheriff, the Lord Lieutenant, and the Present King of England, Then Prince of Wales.

G

cester, the noted historian of Cheshire, living 1600. Jane Brereton, granddaughter of Sir William IX., of Brereton and sister of Sir William Brereton X., of Brereton, maried Richard Clive, of Huxley, Cheshire, and of Stycke, Shropshire; from them was descended Robert, Lord Clive, to whom England largely owes the establishment of her dominion in India. Through the marriage of her grandfather with the Rutland family, she was descended from the Lady Elizabeth Plantagenet, daughter of King Edward I. Robert, Lord Clive, was seventh in descent from Richard and Jane Clive. The present Earl of Powis is a direct descendant from them.

PROFESSIONAL CALLINGS.

During the unsettled and warring times which prevailed throughout the Middle Ages of our history, which embraced the robbing of the lands belonging to the Saxon Thanes or Earls; the crusading expeditions to the Holy Land; the civil Wars of the Roses, between the houses of York and Lancaster; the long continued war between England and France, and the final civil war during the Stuart period, warlike chivalry and tournaments were the main callings of our ancestors. Sir Walter Scott well describes their life in his "Lay of the Last Minstrel."

"They quitted not their armor bright,
Neither by day, nor yet by night;
They carved at the meal
With gloves of steel,
And they drank the red wine through the helmet barr'd."

Those horrible civil wars, in Cheshire especially, were fought out with much family bitterness and fatal sequences. The following old Cheshire ballad well exhibits this, alluding to the awful amount of family blood that was shed at the fight on Blore Heath in 1459 (time of Henry VI.). It is taken from Michael Drayton's Polyolbion, Song XXII ·

53

"There Dutton, Dutton kills; a Done doth kill a Done;
A Booth a Booth; and Leigh by Leigh is overthrown;
A Venables against a Venables doth stand,
And Troutbeck fighteth with a Troutbeck hand to hand;
There Molineux doth make a Molineux to die;
And Egerton the strength of Egerton doth try.
Oh Cheshire! wert thou mad of thine own native gore?
So much until this day thou never shedd'st before;
About two thousand men upon the earth were thrown,
Of whom the greater part were naturally thine own."

Sir Hugh Venables was killed in this fight; he was on the Lancastrian side; his brother, Richard, was on the Yorkist side. After the fight Sir Hugh's fond and devoted wife, Eglanbie, came to the field in search of him and found him dead; she clasped one arm around her warrior's neck and with the other extended in defiance, and with flashing eye, she exclaimed: "Avaunt, and leave me with my dead! Oh, thou, my love, my life, forgive me that I cannot weep for thee. The fount of tears is dry, scorched by the burning heat within my breast. No gentle drops can flow from these strained eyes, but they shall dart forth sparks of fire to light the torch of my so great revenge! Perish! Aye, perish, the flinty-hearted Neville!" (This was Richard Neville, the stout Earl of Warwick and second Earl of Salisbury).

The church embraced a few of the younger sons, and one or two are found in the field of law and literature. In A. D. 1300, we find, from the pedigree, a Gilbert de Brerton, younger son of Sir Ranulphus de Brerton, of Brereton, by his wife, Lady Ada, the Rector of Astbury. In the pedigree of the Venables family is shown a Hugh de Venables, the Rector of Astbury, Eccleston and Rostherne, in 1188. This serves as another illustration of the connection of the Venables and Brereton families in those early days of the family history, Astbury, Eccleston and Rostherne churches being clearly in the patronage of the Baron of Kinderton. In 1344, Hamo de Brerton, a grandson of Sir Randulphus de Brerton, was Rector of Brereton. This is the first record we find of Brereton having a parochial church, as previously it was a chapel attached to the Astbury Parish church. Then we find a John de Brereton (in this case the name is spelt

This is a copy of a Document found in a lumber-room in
SHAW-HOUSE,Newbury,Buckinghamshire,England.In this House
King Charles lst was beseiged by the Rebels.The Document
is a pass,signed by General Thomas Fairfax,3rd Baron,
for Mr.John Brereton of London;his servants and baggage
to pass through and out of the lines round Oxford in 1646.
It is in splendid preservation,framed and hung in the Hall.
The present owner is Mr.Eyre.

Sir Thomas Fairfax *Knight* Generall *of the* Forces *raised by the* Parliament.

SUFFER the Bearer hereof *Mr. John Brereton Cittizen of London* who was in the City and Garrison of OXFORD, at the Surrender thereof, and is to have the full benefit of the *Articles* agreed unto upon the Surrender, quietly and without let or interruption, to passe your Guards with *his* Servants, Horses, Armes, Goods, and all other necessaries, and to repaire unto *London* or elsewhere upon *his* necessary occasions. And in all Places where he shall reside, or whereto he shall remove, to be protected, from any Violence to *his* Person, Goods, or Estate, according to the said *Articles*, & to have full Liberty at any time within Six Months, to goe to any convenient Port, and to Transport selfe, with *his* Servants, Goods, and Necessaries beyond the Seas, And in all other things to enjoy the Benefit of the said *Articles*. Hereunto due Obedience is to be given, by all Persons whom it may concerne, as they will answer the contrary. *Given under my* Hand and Seale the 24th Day of *June* 1646.

all Officers and Souldiers *under my* command, *and to all others whom* *may* Concerne.

Fairfax

G

for the first time with two e's) as Rector of Wallasey, near Birkenhead, Cheshire; he was the great grandson of Sir Randulphus. Then, a little later, in the fourteenth century, there was another John de Brereton, a chaplain, probably of Brereton; he was a great great grandson of Sir Randulphus. In the beginning of the fifteenth century there was a Ralph de Brereton, Rector of Davenham, Cheshire; he was a grandson of Sir William de Brerton V., of Brereton. In 1433, Thomas de Brereton, son of Sir William de Brereton VI., of Brereton, was Rector of Brereton. In the pedigree of the younger family of Malpas, we have record of John, Thomas and Peter, all sons of Sir Randle Brereton IV., of Malpas, being in Holy Orders; the latter was a Catholic priest. Sir William Brereton IV., of the Handford branch of the Malpas family, in his will (1669), left his books to a John Brereton in Holy Orders. In the Burosham branch of the family of Malpas, there was a Thomas Brereton, a great grandson of Sir Randle de Brerton, of Ipstone, and first of Malpas, who, in 1539, was Rector of Northope, and in 1557, of Llandrinio, and in 1566, of Gresford, all in Wales. In the seventeenth century there was a John Brereton, fifth son of William, second Baron Brereton, who was Rector of Beverley, Yorkshire; from him the Bedford Breretons claim descent. In the sixteenth century Sir William Brereton IX., of Brereton, was Chief Justice of Ireland in 1516. His grandson, Sir William Brereton X., of Brereton, was also Chief Justice of Ireland and a member of the Privy Council in 1549 (Froude's History). In 1691 there was a Thomas Brereton, of the Burosham branch of the Malpas family, who was a poet and dramatist; he was drowned in the Saltney, near Liverpool, and left two daughters. Owen Salusbury Brereton, also one of the Burosham branch, was a noted antiquarian and a Fellow of the Royal Society; he died at Windsor and was buried in the royal chapel of St. George's, which was founded by King Edward IV., and completed by King Henry VIII. William, third Baron Brereton, was a literary man, a good mathematician, and one of the founders of the Royal Society. He is highly mentioned in the diaries of Samuel Pepys (1667). Perhaps the most interesting literary member of the family during the fifteenth century was

Humphrey Brereton. He was the third son of Bartholomew Brereton, of Grafton, and cousin of Sir Randle Brereton IV., of Malpas. He is mentioned in the family pedigree as Humphrey Brereton, of Malpas. He lived through the most exciting times of the Wars of the Roses, and was "the only writer among so many fighters." The courage and chivalry he displayed as the go-between agent of the Earl of Derby, the charming Princess Elizabeth of York, eldest daughter of Edward IV., and the Earl of Richmond, afterward Henry VII., were fully equal to that of his armor bearing kinsmen of that period. Miss Agnes Strickland, in her History of the Queens of England, Vol. IV., p. 9, and following, speaks of his literary accuracy in recording the incidents of that period, in the highest terms. He, no doubt, contributed to the issue of that most extraordinary popularity which both branches of the family enjoyed at court and in the County of Cheshire during the Tudor regime. He was well rewarded for his loyal services to the Princess Elizabeth, the Earl of Derby and to Henry VII., and lived and died a lusty, jolly Cheshire squire. His history is written in a metrical style, and his accuracy as to times, names, persons and situations is indirectly most singularly confirmed from various quarters and by many circumstances. It may be interesting to give some quotations and remarks which are to be found in the Archaeologia, Vol. XXXIII., p. 72 (Library of the British Museum). His history was reprinted by T. Hayward, F. R. A., and is published in the works of the Percy Society. The prominent people referred to in this history are Elizabeth, "the faire Bessye," the "Countess Clere." She was Edward IV.'s eldest and favorite daughter; she was, as Humphrey Brereton describes her, of a warm hearted and lovable nature. When her two brothers were murdered by that human fiend, Richard III., she became the indubitable heiress of the vast estates of the Earls of Clare, through her ancestress, who married Lionel, third son of Edward III.; the earldom of Clere, or Clare, was a female fief. The Lord Derby referred to was Thomas, second Lord Stanley, whose second wife was Margaret, daughter and heiress of John, Duke of Somerset, and widow of Edmund Tudor,

Earl of Richmond, and mother of Henry, Earl of Richmond, afterwards King Henry VII. It was Lord Stanley who placed the crown on Henry's head on Bosworth field, after the battle in which Richard III. was killed, August 22, 1485. He was known as "Father Stanley" in the court of Henry VII. The marriage of Henry VII., head of the house of Lancaster, with Elizabeth of York, blended the two Roses into one, and established the Tudor regime in England. Brereton's narrative shows the political plot through which this was brought about and the extremely difficult and dangerous policy which Stanley and Elizabeth pursued.

"SONG OF LADY BESSYE."

It appears that Lord Stanley at first refused to entertain the urgent prayers of the fair Bessye to get her lover, Henry of Richmond, on the English throne, but yielded at last.

"We must part lady," the Earl said then,
"But keep this matter secretly,
And this same night, at nine or ten,
In your chamber I think to be.
Look that you make all things ready.
Your maids shall not our council hear,
And I will bring no man with me,
But Humphrey Brereton, my trusty squire."

It was the winter season, and the Princess' apartment is thus described:

"Charcoals in chimnies there were cast,
Candles on sticks were burning high,
She oped the wicket and let him in,
Saying, 'Welcome, lord and knight so free!'
A rich chair was set for him,
Another for that fair lady.
They eat the spice, and drank the wine;
The lady then so fair and free,
With rudd as red as rose in May,
She kneeled down upon her knee."

Elizabeth had been taught to read and write. Stanley could not write, and so he told her she was a "proper wench." She then wrote at his dictation six dispatches to his kinsmen and followers, which he sealed with his seal. They slept that night in Elizabeth's apartments, but she watched till dawn.

> "And Bessye waked all that night,
> There came no sleep within her eye,
> Soon in the morn, at the day-spring,
> Upriseth the young Bessye,
> And maketh haste in her dressing.
> To Humphrey Brereton gone is she,
> And when she came to Humphrey's bower,
> With a small voice called she;
> Humprey answered that lady bright,
> Saying, 'Who calleth here so early?'
> I am King Edward's daughter right.
> The Countess Clere, young Bessye;
> In all haste with means and might,
> Thou must come to Lord Stanley."

The lady "fair and sweet" guided him to the bedside of his master, who gave him directions for the safe delivery of the six letters written by Bessy. These were delivered by Humphrey to Sir William, brother of Lord Stanley, at Holt Castle; to Lord Strange, at Latham House; to Edward and James Stanley, of Manchester; to their cousin, Sir John Savage; and lastly to Gilbert Talbot, "fair and free," at Sheffield Castle, who, on reading Elizabeth's missive, exclaimed characteristically ·

> When he that letter looked up
> A loud laughter laughed he,
> Fair fall that lord in his renown,
> To stir and strive beginneth he!
> Fair fall Bessye, that Countess Clere,
> That such counsel giveth truly!
> Commend me to that Countess Clear,
> King Edward's child, young Bessye;
> Tell her I trust in Jesu, who hath no peer
> To bring her her love from over the sea."

Humphrey Brereton returns to London and finds Lord Stanley walking in the garden of the palace at Westminster with King Richard III. Lord Stanley looks at his newly arrived esquire a volume of diplomacy. The king questions and *cants* about his dear people, "Our own commonalty." Humphrey is discreet and guarded. Afterwards they repair to "Bessye's bower." When Bessye Humphrey did see anon, "she took him in her arms and kissed him times three," which Miss Strickland calls "receiving him with extraordinary gratitude." It was then decided to send Humphrey to Henry, Earl of Richmond, who was then residing at the Begars Monastery, near Rennes, the ancient capital of Brittany, France. He took with him much gold, an offer of the crown and a valuable ring from the princess for her lover. He sailed from Liverpool, at that time a small port where the Stanleys controlled the shipping. He arrived safely at his destination. The porter, being a Cheshire man, knew Humphrey at sight, and refused his proffered largess of £3, but pointed out where Richmond was to be found, and described him thus:

> "With a long visage, and pale and black,
> A wart he hath, the porter said,
> A little above the chin;
> His face is white, his wart is red!"

Richmond kissed the ring, but "Humphrey of the prince answer got none." He ventured to remonstrate and warmly extolled the charms of the Ladye Bessye. Richmond, with characteristic caution, replied that he would send an answer in three weeks. Humphrey was evidently at the great Bosworth field fight, but his description of it is not luminous. He does not paint the "battlefield" with the same graphic power that he has displayed in delineating home scenes of life and manners; "non omnia possumus omnes."

Humphrey Brereton must have been well satisfied with the implicit confidence shown him by the fair Bessy and Stanley, as he quotes them thus:

> Stanley—"There is no messenger we may trust,
>   Because the matter it is so high."
>   "Humphrey Brereton," then said Bessye,
>   "Hath been true to my father and to me;
>   He shall take the writings in hand,
>   And bring them into the west countrie;

I trust him best of all this land."
Stanley to Humphrey—"My love, my trust, my life, my land,
All this, Humphrey, doth lie on thee."

Michael Drayton, the poet of the sixteenth century, in his Heroical Epistles, written in 1597, writes as follows about the Breretons: "Of the incontestable fact of. the high court favor of the Breretons under the Tudor dynasty, a remarkable instance occurs in the first volume of the state papers, where, in 1521, Wolsey, who had, on good prudential and economical grounds, planned the sending of the Knights of Kent to France on military service, was compelled to yield to the appointment of a Brereton, from Cheshire, on the nomination of the king himself. (This knight was Sir Randle Brereton IV., of Malpas, the father of John Brereton, the founder of the Norfolk branch of the family). Wolsey to King Henry VIII.: 'The knightes of Kent, being neare hand and sonest in aredinesse, were thought right meet; neverthelesse, as it shall stande with your pleasure, so I must and wol be contentyd; thinking Sir Randolph Brereton, with thothyr knightes by your Grace appointed, to be convenient in the lien and place of the knightes of Kent.'" Drayton goes on to remark: "It is very justly observed in the able introduction to the state papers that the predominant influence which Wolsey is usually supposed to have exercised over Henry VIII. is considerably overrated. From this branch of the family are descended the Breretons of Norfolk. A younger son of Sir Randle Brereton, of Malpas, was, by Alicia, his wife, father of the first Brereton of Suffolk." (This was William Brereton, of Hoxne, near Eye, Suffolk).

BRERETON FAMILY IN IRELAND.

Continuing with the record of the professional callings of the family, we find mention of Andrew Brereton, of Moyle Abbey, the founder of the elder line in Ireland, made Governor of Ulster for defeating the Scotch forces in the Irish rebellion in 1549. Captain Andrew Brereton, great grandson of Edward Brereton, of Shannenmullen, the founder of the younger line in Ireland, was highly distinguished in defending Borras Castle in 1646. Major William Brereton of the Royal Artillery, was distinguished at the battle of Culloden Moor, Scotland, in 1746, where the Royalists under the Duke of Cumberland defeated the army of Charles Edward, the Young Pretender; also at Madras, India, in 1759. Lieutenant General Robert Brereton, of New Abbey, Kildare, was Governor of St. Lucia, W. I., from 1800 to 1813, and Commandant of the Southern District of Ireland. Sir William Brereton was made a K. C. B. in 1861 for distinguished services under the Duke of Wellington at the Peninsula (Spain), Waterloo, and in China in 1848, and in the Crimea in 1854. He was the son of Major William Brereton, of Culloden fame. John Brereton, of Rathgilbert and of Ballyadams, was major in the army and High Sheriff of Queen's County in 1780. Edward Brereton, of Shannenmullen, was High Sheriff of Queen's County in 1677. (See notes to pedigree in appendix).

RECENT. TIMES.

Many of the last, present and rising generation of the Brereton family have entered the church, the educational and literary departments, the military, civil and uncovenanted services of India and of the colonies; some also the medical and civil engineering professions. In all of these, several have earned popularity and reputation. The Canada branch of the Norfolk family appears to be the only one whose members have made the medical line a family calling, and in this they have earned a high reputation in the Province of Ontario. Some descendants of the elder line of Brereton have been highly distinguished in the church and in the public schools of England. Canon John Brereton, D. C. L., descended from Rev. John Brereton, fifth son of William, second Baron Brereton, Rector of Beverley, Yorkshire; was head master of Bedford School from about 1811 to 1860. He was succeeded in that position by his second son, Canon Charles Brereton, who died in 1894. Only two of his sons are living, Herbert and William H. Brereton; the latter is a noted singer. Of the Helmingham (Suffolk) family, descended from Thomas Brereton, third son of William, second Baron Brereton, whose grandson, Thomas, was the highly valued agent of Lionel Tollemache, third Earl of Dysart, of Helmingham Hall, Suffolk, Edward William Brereton, Vicar of Kildwick, near Keighley, Yorkshire, of this branch, is one of the leading high churchmen in the county. He has given much time and patient investigation about the old family history, and is probably the best posted authority in that line in England today. Of the Blakeney branch of the Norfolk family, Robert Pearson Brereton was a well known and able civil engineer; he also spent much time and trouble in preparing the family record, but, unfortunately, died before his work in this line was matured and arranged. He was associated with the celebrated civil engineer and naval architect, Isambard Kingdom Brunel, as first assistant in all of his great achievements, which were the following: The Great Western broad gauge railway; the Great Western (in 1838); the Great Britain (in 1845); the Great Eastern (in 1858), steamships; (the latter enabled Cyrus Field, of New York, to accomplish his great enterprise of laying the first Atlantic cable); the notable large and unique bridge at Saltash, across the mouth of the River Tamar, thereby connecting the two counties of Devon and Cornwall; the waterworks of the Crystal Palace at Sydenham; and in assisting the late Lord Armstrong in the development and working of his great inventions in the hydraulic machinery line; and in the models, and experiments in designing and building the first large guns.

Of the Little Massingham branch of the Norfolk family, Joseph Lloyd Brereton, third son of Charles David, was distinguished in his Oxford career by winning the Newdegate prize for his poem on the "Battle of the Nile," the judge of which competition was the Duke of Wellington, of Waterloo fame. He was one of the Minor Canons of Exeter Cathedral; the founder of the county school system in Devon, Norfolk and Durham; also the founder of Cavendish College, Cambridge. Of the same family, Robert Maitland Brereton, sixth son of Charles David, was educated as a civil engineer in Mr. Brunel's office and on his large works. He was afterwards chief engineer of the Great Indian

Peninsula Railroad, connecting Bombay with Calcutta. For his services on the railroad during the Mutiny (1858) period he received the thanks of the Bombay government; and for his services in effecting the early completion of the connection between Bombay, Calcutta and the Northwest Provinces (in 1870) he received the special thanks of the government of India and was presented at the levee held in 1871 by the late Duke of Argyll, then Secretary of State for India, at the personal request of the Viceroy of India, the Earl of Mayo. In 1871 and during the six following years, he designed an extensive system of irrigation in the great valley of the San Joaquin, California, and was sent by the leading men of California, to Washington to get the aid of Congress and of the federal government in forwarding a general system of irrigation on the Pacific coast, which mission he successfully carried out. From 1879 to 1885 he was county surveyor for his native county, Norfolk; on his giving up this position in 1885 he received a very kind and complimentary testimonial from the ratepayers of Norfolk, which was signed by the High Sheriff, the Lord Lieutenant, the Prince of Wales, and by nearly all of the principal landowners and ratepayers in the county, and in addition the officially recorded thanks of the county authority. He was afterwards commissioner to the late Duke of Southerland, in Scotland, and had the entire management of those large estates. Alfred Brereton, second son of Charles, eldest son of Charles David, was a pupil in India of his uncle, Robert Maitland Brereton; served for many years on the government railroad system; he is now Secretary to the Government of India, in the railway department of public works, and received the distinction of the Companionship of the Star of India at the last New Year's Honors, 1904. Of the Briningham branch of the Norfolk family, Henry Cloudesley Shovell Brereton, grandson of Rev. Shovell Brereton, is a rising member of the Government Educational Department. Of the elder line of the Norfolk branch, Robert Pearson Brereton, third son of the late John Brereton V., of Brinton, is head master of the grammar school at Oundle, Northamptonshire. Cuthbert Arthur Brereton, fourth son, succeeded to his uncle, Robert Pearson Brereton's, civil engineering business in London, and is a member of the Council of the Institution of Civil Engineers. Rev. Francis Lloyd Brereton, second son of Joseph Lloyd, is head master of the Northeastern school at Barnard Castle, Durham. Rev. Philip Lloyd Brereton, fifth son of Joseph Lloyd, is a Fellow and lecturer of St. Augustine's College, Canterbury, Kent.

Frederick Sadlier Brereton, of the Rathurless branch of the family in Ireland, was army surgeon with the Scots Guards in South Africa. He is a captain of the volunteers, and a specialist in diseases of the throat; he is a well known writer of fiction stories in connection with the Zulu and Boer wars in South Africa. In the one entitled "In the King's Service," he has written about Brereton Hall and Rathurless in Ireland, in the days of Cromwell's invasion of Ireland, and the storming of the town of Drogheda, on the Boyne, in 1649; he is the fourth son of Frank Sadlier Brereton, who is an old architect and surveyor, of London.

I find another literary member of the family in the present day in Austin W. W. Brereton, of 14 York Chambers, Adelphi, London. He is a descendant of one branch of the Cheshire family, but which, at the present time, I have not been able to trace. He is a journalist and dramatic critic of the Sphere. Born in Liverpool in 1862; came to London in 1881. His last work, "The Lyceum and Henry Irving," is a valuable and interesting history of the English stage. He is the only dramatic writer and critic that I have been able to find in the family since the time of Thomas Brereton, born 1691, died 1772, son of Major Thomas Brereton, of the Queen's Dragoons, who belonged to the Burosham (Welsh) branch of the Malpas family. He was B. A. of Brasenose College, Oxford, 1712, and was drowned in the Saltney, near Liverpool, in 1722. His wife, Jane, daughter of Thomas Hughes, of Mold, Flintshire, wrote a book of poems. Phenix-like, then, Austin Brereton, as dramatist, has arisen from Liverpool, where his kinsman lived and was drowned.

I find I have omitted to mention among the professional members of the earlier times the name of Cuthbert Brereton,

Page 24.   *Tomb of Sir Randle Brereton IV.*

grandson of Rev. John Brereton, the founder of the Norfolk family. He was a famous lawyer of Norwich between 1570 and 1613, and was Sheriff of that city in 1576.

CONCLUSION.

The foregoing pages embrace the history of our ancient family stem and its several branches as far as I have been enabled to trace it out from the information at hand, and I think it will be found fairly accurate. In the appendices will be found the pedigrees of the two main stems—Brereton and Malpas—and of their respective branches, and the notes attached to each will afford some additional information about the families with which the Breretons were allied by marriage. As history has shown how nations of old have arisen, reached their zenith, and finally have been absorbed by others, so has it been with the descendants of distinguished families and individuals. The Celts, the Saxons and the Normans were each of them proud of their so-called individual blood, clan and family, though primarily they were all of one race—the Northmen of Europe. Ever evolving conditions of earthly existence, and the far-seeing designs of an overruling providence have been at work bringing about through the centuries, a reunion of the branches of primary blood, and the furtherance of the higher and nobler perception of the brotherhood of mankind, with all its possibilities for the betterment of human existence on earth. Nowhere on earth is this reunion process more clearly perceivable than it is in the United States of North America and Canada. When our kinsman, John Brereton, first visited North America in 1602, he and his few companions were the first white men the aborigines of the country had ever seen. During the three hundred years which have since passed, and which represent less than one-half of the number of years of the traced existence of our family, has arisen in the United States of North America, from the Atlantic to the Pacific coast, a nation numbering nearly eighty millions of the most progressive, the most intelligent, the most utilitarian, and of the most

65

virile characteristics that has ever appeared on earth. No other great continent on the globe was there to be found where such a nation could so well expand or find so available in the way of vast natural resources for the furtherance of its rapid growth and power. Surely we may perceive in this the design of the All Wise and All Powerful Ruler of the Universe. In a few more decades the term, "Anglo Saxon" in North America will be a misnomer. American will better express the fast mingling blood of the Celt, Saxon, Norman, Roman, Hebrew, Red Indian, Ethiopian and yellow races that is flowing on. The beautiful national flag of "The Stars and Stripes" is about the best that could be designed for such a cosmopolitan and philanthropic nation. As the Norman feudal system in the old country, with its selfish and narrow minded land tenure and power disappeared, so will the "Almighty Dollar" feudalism and unequal poverty of the present day disappear as population increases and the natural resources of the country become less in the hands of the few multi-millionaire barons, and made the most of for the greater well being of the American nation. The present greed for getting rich quickly at the expense of the loss of public and self respect, and the smothering of the innate and divine conscience of right and wrong, is only another form of old time barbarism, which in time must give way to the growing spirit of fraternity and liberty, which is the ennobling motto of the American people. The beau ideal of a republic, worthy of this twentieth century, cannot be, must not be, based upon the minimum of superlative opulence and maximum of superlative poverty. Switzerland exhibits today to Europe a people, as a whole, enjoying comfort, contentment, honesty and peace. The United States, the coming equator of the civilized human race on earth, should shine as the brightest star in Humanism.

Appendix

ANCIENT ORIGIN OF THE BRERETON FAMILY.

The family descent is claimed through Gilbert de Venables, younger brother of Stephen, Earl of Blois, in Normandy, France, who was the father of Stephen, King of England (1100), by his wife, Adela, daughter of William the Conqueror. This Gilbert is mentioned in Domesday, 1086, as the Venator, or Hunter, and Baron of Kinderton, in whose barony were thirty-six dependencies, of which Brereton, then called Bretune, formed a part.

In the Harleian Mss. is found the following list of these dependencies of the barony conferred by Hugh Lupus, first Earl Royal of Chester: Alcumlowe, Alpraham, Astbury, Blakenhall, Bradwell, Brereton, Castle Northwich, Checkley, Davenport, Doddington, Eccleston, Hartford cum Horford, High Legh, Hope (County Flint), Hunsterston, Lea, Lymme (one-half), Marston, Mere, Kinderton (Cimbretune), Moresbarrow-cum-Parme, Moreton, Over Peevor (part of), Radnor, Picmere, Somerford, Sproston, Stanthorne, Utkington, Wettenhall, and a joint share with Hamo and Ranulphus Venables of Baggiley and Sunderland. Besides the above there were Arclid, Bollington (a moiety thereof), Rostherne and Tarporley; making a total of thirty-six territorial possessions. At this period a Rafe de Brerton is found mentioned in existing old charter deeds and land grants, as one of the witnesses to the same, made by the Baron of Kinderton. Sir Richard Brerton is also mentioned in A. D. 1170. They were probably relatives and esquires in the retinue of the baron. Again, in 1156, is found a Rafe de Brerton as witness to another grant of lands in Marston, made by a grandson of the above mentioned Gilbert de Venables to his sister, Amabilia, the wife of Richard Davenport, of Davenport; he was also witness to yet another grant made by the same Venables of the rest of the lands in Marston to his brother Hugh, who was parson or Rector of Eccleston, Astbury

69

and Rostherne. The pedigree of the Brereton family begins with a Sir William de Brerton, of Brereton, who was probably the elder brother of the last mentioned Rafe de Brerton. At this period of the history (1175 A. D.) the name appears to have been spelled with only one "e." Pedigree as follows:

Sir William de Brerton I., of Brereton, 1175. Name of wife not found.

Sir William de Brerton II., second Lord of Brereton. Name of wife not found.

Sir Ralph de Brerton I., third Lord of Brereton. Name of wife not found.

Sir William de Brerton III., fourth Lord of Brereton, died in 1216. Married Margery, daughter of Sir Randle de Thornton, of Thornton, Cheshire.

Sir Ranulphus de Brerton II., fifth Lord of Brereton, living in 1272. Married Princess Ada, fourth daughter of David, Earl of Huntingdon, widow of Sir Henry de Hastings. They had two sons, William, the heir, and Gilbert, who was Rector of Astbury; he had one son, Henry, and one daughter, Sibilla, wife of William, son of Sir Adam de Booths, who had lands in Withershaw, which in the sixteenth century were owned by Robert Tatton, who married Anne Brereton, of the Ashley branch. Their canopied tomb is to be seen in Astbury church yard.

Sir William de Brerton IV., sixth Lord of Brereton, married a daughter of Sir Richard de Sonbach, of Sandbach.

Sir William de Brerton V., seventh Lord of Brereton, 1342, married Rose, daughter of Sir Ralph de Vernon, Baron of Ship brook, Cheshire.

William de Brerton, Esq., eldest son, died during his father's life.. Married Margery, daughter of Sir Richard de Bosley.

Sir William de Brerton VI., eighth Lord of Brereton, 1300, heir to his grandfather. His first wife was Ellen, daughter of Philip de Egerton, of Egerton, sister and heiress of David de Egerton, joint baron with the Cholmondeleys, of Malpas. Through her he became joint Baron of Malpas. His second wife was Margaret, daughter of Henry Done, of Utkington, widow of Sir John Davenport; by her he had Randle, the founder of the

Malpas branch; Elizabeth, wife of William Cholmondeley; and a daughter who became the wife of Spurstow, of Spurstow.

Sir William de Brerton VII., ninth Lord of Brereton, was born in 1350, died in 1426. His first wife was Anyll, daughter of Sir Hugh de Venables, Baron of Kinderton. By her he had six sons and two daughters: 1, William; 2, Nicholas; 3, Hugh; 4, Matthew; 5, John; 6, Henry; 7, Elizabeth, wife of Sir John Savage; 8, Margery, wife of Richard Putten Wanflete, of Wanflete. His second wife was Ellen, daughter of Sir William Masey, of Tatton. By her he had one son, Thomas, born in 1433; rector of Brereton; heir to his mother of the Tatton estates.

William de Brerton, eldest son, died in 1420, at Harfleur, France, during his father's lifetime. He married Alice, sister and heiress of Richard de Corbet, of Leghton, in the barony of Caius, Shropshire. By her he had two sons and two daughters: 1, William; 2, Ralph; 3, Alice, wife of Peter Corbet, of Leghton; 4, Joan, wife of Robert Aston, of Park Hall, Staffordshire.

Sir William de Brerton VIII., tenth Lord of Brereton, succeeded his grandfather; died in 1485. His first wife was Matilda, daughter of John Dutton, of Dutton, widow of Sir William Booth, of Dunham; married in 1478. By her he had six sons: 1, William, died issueless; 2, Andrew; 3, Robert; 4, Roger; 5, Henry; 6, Matthew. William married Katherine, daughter of Sir John Byron, of Horestan Castle, Derbyshire; his second brother, Sir Andrew, succeeded his father as eleventh Lord of Brereton. His second wife was a daughter of Sir Hugh Hulse, of Elwood Hall, Cheshire. By her he had two sons and four daughters: 1, Sir John Brereton, of Lea Hall, whose first wife was Katherine, daughter of Maurice Berkeley, of Beverstone, Gloucester, widow of John, Lord Stourton. By her he had one daughter, Wyburgha, heir of her mother; she married Sir William Compton, knight. His second wife was Joan, daughter and heiress of Sir Geoffrey Masey, of Hatton, widow of Sir William Stanley. By her he had one son, Philip, who died without issue; 2, Hugh of Wimbersley, second son, married Anne, daughter of Robert Done, of Utkington; 3, Elizabeth, wife of John Ratclyffe, of Ordeshall, Lancashire; 4, Jane, wife of Cotton, of Rudware;

5, Eleanor, wife of Hugh Cholmondeley; 6, Matilda, wife of Thomas Needham, of Shavington.

Sir Andrew Brerton, eleventh Lord of Brereton, 1495. He married Agnes, daughter of Robert Legh, of Adlington, ancestor of Leghs, of Adlington. By her he had four sons and six daughters. The sons were: 1, William; 2, John, of Leek, Stafford; 3, Andrew; 4, Matthew. William, the heir, succeeded. Of the younger sons there is no record. The daughters were: 1, Johanna, wife of Lawrence Dutton, of Marshe; 2, Ellen, wife of John Fitton, of Gawsworth; 3, Alice, wife of William Moreton, of Little Moreton; 4, Elizabeth, wife of Philip Legh, of Booths, afterward of John Carington; 5, Catherine, wife of Thomas Smith, of Hough; 6, Matilda, wife of John Davenport, of Davenport.

Sir William Brereton IX., twelfth Lord of Brereton, was Chief Justice and Lord High Marshal of Ireland in 1516; died in 1541, in Ireland. His first wife was Alice, daughter of Sir John Savage, of Rock Savage. By her he had one son, his heir, William, who died in 1505, in his father's lifetime; he married Anne, daughter of Sir William Booth, of Dunham. By her he had six sons and three daughters: a, William, his heir; b, Robert; c, Arthur; d, John; e, Edward, the founder of one Irish branch; married Edith, daughter of William Birche, of Birche, Lancashire; f, Andrew, founder of the other Irish branch; married Catherine, daughter of Sir Andrew Fitz-Simon, Ireland; g, Ellen, wife of John Carington; h, Jane, wife of Richard Clive, of Huxley; i, Margaret, unmarried. His second wife was Eleanor, daughter of Sir Randle Brereton III., of Malpas, widow of Sir Philip Egerton. By her he had three sons and five daughters: 1, Henry; 2, John, a Captain in Ireland; 3, Richard, the founder of the Ashley branch; 4, Margaret, wife of William Goodman, Mayor of Chester, 1554; 5, Katherine, wife of Edward Folleshurst, of Crewe, remarried to Sir Roger Brereton, of Halton, Cheshire; 6, Ellen, wife of Robert Dokenfield, of Dokenfield; 7, Anne, wife of David Kynaston, of Hanney; born in 1547; 8, Mary wife of Sir John Warburton, of Arley.

Sir William Brereton X., thirteenth Lord of Brereton, Sheriff of Cheshire, 1550-1554; died in 1559. Member of the Privy

*Choir of St. Canice's Cathedral, Limerick, Ireland, Where
Sir William Brereton, IX, Chief Justice, is Buried.*

G
9
B

Council in Ireland, 1549; recalled for quarreling with Con Bacach O'Neill, first Earl of Tyrone (Froude's History). He married Jane, eldest daughter of Sir Peter Warburton, of Arley; remarried to Sir Lawrence Smith, of Hough; died in 1561. By her he had one son, William, his heir, and five daughters: 1, Mary, unmarried; 2, Elizabeth, wife of Thomas Venables, of Kinderton; 3, Jane, wife of John Legh, of Booths; 4, Anne, wife of Sir Thomas Smith, Mayor of Chester, 1596, Sheriff of Cheshire, 1600; 5, Susannah, unmarried.

Sir William Brereton XI., fourteenth Lord of Brereton, born 1550; built Brereton Hall, 1586; created first Baron Brereton, of Leighlin, Ireland, May 11, 1624; died in 1631. He married Margaret, daughter of Sir John Savage, K. G., of Clifton, Kent, by his wife Elizabeth, daughter of Thomas, first Earl of Rutland. By her he had four sons and three daughters: 1, William, died without issue; 2, Robert, died an infant; 3, William, died at birth; 4, Sir John, died in 1629, in his father's life time; married Anne, daughter of Sir Edward Fitton, of Gaws worth; by her he had two sons and two daughters: a, John, died without issue; b, William, second Baron Brereton; c, Jane, wife of Sir Robert Holte; 4, Mary, wife of Sir Michael Hutchinson. The daughters of the first Baron Brereton were: 1, Mary, wife of Henry, Lord Fuchiquin; 2, Elizabeth, unmarried; 3, Margaret, unmarried.

The descendants of the first Baron Brereton claim royal Plantagenet descent through this marriage of Sir William Brereton XI., of Brereton Hall, with Margaret Manners, of Belvoir, Castle, as follows: Sir George Manners, twelfth Baron Ros, in 1487 married Anne, only daughter and heir of Sir Thomas St. Leger, knight, by his wife, Anne Plantagenet, sister of King Edward IV., and daughter of Richard Plantagenet, Earl of Cambridge, the son of Edmond Plantagenet, Duke of York, who was the fifth son of Edward III., the grandson of Edward, first king of the Plantagenet line. This Richard Plantagenet, Earl of Cambridge, married Lady Ann Mortimer, daughter of Roger Mortimer, fourth Earl of March, the son of Edmond Mortimer third Earl of March, who married Lady Philippa Plantagenet,

73

the only daughter of Lionel, of Antwerp, Duke of Clarence, the third son of King Edward III. Richard, Duke of York, son of Richard Plantagenet by his wife Lady Ann Mortimer, married Lady Ciceley Nevill, daughter of Ralph, first Earl of Westmorland. Sir William Brereton XI., of Brereton, married Margaret, daughter of Sir John Savage, K. G., of Rock Savage, Cheshire, and of Clifton, Kent, by his wife, Elizabeth, the fifth daughter of Sir Thomas Manners, thirteenth Baron Ros and first Earl of Rutland, who was the eldest son and heir of the above mentioned Sir George Manners, twelfth Baron Ros.

William, Baron Brereton II., fifteenth Lord of Brereton, succeeded his grandfather; born in 1611, died in 1664. He married Elizabeth, daughter of George, Lord Gorringe, Earl of Norwich. By her he had five sons and six daughters: 1, William, his heir; 2, Henry, died without issue; 3, George, died without issue; 4, Thomas, founder of Helmingham family, Suffolk; 5, John, of Beverley, Yorkshire, not in the family pedigree, ancestor of the Bedford family; 6, Margaret, wife of ———— Owen; 7, Anne, unmarried; 8, Mary, unmarried; 9, Elizabeth, unmarried; 10, Jane, unmarried.

William, Baron Brereton III., sixteenth Lord of Brereton, born in 1631, died in 1679, in London; was buried in St. Martin's, in Fields. He married Frances, daughter of ————, Lord Willoughby, of Parham. By her he had three sons: 1, John, his heir; 2, William, died without issue; 3, Francis, succeeded John.

John, Baron Brereton IV., seventeenth Lord of Brereton, died without issue, in 1718. He married Mary, daughter of Sir Thomas Tipping, of Wheatfield and Draycott, Oxfordshire.

Francis, Baron Brereton V., eighteenth Lord of Brereton died in 1722, unmarried.

Here ended the Lords of Brereton, Cheshire. "Sic transit gloria Mundi."

At the decease of Francis, fifth Baron, Brereton Hall and estates passed to the family of Holte, through the marriage of Jane Brereton, daughter of Sir John Brereton, and grand daughter of Sir William Brereton XI., of Brereton, with Sir Robert Holte, Bart., in 1646. Thence through the Holte family it passed

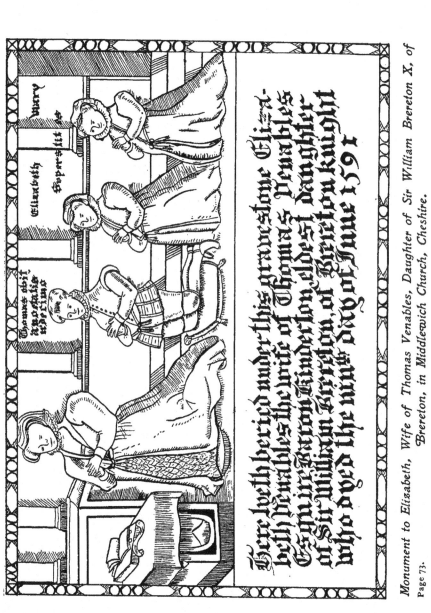

Monument to Elizabeth, Wife of Thomas Venables, Daughter of Sir William Brereton X, of Brereton, in Middlewich Church, Cheshire.

G
9
B

by marriage into the Bracebridge family, of Atherstone, Warwickshire, in 1775, and was afterwards sold by an act of parliament to satisfy the creditors of Abraham Bracebridge. For over six hundred years the Brereton family's main stem had held these estates from father to son or grandson through a succession of eighteen Lords of Brereton, and through twenty primogenital generations of the male line. Brereton Hall, with a portion only of the original manor, now belongs to a Stockport merchant family of the name of Howard. The act of parliament above mentioned, for the dismemberment of the Brereton Hall estates, was obtained in 1817. It seems strange that the peerage titles should have lapsed with the death of Francis, fifth Baron Brereton, seeing that the estates were probably entailed, and so rendered it necessary to obtain an act of parliament in order to satisfy the claims of Abraham Bracebridge's creditors, and that there were existing descendants of William, second Baron Brereton, of the male line. The Rev. E. W. Brereton, Vicar of Kildwick, Yorkshire, one of the descendants of William, second Baron Brereton, has investigated this matter to a considerable extent, and the following is his explanation: "George, second son of William, second Baron Brereton (uncle to Lord Francis), was baptized at Brereton, 26 August, 1638; from the history of Durham by the Surtees Society, George Brereton was appointed Rector of Elwick, alias Elwick Hall, in 1667, and resigned in 1672." In Foster's Alumni Oxonienses there is the following entry: "Brereton, George, S. (for son) of William; Queen's College; mat. 10 Nov., 1654; subscribed himself Baronis fil.; created M. A., 29 Nov., 1660; Fellow All Souls College; Rector of Elwick, Durham, 1668; Canon of St. David's, 1672; third son of William, Lord Brereton. He is said to have died unmarried." We pass on, therefore, to Thomas Brereton, of Brereton, third son of William, second Lord Brereton; he was baptized at Brereton, 23 June, 1639; he married A. D. 1668, Christiana (maiden name unknown); by her (who died 1710) he had one son, Thomas, and two daughters; he died May, 1709, at Brereton. Thomas, the son, was baptized at Brereton, June 4, 1671; he was appointed Domestic Steward of the estates at Helmingham Hall, Suffolk, by Lionel, second Earl of Dysart; he married July 1, 1709, Margaret Newdegate, at Helmingham. It is plainly evident from the foregoing that on the death of Francis, fifth Lord Brereton, A. D., 1722, the title of Baron of Leighlin, together with the Brereton estates, should have descended to his cousin, Thomas Brereton, of Helmingham, the only son of his uncle Thomas, the fourth son of the second Lord Brereton, and, therefore, heir. But on the death of Lord Francis, it is said that Lady Elizabeth Brereton, the last surviving daughter of the second Lord Brereton, occupied Brereton Hall, and held it against her fifth brother, John Brereton, Rector of Beverley, who claimed the property as son of the second Lord. The Rev. John Brereton, whose omission by Ormerod from the family pedigree is said to have been due to the Holte influence, was brought up as a son of Captain John Brereton, of Nantwich, his uncle, and is said to have agreed to that parentage on condition of being presented to the living of Beverley, A. D. 1672, as there seemed but a remote chance, at that time, of his succession. When, therefore, he advanced his claims, he is said to have been confronted by Lady Elizabeth with the affidavit which he had himself made as to his parentage. He was a decided Puritan, and hence an object of abhorrence to Lady Elizabeth, who, like her mother, favored the Roman Catholic religion, and who is also said to have left all her property to the Holtes, who were all known Catholics, and to have destroyed all the documents at Brereton which could possibly lead to a Brereton succession. As the Rev. John Brereton failed to establish his claim, and Thomas Brereton, of Helmingham, for some reason as yet unexplained, did not seem aware of his right of succession, or at least made no claim, the peerage was allowed to fall into abeyance, and the Brereton Hall estates passed to the Holtes, of Aston, in Warwickshire, in right of Jane (Brereton), wife of Sir Robert (John?) Holte, second daughter of Sir John Brereton, Baronet, and therefore great aunt of Lord Francis. Jane died in 1648. It is said that William, third Lord Brereton, left by will the Brereton estates to the descendants of his aunt Jane, if his two sons, John and Francis, died issueless. This will has not yet been found, but the provision seems strange, and even illegal, thus to exclude both his brother, Thomas, and also his nephew, Thomas Brereton, of Helmingham, if it was entailed property. Thomas Brereton died at Helmingham Hall, and was buried in the Dysart family vault, December 8, 1733. The leaden coffin is still visible through the iron grating from the church yard. His age was sixty-two years. His second wife was Mary, daughter of ———— Bulmer; she survived him and was buried at Brereton in 1742. Concerning Thomas Brereton's (of Helmingham) eldest son and heir, Thomas, no trace has as yet been found, nor of the younger children; but Joseph Brereton, the second son of Thomas Brereton, the Steward at Helmingham, became Vicar of Acton, Cheshire, on the presentation of Lionel, Earl of Dysart, the Patron, in 1745; he died in 1787, leaving a son, Thomas William, then ten years old. This Thomas William Brereton was educated at Rugby school, from whence he went to Merton college, Oxford. He became Vicar of Framsden (Suffolk) in 1812, and died in 1858, leaving three sons, Edward William, Esq., of Ipswich; Rev. Thomas Joseph, Vicar of Wyvesdale, Lancashire; Rev. Arthur Henry, late Vicar of Mendham (Suffolk). Thomas Joseph Brereton, Vicar of Wyvesdale, left two sons, Rev. Arthur Thomas, of St. Luke's, Dukinfield, Cheshire, and Rev. Edward William Brereton, present Vicar of Kildwick, Yorkshire, who has kindly furnished me with much information for this history.

From the foregoing history, and from the family pedigrees given by Ormerod, it would appear that William, second Baron Brereton, had only one brother, John Brereton, of Nantwich, born in 1624, died in 1656, age thirty-two years. There is no mention in the pedigree of his marriage. William, second Baron, had eleven children, six sons and five daughters: 1, William, third Baron Brereton; 2, Henry, who died in 1657, issueless; 3, George, who died in 1672, issueless; 4, Thomas, born, in 1639, married in 1668, died in 1709; 5, John, alleged son of Captain John Brereton, of Nantwich, Rector of Beverley 1672, and who is omitted from the family pedigree; 6, Charles, who married Theodosia, widow of Sir Thomas Brereton, of Handford. Daughters·7, Margaret, married an Owen; 8, Anne, unmarried; buried at

Nantwich in 1718; 9, Mary, unmarried; buried at Nantwich in 1716; 10, Elizabeth, unmarried; buried at Brereton in 1723; 11, Jane, unmarried; buried at Nantwich in 1712. Thus we have three of the unmarried daughters living and dying at Nantwich, after their father's death in 1664, and after their uncle John Brereton's death in 1656, which would indicate that there existed a family homestead in Nantwich. Helmingham, Suffolk, seems to have been the original home of the present descendants of Thomas, the fourth son of William, second Lord Brereton; and Beverley Rectory, Yorkshire, of those of John, fifth and youngest son of the same Lord. The Bedford Brereton family, so far as I know, are the only living male line of John, the fifth son, and there are only two of them: 1, Herbert James, born in 1854, India Civil Service; married Eleanor Boddam; has two girls; 2, William Henry, born in 1858, married Sarah Ambler in 1883; has two girls; he is a celebrated singer in London.

PRINCESS ADA'S CELTIC BLOOD DESCENT.

Kenneth I., Celtic King of Scotland, A. D. 850; Donald, Celtic King of Scotland, A. D. 889; Malcolm I., Celtic King of Scotland, A. D. 942; Kenneth II., Celtic King of Scotland, A. D. 971 · Malcolm II., Celtic King of Scotland, A. D. 1005; Duncan I Celtic King of Scotland, A. D. 1034; Malcolm III., Celtic King of Scotland, A. D. 1058; (Canmore).

CELTIC AND SAXON BLOOD.

Malcolm III. married Margaret, grand daughter of Edmund Ironsides, Saxon King of England; their sixth son, David I., was King of Scotland, 1124-1153.

78

SAXON BLOOD.

Egbert I., Saxon King of all England, A. D. 827; Alfred the Great, King of all England, A. D. 871; Edmund Ironsides, King of all England, A. D. 1016; Margaret, grand daughter, married Malcolm III. in 1070. She was sister to Edgar Atheling, the last heir to the Saxon Crown.

NORMAN BLOOD.

David I., King of Scotland, married Matilda, or Maud, daughter and heiress of Waltheof, Earl of Northumberland, Huntingdon, by his wife Judith, niece of William the Conqueror. David I. had only one son, Prince Henry, of Scotland, who married in 1139 Ada, daughter of William de Warrenne, of Normandy, second Earl of Surrey. Their third son, David, Earl of Huntingdon, married Maud, daughter of Hugh Kevelioc, fifth Earl Royal of Chester, who was descended from Margaret, the sister of William the Conqueror, and the mother of Hugh Lupus, first Earl Royal of Chester, and Palatine of Cheshire. Maud, the wife of David, Earl of Huntingdon, was the sister and heiress of Randulph de Blundevill, sixth Earl Royal of Chester. Princess Ada was the fourth daughter of David, Earl of Huntingdon. She married first Sir Henry de Hastings, by whom she had issue; secondly Sir Ranulphus de Brerton, fifth Lord of Brereton, by whom, also, she had issue, Sir William de Brerton IV., sixth Lord of Brereton, who thus, through his father and mother, inherited the Norman blood, and, also, through his mother, the royal Celtic, Saxon and Norman blood, if this royal descent claim has any real foundation.

Hugh Lupus, first Earl Royal of Chester, was called Lupus, or the Wolf, because of his ferocity displayed in the war with the Welsh. He took the estates in Cheshire which belonged formerly to Leofric and Neubold, the Saxon Earls of Cheshire. Richard, second Earl Royal of Chester, married Matilda, daughter of Stephen, Earl of Blois, by Adela, daughter of William the Conqueror and sister of Stephen, King of England. She was a niece of Gilbert de Venables, Baron of Kinderton, from whom the Brereton family claim their original descent. Princess Ada's first husband, Sir Henry de Hastings, derived his descent from a family who took their surname from the seaport of Hastings, in Sussex, through Robert de Hastings, Lord of Fillongley, Warwickshire, who was Steward to William the Conqueror; his grandson was Sir Henry de Hastings, afterwards Baron Hastings. From them are descended the present Earl of Huntingdon, of Ireland.

DOUBTFUL POINTS ABOUT LADY ADA'S SECOND MARRIAGE.

1. In the inscription placed in Brereton church in 1618 by Sir William Brereton, afterwards Baron Brereton, it is stated that his ancestors were buried in the church yard of Astbury, where their tombs still existed, but that after the Chapel of Brereton had been made parochial his ancestors had been buried in the chancel of Brereton Church. If Brereton was made parochial in the time of Richard I., 1189-1199, the Sir Radulphus Brereton canopied tomb could not then have existed, as the pedigree given by Ormerod states he was living in 1275.

2. In Nicolas' Synopsis of the Peerage it is stated that Henry, Baron Hastings, Lady Ada's first husband, died in 1268, and that John Hastings, his son, who was one of the claimants for the crown of Scotland, claimed it in right of his mother. Nicolas makes out in the pedigree that his mother's name was Joane, the sister and heiress of George de Cantelupe, Baron of Bergavenny, and that this same John Hastings was summoned to Parliament in 1295, in right of his mother Joane.

3. In Erdeswick's Survey of Staffordshire, published in 1603, there is the following· "In Henry II.'s time, one Robert de Handsacre was Lord of Handsacre, and in Henry III.'s time, 1215-1272, Sir William de Handsacre had to wife, Ada, widow of Henry, Lord Hastings, and daughter and heiress of David,

Earl of Huntingdon (brother of William, King of Scotland), by Maud, *his wife's eldest sister* and one of the heirs of Ranulph, Earl of Chester, and by her he had issue, Sir William Hands acre."

4. Nicolas, in his Synopsis, Vol. I., p. 339, states that David, Earl of Huntingdon, died in 1219; and if Henry, Baron Hastings, died in 1268, Lady Ada must have been at that time nearly fifty years old, if she was born only a short time before her father died. It seems almost impossible of belief that she, at that age, could have married both Sir William Handsacre and Sir Radulphus Brereton, *and have had issue by both.* There is no record of when or where she died.

EXTRACTS FROM ORMEROD'S HISTORY.

(Vol. III., p. 34.)

The Brereton inscription is correct in the marriage it mentions, because such a marriage appears in several pedigrees.

The honesty of the Brereton is not to be called in question as some have assumed.

The Heralds would have interfered if the Breretons had possessed no title to set up the inscription. (In the tomb at Astbury).

The claim was seemingly substantiated by King James I. in giving the patent to Sir William Brereton XI., of Brereton, as follows: "We, considering with mature deliberation, the free and true services of Sir William Brereton, and that he is sprung from an ancient, noble and most renowned family, inasmuch as he is descended from many illustrious ancestors from Ada, sister to John, surnamed Scot, seventh Earl of Chester, and daughter of David, Earl of Angus and Huntingdon, Lord of Galloway, within our kingdom of Scotland, etc." Sir William Brereton XI., of Brereton, made Baron Brereton of Leighlin, also had royal blood descent through his grandmother, wife of Sir William Brereton IX., of Brereton, who was daughter of the Earl of

Rutland, who was lineally descended from Edward I., King of England. The earliest Breretons, of Brereton, claimed royal descent in, 1, Normandy; 2, Scotland; 3, England; i. e., from the Conqueror's family per the House of Blois; Lady Ada, Princess of the Royal Scotch family; Edward I., of the Plantagenet line, or House of Anjou. Of the first claim there has been no question raised. Very old family traditions maintained this royal descent from Lady Ada, and no doubt Sir William Brereton XI., of Brereton, followed them, especially as the canopied tomb in Astbury is proved to have been in existence before his time, as, also, the inscription over the tomb.. The (3) claim to royal descent on the maternal side from the Plantagenet line holds good.

THE IRISH. BRANCH. OF THE ELDER LINE OF BRERETON HALL.

This branch of the family has been a highly distinguished one in Ireland and in the English army. The first in Ireland of the elder line of Brereton was Sir William Brereton IX., of Brereton, who, in A. D. 1516, was Chief Justice of Ireland, and also Lord High Marshal till his death in 1541. His second son, John, was a Captain in Ireland, and his eldest son, William, who died in his father's lifetime, was the father of two younger sons who were the founders of the two Irish families, viz.: Andrew, second son, the founder of the Carrigslaney family in County Carlow; Edward, sixth son, the founder of the Shannenmullen family in Queen's County. These two families became united by marriage at a later date, and were known as the Breretons, of Carrigslaney. The existing family of Rathurless in County Tipperary, is descended from Andrew Brereton, of Moyle Abbey.

Andrew Brereton, second son of William Brereton, Esq., of Brereton, lived at Moyle Abbey, County Kildare. He was made Governor of Ulster for defeating the Scotch forces in the Irish rebellion in 1549. He married Catherine, daughter of Sir Andrew (James) Fitz-Simon, Knight, of Dublin, in 1617. By her he had two sons and five daughters: 1, William, his heir; 2, John; 3, Mary, married Sir Nicolas White, Master of the

Ruins of Manooth Castle, Ireland.

Page 82.

Rolls; their daughter married Sir W. Walpole, of the Orford family; 4, Jane, married Nugent, son of Lord Trimleston, County Meath; 5, Ciceley, married John Cusock; 6, Alicia, married John Carfa, of Trubly; 7, Eleanor, unmarried. There is no record of the second son, John.

William Brereton, eldest son of Andrew Brereton, married Duncea Pelham, grand daughter of Sir Edward, Viscount Chichester, and Baron, in 1612. By her he had two sons: 1, Henry; 2, William, who married Jane, daughter of Edward Blount, of Bolton, sister of his brother Henry's wife. By her he had four sons: a, Robert, of Rathurless, County Tipperary; b, Blount; c, George; d, William.

Henry Brereton, eldest son, of Moyle Abbey, County Kildare, died in 1670. He was one of the Commissioners appointed to inquire into the cruelties against Protestants in Ireland in 1661. He married Mary, daughter and co-heir of Edward Blount, of Bolton. By her he had three sons and one daughter (Ellen) · 1, William; 2, Edward; 3, George. There is no record of the last two, or of Ellen.

William Brereton, eldest son, of Moyle Abbey, and of Brittas. County Carlow, and of Carrigslaney, which was bought of the Earl of Arran in 1676, died in 1692. He married Jane, daughter of George Webbe, of Harristown, and co-heir of General Webbe. By her he had three sons and three daughters: 1, George, his heir; 2, William, of Castle Grace; 3, Gilbert; 4, Eleanor, who married Bowen Brereton, of Loughteage and Raheenduffe, County Queen, descendant from Edward Brereton, the founder of the Shannenmullen family; 5, Elizabeth; 6, Catherine; both unmarried.

George Brereton, eldest son of Carrigslaney, died in 1720. He married Catherine, daughter of George Percival, Esq., of Templemore, County Sligo, of the Egmont family (the first Earl of Egmont, in 1732 obtained a charter for colonizing the province of Georgia, North America). By her he had two sons and three daughters: 1, William, his heir; 2, Robert, Rector of Burton, who married Elizabeth, daughter of the Dean of Downe, sister of the Bishop of Limerick; 3, Jane, who married ——— Bickersteth, Esq.; 4, Rose; 5, Mary; both unmarried.

William Brereton, eldest son, of Carrigslaney, died in 1777. He married Alicia, daughter of ——— Noecott, Esq., widow of ——— Maunsell, Esq. By her he had four sons and two daughters: 1, George, his heir; 2, William (or Robert), of Bath, Major in the Royal Artillery; served at Culloden in 1745; at Madras in 1759; he married Marion, daughter of ——— Edmonston, Esq., of Scotland. By her he had one son and two daughters: a, Robert, of New Abbey, Lieutenant General, Governor of St. Lucia, Commandant of Southern District of Ireland; died in 1818. By his second wife, name unknown, William had one son, Sir William Brereton, unmarried; born 1789, died in 1864. He was distinguished at Matagorda; Waterloo; Peninsula (Spain); China in 1843; Crimea in 1854; made K. C. B. in 1861; 3, Percival, third son, died in Germany, age twenty-two; married Mary, daughter of General Lee, of Yorkshire; by her he had one son, Colonel William Brereton, of Chichester, died in 1830; he married Mary, daughter of Judge Lill, Court of Common Pleas, and sister of Sarah, wife of first Earl of Castle Stewart. By her he had three sons and two daughters, who all died issueless; Godfrey, third son, was Commander in the Royal Navy, High Sheriff for Sligo in 1874; living 1877; 4, Robert, fourth son of William Brereton, of Carrigslaney, was Captain in the army and served in W. I. and Cape of Good Hope; was married three times; had issue only by his third wife, Anne, daughter of Major Smith; by her he had three daughters: a, Alicia, who married Sir Fortunatus Dwarris, distinguished writer and antiquary, who wrote a paper on the Brereton family of Cheshire (1811); they had five chil dren; b, Anne, unmarried; c, Caroline, who married F. Todd, Esq.; they had eight children. The daughters of William Brereton, of Carrigslaney, were: 1, Mary, who married J. Bailey, Esq.; 2, Rose, who married Rev. J. Naylor. There is no record of their families.

George Brereton, eldest son of William Brereton, of Carrigslaney, married Alicia Fremains, of Cork. By her he had only one child, George, who married his cousin.

Page 86.

Ruins of Borris Castle, Taken by Captain Arthur Brereton.

George Brereton, only son of George Brereton, of Carrigslaney, married Janetta, daughter of Major William (Robert) Brereton, of Bath. By this marriage he had four daughters, but no son, so that at his death the direct male line was extinct. The pedigree follows the line of the second son, Major William Brereton, of Bath, through his eldest son, Lieutenant General Robert Brereton, of New Abbey, County Kildare. He married Mary, daughter of John Dexter, Esq., of Armfield, County Kildare. By her he had one son and three daughters: 1, William Robert; 2, Julia, unmarried; 3, Anna, who married Major J. Kennon, had issue; 4, Mary, who married Le Batt, Esq., had issue.

William Robert Brereton, of New Abbey, born 1816, was living in 1877; Major of 70th Regiment; Adjutant of Brecon Militia. He married Edith, only daughter of Paul Barry, Esq. By her he had two sons and two daughters: 1, William, his heir; 2, Robert, Captain in 46th Regiment; Adjutant of Brecon Militia; he married Josephine Lynch, by whom he had one daughter; 3, Catherine, unmarried; 4, Anne, who married ——— Bourne, Esq., of London.

William, eldest son. died in 1886; Captain in 89th Regiment. Married Maria Elliott, of Holyhead. By her he had two sons: 1, William, the heir, and representative of the elder branch of the Brereton family in Ireland; 2, Robert, born in 1878.

The following pedigree of the younger branch of the Brereton family in Ireland, which descended from Edward Brereton, of Shannenmullen, Queen's County, who was the sixth son of William Brereton, Esq., of Brereton, Cheshire, is taken from Burke's Landed Gentry (1868) and only carries it down to Arthur Brereton, eldest son of William Westropp Brereton, Q. C., of Carrigslaney. Arthur sold Carrigslaney and went to Chicago, U. S. A., where he died. It should be observed that Bowen Brereton, of the younger line, who was of Loughtiage, married Eleanor, the eldest daughter of William Brereton (1692), of Moyle Abbey and of Carrigslaney. There are to be found several descendants of the Irish branches of the family in the United States, but it is very difficult to trace them out.

YOUNGER BRANCH OF THE BRERETON LINE IN IRELAND

Edward Brereton, of Brereton, sixth son of William Brereton, Esq., and younger brother of Andrew Brereton, the founder of the Carrigslaney family, obtained grants of land in Queen's County, Ireland, from Queen Elizabeth, February 28, 1594.

Edward Brereton, sixth son, of Shannenmullen, married Edith, daughter of William Bryche, of Bryche, Lancashire. By her he had one son and one daughter: 1, Henry; 2, Jane, who married Alexander Barrington, of Tymage, Queen's County.

Henry Brereton, of Shannenmullen and Loughtiage, Queen's County, died in 1627. He married Margery, daughter of Robert Bowen, of Ballyadams, Queen's County. By her he had six sons and three daughters: 1, Edward, the heir; 2, Robert, Captain in the army; he had two sons, who died unmarried, and four daughters; of these there is no record; 3, Andrew, of Philipstown, who defended Borris Castle in 1642; 4, William, of Derry; no record of issue; 5, Roger, no record; 6, Francis, of Killumney, died in 1688; had one son, William, of Killumney, and one daughter, wife of Richard Cosby. There is no record of the daughters.

Edward Brereton, eldest son, of Shannenmullen and Loughtiage, was born in 1602, died in 1690; was High Sheriff of Queen's County in 1677. Married Helena, daughter and co-heiress of William Bowen, of Ballyadams. By her he had four sons and one daughter (Bridget, wife of Thomas Piggot): 1, John, the heir, forfeited his property in 1688; 2, Bowen, of Raheenduffe and Loughtiage, Queen's County; married Eleanor, daughter of William Brereton, of Carrigslaney, Carlow County. By her he had two sons and one daughter: a, Edward, the heir of Loughtiage and Rathgilbert, who died without issue; b, second son, not mentioned; c, Catherine, wife of John D'Alton Harwood; 3, Robert, died in 1748, unmarried; 4, Arthur, with whom this pedigree follows.

Arthur Brereton, fourth son, of Raheenduffe, Queen's County, died in 1761. He married Margery, daughter of ———— Lawless, Esq. By her he had one son and three daughters: 1, John, the heir; 2, Jane; 3, Catherine; 4, Helen. Of these there is no record.

John Brereton, of Rathgilbert and Ballyadams, was a Major in the army and High Sheriff of Queen's County in 1780; he succeeded as representative of the ancient family of Bowen. He died at the age of ninety-four. His first wife was Anne, daughter of Pryce Peacock. By her he had two daughters: 1, Anne, wife of Robert Perceval, M. D.; had issue; 2, Jane, wife of Captain William Perceval, of the 104th Regiment, brother of Robert Perceval (Earl of Egmont family); had issue. His second wife was Anne, daughter of Henry Hickman, of Kilmore, County Clare. By her he had two sons and four daughters: 1, Arthur the heir; 2, Henry, Captain in the 4th Dragoons, died issueless; 3, Frances, unmarried; 4, Helen, wife of Richard Adlum, had issue; 5, Letitia, wife of Rev. Thomas Dooley, no issue; 6, Catherine, wife of ———— Moore, Esq., no issue.

Arthur Brereton, of Ballyadams, eldest son, born in 1766, died in 1836. Was Captain in the 71st Regiment. The pedigree proceeds with his fourth son, William Westropp, who married Eliza, daughter of Ralph Westropp, Esq. By her he had four sons and one daughter: 1, Ralph; 2, Henry Hickman, Chaplain in India, married, had issue, F. G. Brereton; 3, George Stamer, had issue, John Hatton Brereton; 4, William Westropp; 5, Mary, wife of her cousin, William F. Perceval, Esq.

William Westropp Brereton, Q. C., of Carrigslaney (which he had owned by the bequest of the last owner of that line) and of Fitzwilliam Square, Dublin; called to the bar in 1836; died 1869. His wife was Geraldine, daughter and co-heiress of Robert Kean, of Hermitage, County Clare. By her he had five sons and five daughters: 1, Arthur, the heir; 2, Robert Kean, Captain in the 81st Regiment; 3, William Westropp; 4, John Westropp: 5, Edward Fitzgerald; 6, Mary Geraldine; 7, Elizabeth; 8, Anne; 9, Adela; 10, Julia Rebecca.

Arthur Brereton, eldest son, was born in 1839. He sold Carrigslaney and went to Chicago, U. S. A., and died there. He married Georgina, daughter of Rev. Edward Woodhouse, of Bognor, Sussex; had no issue.

The representative of the elder branch of the Brereton family in Ireland is William, son of Captain William Brereton, of the 89th Regiment, and grandson of Major William Robert Brereton, of New Abbey, County Kildare. He was in the 70th Regiment, and living in 1877.

BRERETONS OF RATHURLESS NONEGH, TIPPERARY.

Andrew Brereton, second son of William Brereton, Esq., of Brereton, Governor of Ulster in 1549. He married Catherine, daughter of Sir Andrew, or James, Fitz-Simon, Knight, of Dublin. By her he had two sons and five daughters: 1, William, his heir; 2, John. He died in 1617.

William Brereton, eldest son, of Moyle Abbey, County Kildare, married Duncea, daughter of the family of Chichester, Earl of Donegal. granddaughter of Sir Edward, Viscount Chichester, Baron of Exchequer. By her he had two sons: 1, Henry, his heir; 2, William, from whom this pedigree flows.

William Brereton, second son (1660), married Jane, daughter and co-heir of Edward Blount, of Bolton. By her he had four sons: 1, Robert, his heir; 2, Blount; 3, George; 4, William. One of these, first name not known, was Major in the army at the battle of the Boyne, in 1690, and later was killed in a duel. The pedigree follows Thomas Brereton, son of one of these.

Thomas Brereton, of Rathurless Nonegh, County Tipperary. married Mary Carrall, of Bally Crinoed, who from an inscription on a tomb, was born in 1693. By her he had, inter alios, his heir, John Brereton, of Rathurless.

John Brereton, of Rathurless, was born in 1729, and married ———, daughter of George Watson of Garra. By her he had one son, Thomas Brereton, his heir.

88

Thomas Brereton, of Rathurless, eldest son, was born in 1785 and died in 1860. He married Maria Sadlier, who was descended from Sir Ralph Sadlier, a famous diplomatist and soldier and guardian of Queen Mary during the reign of Henry VIII. She was the second daughter of Thomas Sadlier, of Castletown, County Tipperary, by his first wife, Margaret, daughter of J. Watson, of Brook Watson, Tipperary; her father was ninth in descent from Sir Ralph Sadlier, of Stanton, through his second son, Edward Sadlier, of Temple Dinsley, Hertfordshire. By her he had three sons and one daughter: 1, Thomas, his heir; 2, John, Lieutenant Colonel; Paymaster Northern Division of Ireland, at Belfast; he married Margaret, daughter of Edwin Sadlier, his cousin; has one son, John, and one daughter, Maria; 3, Frank Sadlier, born in 1838, living in 1904; formerly in 60th Rifles; architect in London; married Izabella, daughter of F. R. Beeston, of an old Cheshire family; by her he has four sons and one daughter: a, Thomas Bloomfield Sadlier, born in 1866; has two children; b, Frank Sadlier, born in 1867; married; no children; settled in U. S. A.; c, John Sadlier, born in 1870; married; has one child; settled in U. S. A.; d, Fred Sadlier, formerly Army Surgeon in Scots Guards, Captain in Volunteers, now a specialist in throat diseases and writer of war scenes in South Africa; born in 1872; has one son, Allen Sadlier, born in 1899, and one daughter, born in 1900; e, Isabella, born in 1868, died in 1880, unmarried. The only daughter, Margaretta, was born in 1843, and died in 1898; she married Major General Ernest Berger, 10th Regiment, retired. By her he has four sons and two daughters; Ernest, eldest son, is in the Bombay Staff Corps; Thomas, second son, is in London.

Thomas Brereton, eldest son, of Rathurless and Shanbally; Colonel in the army, retired; living, March, 1904. He married Frances Gertrude, second daughter of Edward Townly Hardman, of New Bliss, Monaghan. By her he has issue, of whom I have no information.

John Brereton, second son, Lieutenant Colonel in the army, retired, living in 1904. His daughter, Maria, married a Captain in the Sherwood Foresters.

THE ASHLEY BRANCH OF THE BRERETON FAMILY.

The founder of this branch was Richard Brereton, Esq., the third son of Sir William Brereton IX., of Brereton, by his second wife, Eleanor, daughter of Sir Randle Brereton III., of Malpas, and widow of Sir Philip Egerton, of Egerton. Richard Brereton married Thomasine, daughter and heiress of Sir George Ashley, of Ashley, Cheshire, in 1530.

Richard Brereton I., of Ashley, married Thomasine, daughter of George Ashley.

George Brereton II., of Ashley, the heir, died in 1587. He married Sibilla, daughter and heiress of William Arderne, of Timperley, Cheshire. Both are buried in Bowden Church.

William Brereton III., of Ashley (died in 1630), was High Sheriff of Cheshire. In 1589 he married Jane, third daughter and co-heiress of Sir Peter Warburton, of Arley, Cheshire. Their tomb and monument still exist in Bowden Church. They had four sons and four daughters: 1, Richard, his heir; 2, Thomas; 3, William, unmarried; 4, Peter, unmarried; 5, Frances, wife of Alexander Barlow, of Barlow, Lancashire; 6, Mary, unmarried; 7, Anne, wife of Robert Tatton, of Withershaw, Cheshire, in 1628; Katherine, wife of Raufe Ashton (in modern times spelled Assheton), of Kirkley, Yorkshire, second son of Sir Richard Ashton, of Middleton, Lancashire. Richard Brereton, the heir, never married; he left an illegitimate son, who was living in Chester in 1653. He was High Sheriff of Cheshire in 1632, and died in 1649, aged fifty-nine. Thomas succeeded.

Thomas Brereton IV., of Ashley, in descent, was born in 1594, died in 1660. He was the last of the male line. He married Theodosia, daughter of Sir Thomas Tyrrell, of Castlethorp, Buckinghamshire. By her he had no issue.

He built the domestic chapel at Ashley, and a fair dining room there. He left the whole of his estates to be equally shared by his three married sisters and their heirs. Thus, in these later days, it cometh about that the direct male line descendant of his sister Katharine Ashton, of Assheton, Thomas Assheton, of Ashley Hall, became the owner of the old Cheshire home. He assumed the surname and arms of Smith at the death of his uncle, Captain William Smith, son of the Right Honorable John Smith, Speaker of the House of Commons in the first two parliaments of Queen Anne, and who was also Chancellor of the Exchequer in the reign of William and Mary. This Thomas Assheton Smith was the owner of Tedworth, Hampshire; his daughter, Mary, in 1847, married Robert George Duff, fourth son of Garden Duff, of Hatton, Aberdeenshire, who was descended from Alexander Duff, of Hatton, son of Patrick Duff, of Craigstone, and brother of William Duff, of Braco, the father of William, first Earl of Fife. The widow of Thomas Assheton Smith left her husband's estate of Vaynol, near Bangor, Wales, to his daughter's (Mary) descendant George William Duff Assheton Smith, of Vaynol. It is also to be noticed that the descendant of a daughter of this Ashley branch, viz.: Anne, third daughter of William Brereton III., of Ashley, who married Robert Tatton, of Withershaw, became the owner of the Brereton estates of Tatton by his marriage with Hester Egerton. (See Tatton branch of the Malpas family). Also it is to be noted that the family blood of the old family stem became reunited through the marriage of Sir William Brereton IX., of Brereton, with the daughter of Sir Randle Brereton III., of Malpas, the parents of Richard Brereton I., of Ashley.

THE HELMINGHAM (SUFFOLK) BRANCH OF THE FAMILY.

William, second Baron Brereton, of Leighlin, County Carlow, Ireland, twelfth Sir William Brereton, Knight, and fifteenth Lord of Brereton, married Elizabeth, daughter of George, Lord Goringe, Earl of Norwich. By her he had twelve children, six sons and six daughters: 1, William, his heir, second Baron Brereton, born in 1631; 2, George, born in 1638, died in 1672, without issue; 3, Thomas, born in 1639, died in 1709; 4, John, born in 1645, Rector of Beverley; 5, Henry, 1656, died in infancy; 6, Charles, married Theodosia, widow of Sir Thomas Brereton, of Handford, died without issue; 7, Margaret, wife of ———

Owen, Esq., Oxon; 8, Anne; 9, Mary; 10, Elizabeth; 11, Jane; 12, Frances; the last five died unmarried. In the family pedigree given by Ormerod, the fourth and sixth sons are not entered.

Thomas Brereton, third son of Baron Brereton II., married Christiana, daughter of ———; by her he had one son.

Thomas Brereton was born in 1671 and died in 1733. He was Steward to Lionel, second Earl Dysart, Helmingham Hall, Suffolk; he was buried in the Helmingham Hall family vault. His descent proceeds through his second son, Joseph Brereton, who was born in 1719, died in 1787 at Holford Hall and was buried at Lower Peevor, Cheshire; he was L.L. D. of Cambridge, and Vicar of Acton, Cheshire.

The first wife of Thomas Brereton was Margaret, daughter of ——— Newdegate. By her he had one child, Mary. His second wife was Mary, sister to Isaac Bulmer, of Helmingham, Suffolk. By her he had four sons: 1, Thomas; 2, Joseph, who succeeded; 3, Lionel; 4, Isaac; daughters were Caroline and Hester. Joseph's first wife was Alethea. By her he had one son and two daughters: a, Joseph, born in 1751, died in 1783; b, Alethea, died in infancy; c, Alethea, unmarried; Joseph died without issue. By his second wife, name not given in pedigree, he had one son and four daughters: a, Thomas William, born in 1776, died in 1858; b, Katherine, wife of ——— Ling, of Altringham; c, Nancy; d, Lucy Green; e, Mary.

Thomas William Brereton, Vicar of Framsden, Suffolk, married Mary, daughter of Peter Waylett. By her he had three sons and one daughter: 1, Edward William, born in 1806; 2, Thomas Joseph, born in 1815; 3, Arthur Henry, born in 1818; 4, Emily, died unmarried.

Edward William Brereton, eldest son, first married Maria, daughter of James Studd. By her he had three sons and two daughters. 1, William, born in 1837; 2, Thomas William, born in 1844; 3, Henry Arthur, born in 1845, died in 1890; 4, Emily Maria, wife of David Alexander, of Kettleburgh, Suffolk; had issue; 5, Martha, wife of Francis Carr, of Framsham, Suffolk. His second wife was Anne Palmer, of Helmingham. By her he had four sons and seven daughters: 1, William, died without

Page 93. *Edward William Brereton and Family.*

issue; 2, Edward Arthur, died in infancy; 3, Arthur Edward, of Ipswich, has issue, Cecil Arthur, born in 1890; 4, Edward Arthur, of Kirkley, near Lowestoft; 5, Anne, wife of Captain George Heathcote, has issue; 6, Maria Emily, wife of George Justice, has issue; 7, Mary Jane, wife of Arthur Cove, has issue; others unmarried.

Thomas William Brereton, second son, died in 1887. He married Ellen Elizabeth, daughter of ——— Harris. By her he had one son and one daughter: 1, James Sydney Herbert, born in 1874, the eldest representative of the male line of Breretons, of Brereton Hall; 2, Adelina, wife of Henry E. R. Huber; has issue.

Thomas Joseph Brereton, second son of Thomas William Brereton, of Framsden, Vicar of Wyresdale, Lancashire; died in 1896. Married Sarah, daughter of John G. Mayhew, of Helmingham. By her he had four sons and two daughters: 1, Thomas John, died an infant; 2, Arthur Thomas, born in 1844, died in 1903, without issue; 3, Thomas Joseph, born in 1848, died in 1886, without issue; 4, William Henry, died an infant; 5, Edward William, born in 1855, at Framlingham; 6, Helen Sarah, unmarried.

Edward William Brereton, fifth son of Thomas Joseph Brereton, of Wyresdale, Vicar of Kildwick, Yorkshire, has made a complete study of the history and pedigrees of the entire family of Brereton from the earliest period down to the present time. He married Henrietta Mary, daughter of Albert Charles Att wood. By her he has three sons and two daughters: 1, Cecil Attwood, born in 1881; 2, Sidney Claude, born in 1882; 3, Arthur Douglas, born in 1888; 4, Hilda Mary, born in 1884; 5, Mildred Emma, born in 1886.

Arthur Henry Brereton, third son of Thomas William Brereton, died in 1902, at Great Yarmouth; was Vicar of Mendham, Suffolk. Married Frances, daughter of John Gardiner Mayhew. By her he had one son and three daughters: 1, Henry, born in 1844, died in 1854;. 2, Frances Maud, wife of Captain Richard Thompson, had issue; 3, Julia Kate; 4, Henrietta An nette; both unmarried.

The foregoing completes the record of the Helmingham, Suffolk, family so far as I have been enabled to learn.

THE BEDFORD BRANCH OF THE ELDER LINE OF BRERETON.

John Brereton, fourth son of William, second Baron, was born 'in 1645 and was brought up by his uncle, Captain John Brereton, of Nantwich, who died in 1656, when his nephew was only eleven years old. He was Rector of Beverley, Yorkshire. He married Elizabeth, daughter of ——— Lockwood, Esq. By her he had three sons and five daughters: 1, John, his heir, born in 1674, died in 1740, without issue; 2, Thomas, who succeeded, born in 1684; 3, William, born in 1688; daughters unmarried; no record of third son.

Thomas Brereton, second son; minor canon of Winchester; M. A. Oxford 1704. Married Susannah, daughter of ——— Caxe, Esq. By her he had five sons and four daughters: 1, John, his heir, born in 1717; 2, William, Captain R. N.; 3, Boulter; 4, Daniel; 5, Thomas, born in 1723, Draper, married Mary Holgate, had issue; 6, Anne, wife of Thomas Harding, had issue; rest unmarried.

John Brereton, eldest son; M. D. of Winchester; died in 1778. This is the only doctor of medicine I have come across in the elder line of the family. He married Elizabeth, daughter of ——— White, Esq. By her he had one son and three daugh ters: 1, John, born in 1744, died in 1811; 2, Jane, widow of ——— Dymock; married Rev. H. Blackstone, vicar of Adder bury; brother of Judge Blackstone; had issue; other two daugh ters unmarried.

John Brereton, only son, Rector of Alton Barnes, Wilts. His third son, Thomas, was Vicar of Steeple Morden, Cambridge- shire; died in 1811. Married Mary, daughter of ——— Long- land, Esq: By her he had four sons and two daughters: 1, John, born in 1782; 2, Henry, born in 1783, had two daughters; 3, Thomas, born in 1785, had two sons, Willoughby, a Brigadier

94

St. Mary's Church, Beverley, Yorkshire.

General in the army, and Francis Milbourn, of Sydenham; 4, Francis William, who died without issue; 5, Mary, wife of Francis Swanton, a grandson of Thomas Brereton, Draper, by Mary Holgate, whose daughter, Elizabeth, married Rev. F. W. Swanton.

John Brereton, eldest son, D. C. L. New College, Oxford; died in 1862. Married Elizabeth Humphries. By her he had two sons and one daughter: 1, John, born in 1812; 2, Charles, born in 1814; 3, Elizabeth, wife of George Andrews, of Sudbury, Suffolk.

John Brereton, eldest son; born in 1812, died in 1866; vicar of Poddington, Bedfordshire. His first wife was Emily Edwards. By her he had five sons: 1, John, died without issue· 2, Charles William, born in 1839; Colonel Madras Artillery; left one son, John, born in 1867; 3, Hugh, born in 1841; 4, Ashley Francis, born in 1842, in the India Office, London; 5, Edward, born in 1844, died in 1859, without issue. By his second wife, Eleanor Parker, he had three sons and three daughters: 1, Richard Augustus; 2, John Ronier; 3, Goeffrey; 4, Eleanor; 5, Agnes; 6, Mary Ada. Of this second family there is no further record.

Charles Brereton, second son; B. C. L. of Oxford; Rector of St. Mary's, Bedford; born in 1814, died in 1839. His wife was Emily, daughter of Henry Hill, Esq. By her he had six sons and six daughters; of these sons only three married and have issue; of the daughters four married and have issue: 1, Charles Henry, born in 1840; 2, Herbert James, born in 1854, fifth son; 3, William Henry, born in 1858, sixth son; the other three sons died unmarried. The daughters were: 1, Elizabeth, second daughter, wife of Rev. Francis Brerley Sandberg, had issue; 2, Maud, third daughter, wife of Thomas Beuther, had issue; 3, Mary, fourth daughter, wife of Edmund R. Green, of Bedford; 4, Ethel, sixth daughter, wife of Wilson Ashurst Hetherington, head postmaster at Brighton; both of these two last have issue.

Charles Henry Brereton, eldest son, married Clarissa. daughter of Major (Lala) Kelly. By her he had five sons and two daughters: 1, John; 2, Stewart; 3, Frank; 4, Archibald; 5, William. Of the daughters, Elizabeth Maud, wife of Percy Coakes, has issue; rest unmarried.

Herbert James, fifth son; living in 1904; India Civil Service. Married Eleanor Boddam, his second wife. By her he has two daughters: 1, Phyllis, born in 1885; 2, Marjory, born in 1890.

William Henry Brereton, sixth son; living in London; a celebrated singer. He married Sarah Ambler, of Handworth. By her he has two daughters: 1, Dulcibella, born in 1886; 2, Edith Mary, born in 1889.

The foregoing embraces all the information I possess of the Bedford family. Canon Charles Brereton, of St. Mary's Rectory, Bedford, had a portrait of William, first Baron Brereton, engraved from the original painted by Lucas de Here, in the collection of Owen Salusbury Brereton, of Burosham, with the following inscription attached: "Gulielmus Brereton, Bars de Loughlin, Elizabeth Reg: serviens Gulielmi filius ab Hen. viii; trucidate AE. suae 28."

BRERETONS OF BAWTRY, BEVERLEY. AND HULL, YORKSHIRE.

I have assumed this Yorkshire family to be descended from John Brereton, of Beverley, the younger son of William, Baron Brereton II., of Brereton Hall, Cheshire. This family of Bawtry married into the LeGay family, of Bawtry, Yorkshire, who were descended from Acklow LeGay, who was Governor of Barbadoes at the end of the seventeenth century.

John Brereton, of Bawtry, who was a surgeon, died in 1823 He married Anne, only daughter of John Baxby, of Hull, buried at Bawtry in 1808. By her he had three sons: 1, John, who was in the Royal Navy, died in 1816, unmarried; 2, Thomas LeGay; 3, Charles.

Thomas LeGay Brereton, of Bawtry, second son, was born in 1787, died in 1831; buried at Doncaster. Married Mary Anne Taylor, who died at Ipswich in 1873. By her he had one son, John LeGay Brereton, of Bradford.

Another View of Ruins of Borris Castle.

Page 86.

John LeGay Brereton, of Bradford, born in 1828, died in 1886, in Sidney, Australia; he was a surgeon and an author of poems. In 1857 he married Mary Tongue. By her he had five sons: 1, Victor LeGay; 2, Ernest LeGay; 3, John LeGay; 4, Wilfrid LeGay; 5, Goeffrey LeGay.

The pedigree ends here, and proceeds with that of Charles Brereton, third son of John Brereton, of Bawtry.

Charles Brereton, of Beverley, who was a surgeon, was born in 1788, and died in 1872. He married Caroline Osborne, born in 1792, died in 1881. By her he had one son, Charles LeGay, and four daughters: 1, Caroline, who married John Hartley, of Beverley; 2, Mary, who married Charles Peach, Rector of Evenlode, Worcestershire; 3, Ada, who married T. A. Hudson, of Longcroft, Beverley.

The pedigree does not extend beyond the above. The son, Charles LeGay Brereton, of Morpeth street, Spring Bank, Hull, was living in 1893.

THE YOUNGER BRANCH OF THE BRERETON FAMILY, OF IPSTONE, MALPAS AND SHOCKLACH.

The founder of this branch was Sir Randle, or Ranulph, de Brerton, only son of Sir William de Brerton VI., of Brereton, by his second wife, Margaret, daughter of Sir Henry Done, of Utkington, Cheshire. He married Alicia, daughter and heiress of Sir William Ipstone, of Ipstone, Cheshire, and assumed the name of Sir Randle Brereton, of Ipstone, at her father's death in 1399. Her mother was Maude, daughter and heiress of Sir Robert de Swinnerton, Knight, of Staffordshire. She was a veritable pluralist in husbandship: 1, widow of Sir John Savage, of Rock Savage; 2, widow of Sir Piers Leigh, the ancestor of the Leighs of Lyme; 3, widow of William de Ipstone; 4, widow of Richard Peshall. By her Sir Randle de Brerton had two sons and one daughter: 1, Randle, his heir; 2, William, the founder of the first offshoot of the Malpas branch, viz.: the Brereton family of Burros, or Burosham, Denbighshire; 3, ————, wife of her cousin, Randall Spurstow, of Spurstow.

Sir Randle de Brereton II., of Ipstone and Malpas, married Joanna, daughter of William Holford. By her he had two sons: 1, Randle Brereton, founder of the Eccleston and Wettenhall branch; 2, Owen Brereton, of Bar Hill, the ancestor of Brereton of Coddington. His second wife was Katherine, daughter of William Butheley, of Eaton, Cheshire. By her he had three sons: 1, Randle, his heir, of Ipstone and Malpas; 2, Ralph Brereton, of Iscoyd Castle, Shropshire, who had one daughter, wife of John Holford; 3, Bartholomew Brereton, of Grafton who had three sons: a, Bartholomew; b, John; c, Humphrey, of Malpas, the historian of the War of the Roses.

Randle Brereton III., of Ipstone, died in Burgundy, France. His wife was Emma, daughter and heiress of John Carington, of Carington. By her he had two sons and two daughters: 1, Randle, his heir; 2, Humphrey, of Malpas; 3, Ellen, wife of Nicholas Bruyn, of Tarwin, Cheshire; 4, Eleanor, wife of Philip de Egerton, afterwards wife of Sir William de Brerton IX., of Brereton.

Sir Randle Brereton IV., of Ipstone and Malpas; Chamberlain of Chester 1506 to 1532; Knight of the Body to Henry VII. and Henry VIII.; made a Knight Banneret by Henry VIII., at Boulonge, for Terrouenne and Tournay; built the Brereton Chapel in Malpas Church in 1522, in which he was buried in 1532. He married Eleanor, daughter of Sir Piers Dutton, of Halton Castle, Cheshire. By her he had nine sons and three daughters: 1, Randle, his heir; 2, Richard, founder of the Tatton branch; 3, John, founder of the Norfolk branch; 4, Thomas; 5, Peter; 6, Roger, founder of the Halton branch; 7, William, succeeded his father as Chamberlain of Chester; was beheaded by Henry VIII. with Queen Anne Boleyn, in 1536; 8, Robert; 9, Urian, founder of the Handford branch. The daughters were: 1, Anne, wife of John Harcourt; afterwards was wife of John Pershall, of Hordesley; 2, Elizabeth, wife of Richard Cholmondeley; afterwards was wife of Randle Mainwaring, of Over Peevor, Cheshire; 3, Jane, wife of Sir Thomas Hanmer, of Hanmer, Flintshire. (See Burosham branch).

Page 23   *Altar—Tomb of a Priest.*

Sir Randle Brereton V., of Ipstone, Malpas and Shocklach, married Eleanor, daughter of Sir Philip Egerton, of Egerton. By her he had one child, Anne, wife of Randall Dod, of Edge. His second wife was Izabel, daughter of Thomas Butler, of Bewsey. By her he had one son, Randle, his heir, and one daughter, Elizabeth, wife of James Starkey, of Darley.

Sir Randle Brereton VI., of Malpas and Shocklach, married Mary, daughter of Sir William Griffith, who was afterwards wife of Sir Hugh Cholmondeley. By her he had three sons: 1, Randle, his heir; 2, Richard, of Mitcham, Surrey; 3, Sir Thomas, of Yard, Somersetshire. (See these branches).

Sir Randle Brereton VII., of Malpas, died in 1811. He married Frances, daughter of Sir Robert Throgmorton, of Coughton, Warwickshire. By her he had Mary, sole daughter and heiress, born in 1576, married Sir Richard Egerton, of Egerton.

By this marriage the whole of the immense estates of Ipstone, Malpas and Shocklach, with the family chapel in Malpas Church, passed into the possession of the Egerton family. The foregoing pedigree represents the direct male line from father to son for a period of two hundred years, through seven generations. It represents a direct male descent of sixteen generations from Sir William de Brerton, first Lord of Brereton. The Shocklach estates were purchased by Sir Randle Brereton V., of Malpas, from Sir Richard Corbet, of Leghton. Humphrey Brereton, the historian of Princess Elizabeth, of York, had three daughters: Emma, wife of John Dod, of Edge; Anne, wife of John Stringer, of Crewe; Catherine, wife of Rawlin Warburton, of Edge. The pedigree shows that Sir Randle Brereton V.'s daughter, Anne, by his first wife, married Randall Dod, of Edge. This Dod family were living in the time of Edward III., and the descendants were living in 1852. They were connected by several marriages with the family of Eyton, of Eyton, with which the Brereton families of Burosham and Eccleston were also connected by marriage; also, with the Mainwaring family. The Starkey family were descended from the ancient family of Starkey, of Stretton, Cheshire, in the time of Richard II.; this family can be traced down to 1811. The Throgmorton family was also of ancient ancestry. Thomas Throgmorton, son of Sır John, who was Sub-Treasurer of England in 1440, married in 1409 the daughter and heiress of Sir Grey Spiney, of Coughton, and was the ancestor of Sir Robert Throgmorton. The Eyton family was descended from Robert de Eyton, Lord of Eyton, in the time of Domesday; several of his descendants were High Sheriffs of Shropshire. The Eytons, of Leeswood, Flintshire, with whom the Breretons of Burosham were connected by marriage, were descended from the tribe of March, whose ancestor was Cynic Efell, son of Madoc, last Prince of Powys. The Savage family was a noted one in Cheshire from the earliest time, and both of the main branches of the Brereton family were connected with it by intermarriages. Sir John Savage, in 1422, married Katherine, daughter of Thomas, Lord Stanley, and sister of Thomas, first Earl of Derby.

BRERETONS OF BUROSHAM, COUNTY DENBIGH, WALES.

This was the first offshoot of the family descended from Sir Randle de Brerton, of Ipstone and Malpas, at the very beginning of the fifteenth century. Ipstone, of Ipstone, was one of the ancient family of Knights in the Palatinate of Cheshire, and which was closely allied to the ancient family of Corbet, of Morton Corbet. Maude, the mother of Alice, Lady of Ipstone, wife of Sir Randle de Brerton, was the daughter and heiress of Sir Robert de Swinnerton, in the County of Staffordshire, bv Elizabeth, his wife, daughter and heiress of Sir Nicholas de Beche. Maude had married four times: 1, Sir John Savage, of Rock Savage, Cheshire; 2, Sir Piers Leigh; 3, William de Ipstone; 4, Richard Peshall.

Sir Ranulph, or Randulphus, de Brerton, of Malpas, second son of Sir William de Brerton VI., of Brereton, by his second wife, Margaret, daughter of Henry Done, of Utkington, widow of John de Davenport, of Henbury, married Alice, daughter and heiress of William de Ipstone, of Ipstone, who died in 1399. By her he had his second son, William, of Burosham.

William Brereton, of Burosham, died in 1450. He married Catherine, daughter and co-heir of Thomas de Wylde, of Burosham. By her he had one son, Edward, who had two wives: Elizabeth Roydon, of Pulford, and Dorothy Hanmer, of Hanmer. The arms of the Wylde family were, Argent, a chevron sable, on a Chief of the second; three martletts (a bird on the shield with wings closed, without feet) of the field.

Edward Brereton I., of Burosham, first married Elizabeth, daughter of John Roydon, of Pulton, by his wife, ———, daughter of Thomas Hanmer, of Bettisfield. By her he had two sons 1, Randolph; 2, John. His second wife was Dorothy, daughter of Richard Hanmer and sister of Sir Thomas Hanmer, who was knighted at the taking of Tourney, under Sir Randle Brereton IV., of Malpas. By her he had one son and three daughters.

Randolph Brereton, of Burosham, married Margaret, daughter of Ellis, ap. Ellis Eyton. By her he had only one daughter, Jane, who married Robert, son of Eow Puleston, of Exlusham.

John Brereton, second son, of Burosham, successor to his brother, married Margaret, daughter and heir of Richard, ap. Tenan, ap. David, ap. Ithel Fychan, of Llanewgain, descended from Ednowain Bendew, chief of one of the noble tribes of Wales. By her he had one son, Owain, who had two wives, Elizabeth Salusbury and Catherine, daughter of Harry Gooch Salusbury, of Llewesog, and widow of John Lloyd, of Bodidris, by whom he had no issue.

Owain Brereton, of Burosham, was High Sheriff of Denbigh in 1580 and 1588. He married Elizabeth, his first wife, who was a daughter of John Salusbury, of Lleweny, M. P. for Denbigh in 1554, by his wife Catherine, daughter and heiress of Tudor, ap. Robert Fychan, of Berain. By her he had two sons: 1, Edward II., of Burosham; 2, John, of Exlusham. Edward was High Sheriff in 1598, in which year he died. The daughters of Edward Brereton were: 1, Elizabeth, who married James Eyton, of Eyton; 2, Joanna, who married Cynwig, ap. Richard, of Penachlech; 3, Catherine, who married Lancelot Lloyd, of Tref Alun (Allington)

Edward Brereton I., of Burosham, married as his second wife, Dorothy, daughter of Richard Hanmer and sister of Sir Thomas Hanmer, son-in-law of Sir Randle Brereton IV., of Malpas. By her he had one son, Thomas, and three daughters: 1, Elizabeth, who married James Eyton, of Eyton; 2, Joanna, who married Cynwig, ap. Richard, of Penachlech; 3, Catherine, who married Lancelot Lloyd, of Tref Alun (Allington).

Thomas Brereton, son of Edward Brereton, of Burosham; rector of Northope in 1539, of Llandrinio in 1557, of Gresford in 1566. Married Margaret, daughter of Ithel, ap. Gruffydd, ap. Belyn. By her he had one son, Peter, who married Jane, daughter of Owen, ap. John, ap. Howell Fychan.

Peter Brereton, B. A., Vicar of Llannyhangett in 1597. No record of issue obtainable.

Edward Brereton, eldest son, of Burosham, was High Sheriff of Denbigh in 1598; died in 1598. He married Anna, sister to Sir Jevan Lloyd, of Yate. By her he had one son, Owen Brereton, of Burosham.

PEDIGREE OF JOHN BRERETON, OF EXLUSHAM.

John Brereton I., of Exlusham, second son of Owain Brereton, of Burosham, died in 1622. He was married, but the name of his wife is not given. By her he had two sons and one daughter: 1, John, his heir; 2, Edward, of Burosham, who married Anne, daughter of John Lloyd, of Bodidris. John Brereton II., of Exlusham, married Margaret, daughter of Hugh Wynn, of Wigfair. By her he had two daughters: a, Elizabeth, who married Thomas Bulkeley, of Coedan; b, Jane, who married, first, John Ffachnallt, of Ffachnallt, Flint, no issue; second, Owain Lloyd, second son of William Lloyd, of Plas Madog, by his wife, Catherine, daughter of John Brereton, of Exlusham. They had one son, Thomas, who died without issue, and one daughter, who married her cousin, Edward Lloyd, of Plas Madog; 3, Catherine, who married William Lloyd, of Plas Madog, Denbigh, by whom she had two sons: a, Edward Lloyd, of Plas Madog; b, Owain Lloyd.

Inscription Within Canopied Tomb.

OWEN SALUSBURY BRERETON, OF BUROSHAM AND SHOTWICK HALL.

Edward Brereton II., the elder son of Owain Brereton, of Burosham, who died in 1598, had by his wife, Anna, daughter of Sir Jevan Lloyd, of Yate, one son, Owen Brereton, of Buro sham. The pedigree follows his son or grandson, Thomas Brere ton, of Burosham.

Thomas Brereton, of Burosham, died in 1756. His first wife was a daughter of Sir Jonathan Trelawney, of Trelawne, Cornwall. By her he had one son, Owen Brereton, born in 1715, died in 1798, without issue. He was F. R. S. and R. A. and M. P.; Constable of Flint Castle; Recorder for Liverpool; buried in Royal Chapel, Windsor. On the death of his father he took the name of Salusbury (Owen Salusbury Brereton). The second wife was Catherine, daughter and heir of Salusbury Lloyd, of Llewenny; he had no issue. Through her he received Shotwick Hall, in Cheshire. On the death of Owen Salusbury, Shotwick Hall passed to Colonel Charles Trelawney, nephew of Thomas Brereton's first wife.

ECCLESTON AND WETTENHALL BRANCH OF THE MALPAS FAMILY.

Randle Brereton, the founder of this branch, was, according to Ormerod, the base or illegitimate son of Sir Randle Brereton II., of Malpas. He was also Escheator or Holder of the Escheat Lands of the Crown, as was Sir Urian Brereton, of Handford. In those days the stain of illegitimacy did not hold the disparagement pertaining to a later period.

Ormerod, in his pedigree of the Malpas family, gives Randle Brereton, of Eccleston, as the eldest son of Sir Randle Brere ton II., of Malpas, by his wife Joanna, daughter of William Hol ford, of Holford, which seems to contradict his designation of "base" son. I assume he was legitimate.

Randle Brereton I., of Eccleston, was the eldest son of Randle Brereton II., of Malpas, by his wife Joanna, daughter of William

Holford, of Holford. He died in 1537. His wife was Katherine, daughter of Richard Manley, of Pulton. By her he had two sons: 1, Thomas, his heir, who died without issue; 2, John.

John Brereton II., of Eccleston, heir to his brother, died in 1568. His first wife was a daughter of ——— Tarrance, of Holt, Denbighshire. By her he had one child, Jane, wife of Thomas Holme, of Coddington, Cheshire. His second wife was Katherine, daughter of Louth Dutton, Alderman of Chester. By her he had two sons and three daughters: 1, Richard; 2, Randle John, of whom there is no record; 3, Ursula, wife of John Anson, of Middlewich, Cheshire; 4, Dorothy, unmarried; 5, Mary, wife of William Aldersey, of Chester.

Richard Brereton III., of Eccleston, was born in 1548, died in 1630. He married Maud, daughter of Richard Hurlestone, of Picton. By her he had eight sons and eight daughters. The pedigree only mentions four of these: 1 John, his heir; 2, Edward; 3, Hugh; of these there is no record; 4, George, who died young; 5, Elizabeth, wife of Edward Cotton, of Cotton.

John Brereton IV., of Eccleston, was born in 1613. He sold the manor of Wettenhall. His wife was Atlanta, daughter of Thomas Piggot, of Chetwynd, Shropshire. By her he had one son, Richard, and one daughter, Dorothy. Of them there is no record.

The Breretons held these estates for over one hundred years. Eccleston now forms a part of the Eaton Hall estates, belonging to the Duke of Westminster. There was a Joseph Brereton who was Mayor of Chester in 1623; he was probably one of the eight sons of Richard Brereton III., of Eccleston. There was, also, a Henry Brereton, of Eccleston, of about the same time, one of whose wives was Margaret, daughter of Richard Grosvenor, of Eaton Hall, who was Sheriff of Cheshire in 1602, and whose wife was Christian, daughter of Sir Thomas Brooke, of Halton (Norton Abbey), Cheshire, whose father, Thomas Brooke, married Margaret, daughter of Henry (Richard?) Brereton, of Eccleston. (This is given in the National Biography). The Piggot family was paternally descended from the ancient Cheshire fam ily founded by Gilbert, Lord of Broxton, in the time of the Con queror. He married the heiress of Sir Richard de Peshale, Lord of Chetwynd, Shropshire. Atlanta's father, grandfather and great grandfather were Sheriffs of Shropshire. The Cotton family was descended from Sir Hugh Cotton, of Cotton, in the time of Henry II. (1154); his descendants, the Cottons of Adlington, intermarried with the Stanley and the Dod families. Among the Eccleston Church records is found mention of the burial of Jane, wife of John Eyton, son of Thomas Eyton, in 1654, who had been the widow of Henry Brereton, of Eccleston.

THE TATTON BRANCH OF THE MALPAS FAMILY.

William Stanley (family of Stanley, Cheshire) of Tatton, died in 1498. Joan, his widow, afterwards married Sir Edward Pickering, in 1500, and lastly Sir John de Brereton, of Lea Hall, Cheshire, by whom she had one son, Philip, who died without issue. She was the daughter and heiress of Sir Geoffrey Masev. Her only child by her first husband was Jane, or Joan, the heiress of Tatton. She had two consorts. The first was John Ashton, son and heir of Sir Thomas Ashton, of Ashton, super Mersey, Cheshire; she was then but eight years old; he died young without issue by her, in 1511. Her second husband was Sir Richard Brereton, second son of Sir Randle Brereton IV., of Malpas.

Sir Richard Brereton I., of Tatton, died in 1557, at Islington, London. He married Jane, daughter of Sir William Stanley, of Tatton; she died in 1570, aged seventy-seven. By her he had two sons and one daughter: 1, Richard, his heir; 2, Geoffrey; 3, Anne, wife of John Booth, of Barton, Lancashire.

Richard Brereton, of Tatton, died in 1551, during his father's life. He married Dorothy, daughter of Thurstan de Tildesley, of Lancashire. By her he had no issue.

Geoffrey Brereton II., of Tatton, second son, was born in 1535, died in 1565. He married Alice, daughter of Piers Leycester, of Nether Tabley, Cheshire. By her he had one son, Richard, his heir, and one daughter, Anne, who died issueless.

Richard Brereton III., of Tatton, died in 1598. He married Dorothy, daughter of Sir Richard Egerton, of Ridley, Cheshire, great grandson of Sir Philip Egerton, by his wife, Eleanor, daughter of Sir Randle Brereton III. By her he had no issue.

Richard Brereton, the last of the male line of this branch, settled all his estates on his relative, Sir Thomas Egerton, Lord Chancellor of England in 1603-1617, from whom the Earls of Bridgewater were descended, and who were the owners of Tatton in 1667. Sir Thomas Egerton, afterwards Baron Ellesmere and Baron Brackley, died in 1617; he was ninth in descent from Philip the Red, founder of the Egerton family of Egerton and Oulton. The Brereton family were connected with Tatton in 1445 by the marriage of Sir William de Brerton VII., of Brereton, with Ellen (his second wife), daughter and heiress of Sir William Masey, of Tatton, their son Thomas de Brerton, Rector of Brereton, being his mother's heir to Tatton. It is interesting to note that the present family of Baron Egerton, of Tatton Park, who are descended from the Bridgewater family who inherited the Tatton estates from Richard Brereton, are descended from William Tatton, of Withershaw, Cheshire, by his wife, Hester Egerton, grand daughter of John Egerton, third Earl of Bridgewater. This William Tatton, on his marriage with Hester, in 1747, assumed the name of William Tatton Egerton. His ancestor, Robert Tatton, of Withershaw, married Anne, third daughter of William Brereton III., of Ashley. The Leycester family, of Cheshire, as also the Mainwaring family, claim descent from a common ancestor of the Conquerer, through Gumora, Duchess of Normandy, and Robert de Bellamont, Earl of Leicester, in 1118. They also claim common descent from Hugh de Cyveliog, or Kiveliog (the father of Maud, wife of David, Earl of Huntington, and the maternal grand father of Lady Ada de Brerton) who was second Earl Royal of Chester, through his illegitimate daughter, Amice. Sir Peter Leycester, the Cheshire historian in 1600, was a brother of Alice, who married Geoffrey Brereton. It will be seen from the above pedigree that the Tatton branch were well connected with the best families of Cheshire.

Canopied Tomb in Astbury Churchyard.

THE HANDFORD BRANCH OF THE FAMILY IN CHESHIRE.

This is a very interesting branch of the Malpas family, dating from about A. D. 1500 to A. D. 1673. It embraces the reigns of Henry VIII., Edward VI., Mary, Elizabeth, James I., Charles I. and Charles II., all of them very important times in English history. Sir Urian Brereton, the founder of this branch, was the ninth son of Sir Randle Brereton IV., of Malpas. Urian was a family name in the Malpas Hall branch of the Brereton family, being derived from the early barons of Malpas. It is a singular coincidence that Queen Anne Boleyn's favorite Italian greyhound was called "Urian." It is remarkable that though Henry VIII. beheaded his Groom of the Chamber, Sir William Brereton, in 1536, he appointed his brother Sir Urian to the same office in 1541. It is also a remarkable fact that in 1529 Henry VIII. granted to the ill fated Sir William Brereton and to his brother Sir Urian, for their joint lives, the rangership of Shotwick Park, with a fishery on the River Dee, and its appurtenances, and that Shotwick Park should have again come into possession of the Brereton family through the marriage of Owain Salusbury Brereton, of Burosham, with the daughter and heiress of John Salusbury, of Lleweny, in 1570, the later owner. This is probably the reason why Ormerod, in his pedigree of the Handford branch, calls Sir Urian Brereton "Escheator." (Vol. III., p. 327). The pedigree of the Honford family extends back to the beginning of the fourteenth century. The mother of Sir Urian's first wife was the daughter of Sir John Savage, of Rock Savage, and her aunt was the wife of Sir John Mainwaring, of Over Peevor. The pedigrees are derived from Sir Peter Leycester's manuscripts and from Le Neve's manuscripts of Baronetage. The coat of arms is from the same sources, and from Richard Brooke's "Visits to Fields of Battles" in 1850. The arms of Brereton are Argent, two barrs sable, a crescent gules (on the first barr); crest, a bear's head and neck, erased (torn off) sable, muzzled gules. The arms of Honford, or Handford (which are impaled with those of Brereton) are first and fourth, sable, a star argent pierced of the field, for Handford proper.

Sir Urian Brereton I., of Handford, Escheator of Cheshire, Groom of the Chamber to Henry VIII., in 1541, died in 1577. His first wife was Margaret, sole child of William Honford, of Honford, who died in 1513; widow of Sir John Stanley, who died in 1527. By her he had six sons and two daughters: 1, Randle, his heir, died in 1584, without issue; 2, William, successor; 3, Edward; 4, Richard; 5, John; 6, Cuthbert; (there is no record of the last four); 7, Jane, wife of Edward Legh, of Baggilegh; 8, Sibilla, wife of Thomas Legh, of Adlington. His second wife was Alice, daughter of Sir Edmund Trafford, of Trafford, Lancashire. By her he had one son and two daughters: 1, Urian; 2, Mary, wife of Alexander Barlow, of Barlow, Lancashire, whose father married Frances, daughter of William Brereton III., of Ashley; 3, Dorothy, wife of George Redish.

William Brereton II., of Handford, second son of Sir Urian, born in 1553, died in 1601. In 1578 he married Katherine, daughter of Roger Hurlestone, of Chester. By her he had four sons and one daughter: 1, William, his heir; 2, Randle; 3, Urian; 4, Richard; the last three died without issue; 5, Dorothy, wife of Charles Wishes, of Copgreve, Yorkshire.

William Brereton III., of Handford, died in 1610. He married Margaret, daughter of Richard Holland, of Denton, Lancashire. By her he had three sons and one daughter: 1, William, his heir; 2, Richard, of whom there is no record; 3, Urian; 4, Margaret, wife of Richard Egerton, of Ridley, who sold and wasted his estates in Cheshire.

Sir William Brereton IV., Bart., of Handford, was born in 1604, died in 1661; was created a Baronet by King Charles I., in 1626; Commander-in-Chief of the Parliamentary forces in Cheshire, Shropshire and Staffordshire during the civil wars of the Stuarts' time. His first wife was Susan, daughter of Sir George Booth, of Dunham-on-the-Hill, Cheshire. By her he had one son and three daughters: 1, Thomas, his heir; 2, Frances, wife of Edward, second Baron Ward of Birmingham and first Earl of Dudley and Ward; 3, Susannah, wife of Edmund Lenthall, grandson of William Lenthall, Speaker of the House of

Commons, of Lachford, Oxfordshire; 4, Catherine, unmarried. His second wife was Cicely, daughter of Sir William Skeffington, Bart., of Fisherwick, Leicestershire; widow of Edward Mitton, of Weston, Staffordshire. By her he had two daughters: 1, Cicely, wife of Edward Brabazon, son of Edward, second Earl of Meath; 2, Mary, unmarried.

Sir Thomas Brereton V., Bart., of Handford, was born in 1632, died in 1673, issueless. He married Theodosia, youngest daughter of Humble, first Baron Ward, of Birmingham; she afterwards married Hon. Charles Brereton, of Brereton, by whom she had one son, Charles, baptized at Brereton February 23, 1677. Charles Brereton, the father, must have been a younger son of the second Baron Brereton, who died in 1664, but he is not mentioned in the pedigree given by Ormerod, who has, also, omitted the name of another younger son, John, who was Rector of Beverley, Yorkshire. And yet Ormerod enters Charles and his son, as above, in this Handford pedigree. The son died without issue.

The Handford estates had been held by this branch of the family for over one hundred and thirty years, through five consecutive generations. Sir William Brereton IV., of Handford, in the reign of Charles II., settled these estates, in default of male issue by his only son Thomas, on Nathaniel Booth, of Mottram St. Andrew, Cheshire, in tail male, but it was not long held by that family; it was subdivided and sold to various parties. He settled his estates of Ashton Super Mersey, Cheshire, upon his daughter, wife of Edmund Lenthall. To his unmarried daughter, Mary, he bequeathed "his best bed." To his brother, Richard Brereton, he donated fifteen pounds per annum for his life. To Mr. John Brereton, minister of the gospel, certain divinity books in his library. He died at Croydon, Surrey, in the Archepiscopal palace, and his body was taken to Handford for burial; but tradition has it that it was lost in a flood. There is found no record of any burial in the Cheadle Church registers, only a mention of his death. He was well rewarded by parliament for his brilliant military services during the civil war. He received the chief Forestership of Macclesfield Forest, with the Seneschalship (the royal officer who presided over the meeting of the magistrates of the district or hundred) of the Hundred of Macclesfield, besides money and lands from estates sequestered by parliament, and had a grant for his life of the Archbishop's palace at Croydon. It is worthy of notice that whilst he was fighting under Cromwell against King Charles I., his kinsman, Lord Brereton, of the elder line of Brereton, was fighting for King Charles. This was the third Lord Brereton who highly distinguished himself in raising troops, and who ventured his life and property in his devotion to the royal cause. He was taken prisoner with his wife and son. He suffered sequestration of his estates and was ultimately reduced to compound for them and to pay a composition for his son. These losses crippled him and his family terribly. After the restoration of the Stuart regime he was associated with the Earl of Derby in the Lord Lieutenancy of Cheshire, and was also member for the county in the first parliament ensuing. He was one of the founders of the R. S.

Sir William Brereton IV., of Handford, "the Warrior," obtained, in or about 1630, a large grant of lands in Massachusetts, U. S. A., near where Boston now is, from Sir Fortunatus Gorges, the Father of the Plymouth Colony (1620). He was also interested with Sir Walter Raleigh in the colonization of Virginia.

BRERETONS OF SURREY, GLOUCESTERSHIRE, AND SUSSEX BRANCHES THEREFROM.

These pedigrees are derived from Harleian Mss., 1559, fol. 139, and 1141, fol. 57 A. B., and 1064, 4 B, and 1433, 42 B, of the Heralds' Visitation in Somersetshire.

Richard Brereton, second son of Sir Randle Brereton VI., of Malpas, married Johanna, daughter of ———— Beyle, Esq., of Newmarket, Suffolk. By her he had Theophilus Brereton, his heir, of Mitcham, Surrey, and of Aldermanbury, London; (died December 8, 1638); he married Maria, daughter of ———— Rowland, Esq., of London. By her he had Robert Brereton, his heir, of London and Worcester (died at Worcester in 1672); he

Brereton Monument in Ross Church.

married Mary, daughter of Francis White, Esq., of Fiffele, Berkshire. By her he had two sons: 1, Theophilus, his heir; 2, Robert, of Gloucester City, of whose wife there is no record; they had one son, Theophilus Brereton, born in 1668, of St. John's College, Oxford, 1686; B. C. L., 1692. The following pedigree is that of the elder son, Theophilus Brereton:

Theophilus Brereton, eldest son, of Charlton Kings, Gloucestershire. Wife's name and family not given. By her he had one son, Charles.

Charles Brereton, of Gloucester (born in 1685), of University College, Oxford. Wife's name and family not given. By her he had one son, Richard.

Richard Brereton, of Wotton, Gloucestershire, born 1723; buried at Edgeworth, Gloucestershire; B. A. of Pembroke College, Cambridge, and M. A. of All Soul's College, in 1748; Rector of Edgeworth. Wife's name and family not given. By her he had one son, Thomas.

Thomas Brereton, of Edgeworth, Gloucestershire; (born in 1760, died in 1814), of Christ Church College, Oxford, 1777; buried at Edgeworth. He assumed the name and arms of Westfaling. A monument and epitaph in Latin to him is in Ross Church, Herefordshire. He married Mary Westfaling, only child of Rev. James Westfaling, and niece of Philip Westfaling, Esq. She was sole heiress and lineal descendant of the families of Rudhall and Westfaling. She died at Rudhall in 1830.

The pedigree does not run beyond the above. The Edgeworth property was, at a later time, purchased by my first cousin, Henry Grace Sperling, who married my eldest sister, Anna Margaretta, of Little Massingham, Norfolk, and afterwards his cousin, Mary Wilson, of Stowlangtoft Hall, Suffolk, by whom he had, inter alios, a son, Henry, the present owner of Edgeworth.

BRERETONS OF SUSSEX.

From Thomas Brereton, the third son of the above Theophilus and Maria Brereton, of Mitcham, Surrey, who was of Stoughton, near Emsworth, Sussex, were descended two generations, but the names of the wives and children are not recorded; these could probably be found in the Parish book of Stoughton, West-bourne and Warbleton, Sussex. The pedigree shows that the above Thomas Brereton, of Stoughton, left one son, Richard Brereton, of Chilgrove, Sussex, born in 1664; B. A. of Trinity College, Oxford, in 1684; M. A. in 1687; Rector of Westbourne, Sussex, in 1687, and of Warblington, Hampshire (Warbleton, Sussex?) in 1688. The pedigree gives him one son, Thomas Brereton, born in 1698, of Trinity College, Oxford, in 1716. No further record of this Sussex family is available.

NORFOLK BRANCH OF THE MALPAS FAMILY.

Sir Randle Brereton IV., of Malpas, was fifth in direct male descent from Sir Randle de Brerton, of Ipstone, and fourteenth from Sir William de Brerton, first Lord of Brereton, about A. D. 1175, acccording to the old pedigree furnished by Ormerod. His third son, John Brereton, was the founder of the Norfolk and Suffolk Brereton branch, the first members of his family having moved to Hoxne, near Eye, Suffolk, and from thence into Nor-folk during the sixteenth century. The following pedigree has been gleaned from Ormerod, Vol. II., p. 377; from Blomefield's History of Norfolk; from Farrer's Church Heraldry; and from Norfolk Archaeology. During the seventeenth century the fam-ily centered in and around the City of Norwich. This pedigree embraces mainly the direct elder line, which, during the eigh-teenth century, settled in Brinton, near Holt.

John Brereton, Rector of Malpas, Astbury, Bebrinton, and St. Mary's, Chester, died in 1542. His wife's name was Alicia, but her parentage is not recorded. William Brereton, of Hoxne, Suffolk, the first son died in 1561. He married Elizabeth, daugh-ter of ——— Green, of Hoxne. By her he had four sons: 1, John of Tharston, Norfolk, died in 1585; 2, William, died in 1599; 3, Sebastian; of these there is no record; 4, Cuthbert, whom the pedigree follows.

Sketch Map of Norfolk, Showing Places With Which the Family Had Ties.

Cuthbert Brereton, of Norwich, a lawyer, Alderman and Sheriff of the city in 1576; died in 1612. He married Joan, daughter of John House, Alderman of Norwich. By her he had three sons: 1, John, his heir; 2, Thomas, who died in 1632, no record; 3, Simon, who married Frances Carsan, by whom he had one son, Henry.

John Brereton, eldest son of Cuthbert, in Holy Orders at St. Peter Mancroft Church, Norwich, died in 1632. He married Margaret, whose parentage is not known. By her he had one son, John, of Shottesham.

John Brereton, of Shottesham, Norfolk, died in 1684. He married Mary, parentage not known. By her he had two sons: 1, Cuthbert, born in 1645, died in 1708. He married Lydia Clax ton, by whom he had one son, Cuthbert, who died in 1724 without issue; 2, John, who succeeded.

John Brereton, second son (first of Brinton), was born in 1650 and died in 1735. He married Cicely, daughter and heir of Robert and Mary Cook, of Brinton. By her he had three sons and two daughters: 1, John, his heir, died in 1772 without issue; 2, William, successor to John (second of Brinton); married Anne Bainbridge. By her he had three sons and two daugh ters; all died issueless; 3, Robert, married daughter of Rev. Fran cis Brooke, of Ashby; 4, Elizabeth, married M. H. Paul, of Sloley; 5, Lydia, married M. Goldsmith.

William Brereton, second son of John I., of Brinton; first William Brereton, of Brinton, lawyer; born in 1688, died in 1777. He married Anne, daughter of Thomas Shorting, of Cley, Collector of Customs; she was niece to Admiral Sir Cloudisley Shovell. By her he had three sons and two daughters: 1, Shovell, his heir, who had no male issue; he married Mary Middleton, who died 1780; 2, John, successor to Shovell; 3, Thomas, died in 1794, without issue; 4, Anne, who married William Guybon, of Thursford, Norfolk; 5, Mary, who married David Lloyd, of Llanvaughan, Cardigan.

John Brereton, second son of John III., of Brinton, died in 1785. He married Bridget, daughter of Abel John Brett, of Admiral Sir Percy Brett's family. By her he had four sons and five daughters: 1, John, his heir; 2, Abel, who married his cousin Elizabeth Lloyd; by her he had Cloudesley Shovell Brereton, founder of the Canada family; 3, William, lawyer, who died in 1796, without issue; 4, Robert, of Blakeney, who married Ann Hudson, of Tottenham; 5, Mary, unmarried; 6, Anne, who married Jeremiah Sharpe, Master of Weasenham Grammar School, Norfolk; 7, Bridget; 8, Sarah; 9, Margaret, all unmarried. John and Abel were twins.

John Brereton IV., of Brinton, merchant, was born in 1753 and died in 1823. He married Anna Margaretta, daughter of David Lloyd, his cousin. By her he had four sons and one daughter, Mary, who married Thomas Seppings of Syderstone; the sons were: 1, William John, his heir; 2, Charles David, of Little Massingham Rectory; 3, Randle, of Blakeney; 4, Shovell, of Briningham.

William John Brereton, William II., of Brinton, J. P. and D. L. of Norfolk, married Elizabeth, daughter of John Hale, of Worcester, descended from Sir Matthew Hale, Lord Chief Justice. By her he had one son, John, and four daughters: 1, Anna Margaretta, who married Robert Pearson Brereton, C. E., of Blakeney and London, no issue; 2, Elizabeth, who married Richard Ward, C. E., of London; issue surviving; 3, Mary Brecknell, who married Rev. Randle Barwick Brereton, of Stiffkey, no issue; 4, Emma Frances, who married Rev. William Buckle; issue surviving.

John Brereton V., of Brinton, was born in 1813, and died in 1861; he was the last of the owners of the Brinton Manor estates. He married Elizabeth Anne, daughter of Robert John Brereton, of Blakeney. By her he had four sons and one daughter, Elizabeth Anne, unmarried; 1, John Lloyd, born in 1843, P. C. of St. Peter's church, Barnsley, Yorkshire, unmarried; 2, William John, born in 1845, unmarried; 3, Robert Pearson, born in

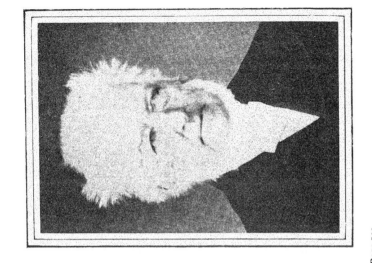

Page 122. *Shovell Brere on, o Briningham.*

Page 4. *John Lloyd Brere on, o Brinton.*

1848, unmarried; he is Classical Master at Arundel School, Oundle, Northamptonshire; 4, Cuthbert Arthur, is the only married one of the four sons, and has issue; born in 1850; M. I. C. E.; married Frances, daughter of Captain Jenner, of Bridgend, Glamorgan, South Wales.

The foregoing completes the direct elder male line pedigree of the Brereton family of Brinton, Norfolk. The several off-shoots from John Brereton IV., of Brinton, are shown in the following pedigrees. Extracts from Blomefield's History of Norfolk, Farrer's Church Heraldry of Norfolk, and from Norfolk Archaeology, are also furnished. These refer to many members of the family in Norfolk who were near kinsmen, but who are not mentioned in the direct elder male line pedigree. William Brereton I., of Brinton, who died in 1777, had a second wife, Margaret, who survived him, and died in 1784. There is a monument to her in Brinton church. Cuthbert Brereton, Sheriff of Norwich in 1576, had a first wife, daughter of George Bolinge, of Norwich; by her he had one child, Thomas, his heir, who died without issue. John Brereton IV., of Brinton, was twenty-first in descent from Sir William de Brerton, first Lord of Brereton, seventeenth from Sir Ranulphus and Lady Ada Brereton, twelfth from Sir Randle de Brerton I., of Ipstone and Malpas, and ninth from Sir Randle Brereton IV., of Malpas. Cuthbert Arthur Brereton's only son is now the twenty-fifth in descent from the first Sir William de Brerton, of Brereton, of the elder line of the Norfolk family.

John Brereton IV., of Brinton, had inherited the red hair of the elder line; his nose was a prominent feature, so that he was known to the family by the sobriquet, "the Nose." He used to tell the funny story of how he and his twin brother, Abel, had a pre-natal struggle as to being the first born. John getting the mastery received a parting kick of rage from Abel, the mark of which John had to bear till his death. This is analogous to the story told in Genesis xxxii. of the pre-natal struggle between Esau and Jacob, and as Esau and John were both of the red type it makes the story the more apposite.

LITTLE MASSINGHAM BRANCH OF THE NORFOLK FAMILY.

John Brereton IV., of Brinton, born in 1752, died in 1823. He married Anna Margaretta, daughter of David Lloyd, Esq., of Llanvaughan, Cardigan.

Charles David, second son, born 1790, died 1868; Rector of Little Massingham, Norfolk. Married Frances, second daughter of Joseph Wilson, Esq., of Highbury Hill and Stowlangtoft Hall, Suffolk. By her he had six sons and five daughters.

Charles David, eldest son, born in 1820, died in 1875; Rector of Framingham Earl, Norfolk. Married Eliza, daughter of William Kent, Esq., of Isle of Wight.

Henry, second son, born in 1821, E. I. C. S., died in 1858, at Bustee, India, during the mutiny. Married Emily, daughter of Henry Boulderson, Esq., E. I. C. S.

Joseph Lloyd, third son, of Little Massingham Rectory; Minor Canon of Exeter; born in 1822, died in 1901; married Frances, daughter of Rev. William Martin, of Staverton, Devon.

John Alfred, fourth son, born in 1827, living in 1904; Major General Bengal Army, retired. Married Marion, daughter of Thomas Gillespie, Esq., of Ardachie, Invernesshire.

William Wilson, fifth son, born in 1830, died in 1854, at Sarawac, Borneo; unmarried.

Robert Maitland, sixth son, born in 1834, living in 1904, at Woodstock, Oregon, U. S. A. Married Alice, daughter of Isaac Fairchild, Esq., of Waterloo, New York, descended from a Revolutionary sire.

The daughters of Charles David were: 1, Anna Margaretta, eldest daughter, who married Henry Grace Sperling, Esq., and died in 1847, without issue; 2, Frances Mary, unmarried; 3, Mary Anne, unmarried; 4, Emma Matilda, unmarried; 5, Henrietta Lucy, born in 1835, died in 1898. She married Frederick Napleton Dew, youngest son of Tompkyns Dew, Esq., of Whitney Court, Hereford, Major 88th Connaught Rangers, Adjutant Herefordshire Militia, living in 1904.

Charles David, Rector of Framingham Earl, Norfolk, eldest son of Charles David, of Little Massingham, had four sons and

Page 116. *Charles David Brereton, Junior.*

Page 6. *Charles David Brereton, Senior.*

Page 7.   *Joseph Lloyd Brere on.*

Page 7.   *Henry Brereton, E. I. C. C. S.*

two daughters: 1, Clement, unmarried; 2, Alfred, born in 1850, who married Haidie Maud, daughter of Colonel Shaw, of the Bengal Army, by whom he has one child, Clement Shaw, born in 1895; 3, Charles Harold, unmarried; 4, Cecil, born in 1856, Rector of Hardham, Sussex who married Rose Emily Temple, adopted daughter of Charlotte, Lady Glamis, by whom he has one son and one daughter: a, Charles Cecil Trelawny, born in 1889; b, Frances Dora, born in 1887; 5, Alice, eldest daughter, who married Rev. Erskine William Langmore, son of General E. G. Langmore, Vicar of Pirton, Herts; no issue; 6, Amy, unmarried. Clement and Harold died in India, unmarried.

Henry, second son of Charles David, had one child, Frances Anna, who married Hume Dudgeon, of Black Rock, Dublin, and died in 1881, without issue.

Joseph Lloyd, third son of Charles David, had five sons and six daughters: 1, William Lloyd Brereton, eldest son, was B. A. at Cavendish College, Cambridge, before he was twenty years old; Colonel in Royal Munster Fusiliers Regiment; was through the Afghan war, under Lord Roberts; was the youngest colonel in the English Army. He married Ethel Alice, daughter of Colonel ——— Clay, of the Bengal Army. By her he had one son, William Munster, born in 1894; 2, Francis Lloyd Brereton, second son, was born in 1859; M. A. at Cavendish College, Cambridge, 1882; ordained Priest, 1893; Head Master Northeastern School, Barnard Castle, Durham, from 1893. He married Maude Louise, daughter of ——— Dixon, Esq. By her he has two sons: a, Joseph Lloyd, born in 1901; b, Henry Lloyd, born in 1903; 3, Henry Lloyd, born in 1864, unmarried; 4, David Lloyd, born in 1875, unmarried; 5, Philip Lloyd, born in 1877, unmarried. The daughters are: 1, Anna Frances, eldest, who married Rev. J. H. Thompson, Rector of Romansleigh, Devon, by whom she had one son, Arthur, born in 1892; 2, Henrietta Mary; 3, Margaret; 4, Jane; 5, Eleanor; 6, Cicely; all unmarried and living in 1904, at Little Massingham, with their brother, Henry Lloyd, the Rector. William-Lloyd, eldest son, died 1898.

John Alfred, fourth son of Charles David, has two sons and four daughters: 1, Randle Areange, born in 1877, Auditor R.

R. Department, Burmah, India, unmarried; 2, Charles Gillespie, born in 1880, clerk in London Bank, unmarried; 3, Frances Marion Emma, born in 1875, unmarried; 4, Rosalie, unmarried; 5, Mary, unmarried; 6, Violet, born in 1886, unmarried; all living in 1904.

Robert Maitland Brereton, sixth son of Charles David, has three sons and one daughter: 1, Maitland, born in 1874; M. E. at Minas Prietas, Mexico; married Susanna, daughter of —— Lovenich, Esq., of Minas, Prietas. They have two children, Blanca Alicia, born in 1901, and Margarita, born in 1902; 2, Ralf Hereford, born in 1877, unmarried; 3, Cloudesley Shovell, born in 1885; 4' Katharine Fairchild, born in 1880, unmarried.

Henrietta Lucy, fifth daughter of Charles David Brereton, of Little Massingham, married Frederick Napleton Dew, by whom she had two sons and five daughters: 1, Armine, born in 1867; Captain in India Staff Corps; political agent, Beloochistan; married Esnie Mary, daughter of Colonel Sir Adelbert Talbot, K. C. I. E.; 2, Roderick, born in 1872; unmarried; in Holy Orders; 3, Gertrude Frances, eldest daughter, born in 1863; married Arthur Stratten, Esq., of London; no issue; 4, Izabel Mary, born in 1864; married John Cockburn, Esq., of Edinburgh, by whom she has three children, a, Archibald Frederick, born in 1890; b, Izabel Stella, born in 1892; c, Laelia Armine, born in 1894; 5, Annette Beatrice, born in 1865; married Moncrief Cockburn, Esq., of Edinburgh, by whom she has two children, a, Archibald Moncrief, born in 1900; b, Frederick Armine, born in 1902; 6, Alice Henrietta, born in 1869, unmarried; 7, Margaret Louise born in 1871; married in 1903 Lieutenant Philip James Stopford, R. N., son of Colonel James Stopford and Mary Waller, his wife.

The foregoing represents all the members of the family of Charles David Brereton, of Little Massingham, and of their descendants alive in 1904. Henry, the second son, died in India during the mutiny. He was Commissioner of Goruckpore. In 1848-50 he was Deputy Commissioner in the Punjab, during the Sikh war, when Runjeet Singh, the King of Lahore, was taken. He had charge of the celebrated diamond, known as the Koh-i-

Page 124.

Thomas George Brereton.

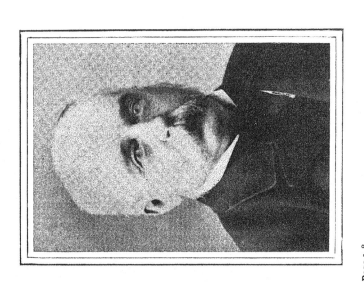

Page 18.

Major-General John Alfred Brereton.

noor, now the largest diamond in the English crown. It had belonged to Nadir Shah, the Shah of Persia, in 1739. William Wilson, the fifth son, entered the Royal Navy in 1843, and served under the late Admiral of the fleet, Sir Henry Keppel, in the China sea; the ship was wrecked off the coast of Sarawac, Borneo, where Sir James Broke was established as rajah; he took a liking for the young "middy," and so William left the navy and joined Sir James in 1845. He died in Sarawac in 1854.

WILSON FAMILY.

As Joseph Wilson, of Highbury Hill, Islington, London, was my grandfather on the maternal side, I give the following brief history of the Wilson family descent, though it appears quite modern as compared with the Brereton history. For several generations the Wilson family had been settled at Stenson, a hamlet of Barrow-cum-Twyford, near Derby. They were landowners in their own right and freeholders of the county. John Wilson, of Stenson, born in 1693, died in 1747, was the father of eight children. Thomas, the fourth son, married Mary Remington. By her he had two sons and one daughter: 1, Thomas; 2, Joseph, my grandfather; 3, Mary, wife of Samuel Mills, of London. Thomas Wilson, the father, was born in 1731, died in 1794. Thomas, the first son, was born in 1764, died in 1843; he married Elizabeth Clegg. By her he had two daughters and one son: 1, Rebekah, wife of Rev. James Stratten, Minister of Paddington Chapel, Islington; 2, Eliza, wife of Joshua Coombs; 3, John, who married Mary Buley. Joseph Wilson, the second son, married Frances, daughter of Robert Maitland (after whom I was named), of Blue Style, Greenwich; her only brother, Ebeneza Maitland, was the owner of Stanstead Hall, Essex, and his son, William Fuller Maitland, of Standstead, was the noted picture connoisseur and collector. Ebeneza was also the owner of the beautiful Park Place, near Henley-on-the-Thames. Joseph Wilson, by his wife Frances Maitland, had two daughters and one son: 1, Mary, wife of Rev. Henry Grace Sperling, Rector of Papworth, Huntingtonshire; by her he had one son, Henry Grace, who married my eldest sister, Anna Margaretta, they had no issue; 2, Frances, wife of my father, Charles David; 3, Henry Wilson, of Stowlangtoft Hall, Suffolk, who was M. P. for West Suffolk. Joseph Wilson owned Highbury Hill, Islington; Stowlangtoft Hall and estates in Suffolk; the parish of Little Massingham, with the Advowson, in Norfolk, which latter my paternal grandfather, John Brereton IV., of Brinton, purchased for him. Joseph Wilson died at Highbury in 1851. He and his brother Thomas were the largest silk merchants and manufacturers in London for many years; they were wealthy and greatly esteemed in the City of London. Their first cousin, Samuel Wilson, was Lord Mayor of London in 1839. Daniel Wilson, Bishop of Calcutta, was also their first cousin. Arthur Stratten, son of Rev. James Stratten, by his wife Rebekah Wilson, married Gertrude Frances Dew, the eldest daughter of my youngest sister, Henrietta Lucy. My grandmother, Frances (Maitland), was descended from the Maitland family of Thirlestone, Berwickshire, Scotland. Her niece, my mother's first cousin, Frances Sarah Maitland, of Park Place, married in 1834, John Colquhoun, of Rossdhu, Luss, Dumbarton, Scotland, who wrote "The Moor and the Loch."

PEDIGREE OF ROBERT. MAITLAND BRERETON'S FAMILY FROM 1175 TO 1904.

A. D.

1st generation—Sir William de Brerton I. _____1175
2d generation—Sir William de Brerton II. _____
3d generation—Sir Ralph de Brerton _____
4th generation—Sir William de Brerton III. _____1216
5th generation—Sir Ranulphus de Brerton and Lady Ada_1275
6th generation—Sir William de Brerton IV. _____1300
7th generation—Sir William de Brerton V. _____1342
8th generation—William de Brerton, Esq. _____
9th generation—Sir William de Brerton VI. _____1400

Page 12   *Maitland Brereton, M. E.*

Page 120.   *Robert Maitland Brere on, C. E.*

10th generation—Sir Randle de Brerton I., of Malpas_____1400
11th generation—Sir Randle Brereton II., of Malpas_____
12th generation—Sir Randle Brereton III., of Malpas_____
13th generation—Sir Randle Brereton IV., of Malpas, died_1530
14th generation—Rev. John Brereton, of Malpas, died_____1542
15th generation—William Brereton, of Hoxne, Suffolk, died.1561
16th generation—Cuthbert Brereton, of Norwich, died_____1612
17th generation—John Brereton, of Norwich, died_____1632
18th generation—John Brereton I., of Brinton, died_____1684
19th generation—John Brereton II., of Brinton, died_____1725
20th generation—William Brereton, of Brinton, died_____1777
21st generation—John Brereton III., of Brinton, died_____1785
22d generation—John Brereton IV., born 1752, died_____1823
23d generation—Charles David Brereton, born 1790, died__1868
24th generation—Robert Maitland Brereton, born 1834____
25th generation—Maitland Brereton, born 1874 _____
26th generation—Alicia Brereton, born 1901 _____

BRERETONS OF BLAKENEY, NORFOLK.

Robert Brereton, third son of John Brereton III., of Brinton, born in 1760, died in 1831; married Elizabeth Ann, daughter of Thomas Hudson, of Tottenham, Middlesex, born in 1756, died in 1821. By her he had one son, Robert John.

Robert John Brereton of Blakeney, born in 1796, died in 1858; married Sarah, daughter and co-heiress of Pearson Walton, Esq., of Walton House, Yorkshire. By her he had one son, Robert Pearson, and one daughter, Elizabeth Anne, who married her cousin, John Brereton V., of Brinton; 2, Walton, born in 1824, died in 1826.

Robert Pearson Brereton, C. E., of London, died without issue; he married Anna Margaretta, daughter of William John Brereton, of Brinton, his second cousin.

RANDLE BRERETON OF BLAKENEY.

Randle Brereton, third son of John Brereton IV., of Brinton, grain merchant, died in 1871; married Sarah, daughter of William Barwick, of Holt Lodge, Norfolk. By her he had one son, Randle Barwick, and four daughters: 1, Anna Margaretta, died unmarried; 2, Mary, who married Rev. Edward W. Dowell, Vicar of Dunton, Norfolk; both dead; they had one son and three surviving daughters, one of whom is married and has issue; 3, Harriet, who married Rev. Robert Hooper, of Brighton; both dead; left issue, sons and daughters; 4, Augusta, who was married but no knowledge of whether there was issue.

Randle Barwick Brereton, Rector of Stiffkey, Norfolk, died in 1897, without issue; in 1842 he married Mary Brecknell, daughter of William John Brereton, of Brinton.

BRERETONS OF BRININGHAM, NORFOLK.

Rev. Shovell Brereton fourth son of John Brereton IV., of Brinton, died in 1886. He was Rector of Poringland, Norfolk, also of Briningham, and a land owner. He married Maria, daughter of Edward Colwell, of London. By her he had two sons and one daughter: 1, Shovell Henry; 2, Charles John, Rector of Thornage-cum-Brinton, who died unmarried in 1898; 3, Anna Margaretta, who married Rev. Henry Brereton Foyster Rector of St. Clement's, Hastings, Sussex, and Prebendary of Chichester Cathedral. Both living in 1904; have issue.

Shovell Henry Brereton, born in 1833, died in 1899, was Captain in Norfolk Militia; his widow is living at Briningham. He married Emma, daughter of Rev. —— White, of Norwich. By her he had two sons and one daughter: 1, Henry Cloudesley Shovell, living in 1904, in the Government Education Department, unmarried; 2, John Lloyd, estate agent, unmarried; 3, Katherine, Army Nurse Corps, unmarried

Wi fred Procter Brere on.

Charles Herber Brereton.

CANADA BRANCH OF THE BRERETON FAMILY.

This family, which settled in the Province of Ontario, Canada, is descended from Abel Brereton, Esq., of Brinton, Norfolk, England, by his wife Elizabeth, second daughter of David Lloyd, Esq., of Llanvaughan, County Cardigan, Wales. He was born in 1773 and died in 1818; he was twin brother of John Brereton IV., of Brinton Hall and Manor, who married Anna Margaretta, the eldest daughter of the same David Lloyd from whom are descended the families of Charles David Brereton, of Little Massingham; of Randle Brereton, of Blakeney; of Shovell Brereton, of Briningham, and the elder line of Brinton. This Abel Brereton had three brothers and five sisters, viz.: John, of Brinton Hall; William, who died in 1790, without issue; Robert, of Blakeney, who died in 1831, leaving issue; Mary, who married John Dew, Esq., of Norwich; Anne, who married Jeremiah Sharpe, Esq.; Bridget, who married Thomas Hewett, Esq.; Sarah and Margaret, who died unmarried. Abel Brereton married twice. By his first wife, Anne Rous, he had seven children, who all died issueless. By his second wife, Elizabeth Lloyd, he had one son and two daughters, viz: Cloudesley Shovell, Elizabeth and Margaret, both daughters died unmarried. The family home is at Bethany, Ontario, Canada. The pedigree proceeds as follows:

Cloudesley Shovell, only son of Abel Brereton, married Charlotte, daughter of John Fisher. By her he had four sons and two daughters: 1, Charles Herbert; 2, William John; 3, Cloudesley Picton; 4, Thomas George, all living in 1904; 5, Elizabeth, married W. H. Lowery, Esq.; 6, Margaret, married William Copland, Esq., of Toronto.

Charles Herbert, M. D., of Bethany, married Eliza Lydia, daughter of Thomas Proctor, M. D. By her he had three sons and two daughters, all living and unmarried in 1904: 1, Wilfred Proctor; 2, Thomas Cloudesley; 3, Lloyd Randolph; 4, Winnifred Margaret; 5, Lilian Myra.

William John, M. D., second son, of Shomberg, Ontario, married Annie, daughter of H. Lount, Esq. By her he has two sons and one daughter: 1, Cloudesley Herbert, married a daughter of Dr. Bonner; 2, Ewart Lount, married a daughter of Dr. Davis; 3, Clara, the only daughter, is unmarried; both of the sons are M. D's.; they have no children in 1904.

Cloudesley Picton, third son, of Oak River, Manitoba, married Annie Fraser, daughter of Alexander Black, Esq. They have four sons and one daughter, all in their teens: 1, Cloudesley; 2, Alexander; 3, George Randle; 4, James Brodie; 5, Charlotte Isabella.

Thomas George, M. D., fourth son, of Bethany, Ontario, married Letitia, daughter of John Hulse, Esq. They have three sons and one daughter, all in their teens: 1, Frederick Elvin; 2, Charles Hulse; 3, Frank Marvin; 4, Lilly Letitia.

Charles Herbert Brereton, M. D., the eldest son, was for six years a member of the Ontario Legislature for the east riding of the County of Durham; William John Brereton, M. D., second son, Coroner for the County of York, Ontario; Cloudesley Picton Brereton, third son, farmer in Manitoba, Canada; Thomas George Brereton, fourth son, M. D., etc., of Trinity University, Toronto; Cloudesley Herbert Brereton, M. D., etc., of Chesley, Ontario; Ewart Lount Brereton, D. D. S., of Barrie, Ontario; William Proctor Brereton, B. A. S., at Pittsubrgh, U. S. A.

The families of the daughters of Cloudesley Shovell Brereton, are: 1, Elizabeth Brereton, who married W. H. Lowery Esq.; their children are Thomas, Dalton, Cloudesley and Elsie; 2, Margaret Brereton, married William Copland, Esq.; their children are Alice and Willa.

SHARPE AND BRERETON.

Anne, second daughter of John Brereton III., of Brinton, by his wife, Bridget, daughter of Abel John Brett, Esq., married Jeremiah Sharpe, Esq., of Weasenham, Norfolk, by whom she had three sons and one daughter: 1, Abel, who married Sophia

Louisa Trash; they had two sons and one daughter, *a*, George Brereton Sharpe; *b,* John Brereton Sharpe; *c*, Anne Sharpe; 2, James.

Abel Sharpe, eldest son of Jeremiah Sharpe, married Sophia Louisa Trash, by whom he. had two sons and one daughter: 1, George Brereton Sharpe; *2*, John Brereton Sharpe; 3, Anne Sharpe.

James Sharpe, second son of Jeremiah Sharpe, married Catherine, daughter of M. Atkinson, by whom he had issue.

Samuel C. Sharpe, grandson of Jeremiah Sharpe, married Maria, daughter of J. P. Palmer, Esq., by whom he had issue.

W. D. Atkinson Sharpe, married Katherine, daughter of Henry Loftie Rulton, Esq., by whom he had two sons: 1, Henry Curtis Sharpe; 2, Charles Brereton Sharpe.

John Brereton Sharpe, grandson of Jeremiah Sharpe, married Martha, daughter of ——— Hand, Esq., by whom he had issue.

Margaret Sharpe, daughter of Jeremiah Sharpe, by his wife, Anne, daughter of John Brereton, of Brinton, married Henry Percy Banks, Esq., by whom he had issue.

Anne Banks married William Withers, Esq., of Norfolk, by whom she bore Henry Percy Withers and two others.

BRERETONS OF NORFOLK.

(Extracts from Blomefield's History of Norfolk).

Andrew Brereton, of Catton, monument in the north aisle of Catton Church. Died May 5, 1703. Vol. X., p. 408.

Catherine Brereton, wife of William Brereton, presented Rev. Edward Yovell to Catton Vicarage, 1699. Vol. X., p. 122.

٠ Catherine Brereton, wife of William Brereton, of Caistor St. Edmund, died August 8, 1708. Vol. V., p. 429.

Cuthbert Brereton, or Briarton, Sheriff of Norwich in 1576. Alderman, Attorney. Vol. III., p. 359.

Cuthbert Brereton, presented Rev. Edward Yovell to the Rectory of Ashby in 1685. Vol. X., p. 95.

Cuthbert Brereton, presented Samuel Conold to Catton Vicarage in 1701. Vol. X., p. 122.

Cuthbert Brereton, presented Rev. Francis Brook to Ashbv Rectory in 1723. Vol. X., p. 95.

Elizabeth Brereton, wife of William Brereton, of Caistor St. Edmund, daughter of William Clark, of Wroxham, died September 2, 1660. Vol. V., p. 429.

Elizabeth Brereton, wife of William Brereton, of Caistor St. Edmund, grave stone in the Chancel, Caistor Church. Vol. XI., p. 213.

John Brereton, Verger Norwich Cathedral for fifty years; died September 13, 1680, age eighty-six. Above is given in list of plain flat stones in the Cathedral. Vol. IV., p. 22.

John Brereton, Apothecary, of Norwich, died August 26, 1710; buried in Arminghall St. Mary's church; arms of Brereton. Vol. V., p. 420.

John Brereton. Inscription in Chancel of Caistor St. Ed mund's church, Brereton impaling an inescutcheon in an orle of Mullets: "Memoride Johannis Brereton de Catton; Gulielmi (William) quondam de Caistor Gen. Filij, qui objt iii die Dec. A. D. MDCLxxxvl (1686), necnon Rosae uxoris Johannis Lynes de Caistor, Gen. Filiae, quae objt——et Johannis eorum Filij, qui objt——" (—— represent portions obliterated by age). (Second inscription). "Domitorium Johannis Lynes qui ob. 1 Augus 1650 superstitem relinquens unicam prolem Rosae uvorem Johannis Brereton." (Mother of Rose). Vol. V., p. 429.

Peter Brereton. Inscription in the chancel of Caistor church: "Expectans horam Domini, Petrus Brereton de Trowse, Gulielmi, de Caistor, F. Gen. xiii die Nov. A. D. MDCLxv (1665)—Crest, a Nag's head—Brereton impales Clerk (Clark of Wroxham?) gule, two barrs vert, on the uppermost, two plates on the lowermost." Vol. V., p. 429.

Reginald Brereton, of Islington (near Lynn). Queen Elizabeth on June 7 in her twelfth year (1570) demised the Manor of New Hall, valued at £10, 14s, 1d per annum (part of the lands assigned to Queen Mary before she came to the crown) to John Lovell, Gent., with the site of the Manor of New Hall in Isling-

Little Massingham Church, Norfolk, Where, in the Churchyard on the East Side, Charles David Brereton and Members of His Family Lie Buried.

Page 119.

ton; demised to Reginald Brereton under the Great Seal on Jan. 23; time, third and fourth of Philip and Mary. (1692). Vol. VIII., p. 476.

Richard Brereton. Inscription in Arminghall Church: "Ric. Brereton, 17 August, 1708, age 39." Vol. V., p. 420.

Robert Brereton. Vol. XI., p. 213.

Rose Brereton, see John Brereton. Vol. V., p. 429.

Samuel Brereton. Inscription in the bellows blower to the organ in St. Peter Mancroft Church (Norwich): "To Sam. Brereton, whose stipend is 40s per annum." Vol. IV., p. 191.

Susan Brereton. Inscription in chancel of Caistor Church· "Susan, wife of John Inman, dau. of Peter Brereton, late of Trowse, Gent., 1686, age 22." Vol. V., p. 429.

Susanna Brereton. Inscription in Arminghall Church, Arms of Brereton: "Susanna, wife of William Brereton, August 17, 1714, age 66." Vol. V., p. 420.

Thomas Brereton. Was Lord of Claxton (Manor) in 1697, and is said to have purchased it of Thomas Gawdy. Vol. X., p. 116.

Ursley Brereton. In list of plain flat stones in Norwich Cathedral is: "Ursley his wife (John Brereton, Verger) May 23, 1663."

William Brereton. Inscriptions in the chancel of Caistor Church: "William Brereton, of Norwich, Gent., April 25, 1691, age 83." (The same inscription as that given under Peter Brere ton). Vol. V., p. 429.

William Brereton. Inscription in Arminghall Church, Arms of Brereton: "William Brereton, Gent., 5 April, 1700, (age) 71." Vol. V., pp. 420, 429.

William Brereton. Inscription in the chancel of St. Peter Mountergate Church, Norwich: "Brereton, argent two barrs sable, impaling a stag's head in a bordure ingrailed, a crescent for difference: William Brereton, 1682, act. 1 year 15 days." Vol. IV., p. 94.

William Brereton. Chapter 32 of the City (Norwich) in the time of King James the Second (1685-8) William Brereton. (In list of Common Council ejected). Vol. III., pp. 423 and 436.

(Cuthbert) Mr. Brereton, attorney at law, left a house situate between Mr. Mickelburgh's and Mr. Randal's, now let at £5 a year, to be distributed to the poor in coals, candles, bread and money. (The above is mentioned under the heading of St. Michael's-at-Plea Church, Norwich). Vol. IV., p. 329.

(Some of the Brereton family held Manors in Ashby, Claxton, Helgeton, Holveston, Rockland, Thurton and Carleton, with the advowsons of Ashby and Helgeton, in the seventeenth century).

Ashby. In the next year (i. e. 26th Edward I., A. D. 1298) he (Sir William de Kerdeston) purchased of John de Helgeton 24 messuages, 3 mills, 320 acres of land, 9½ acres of meadow, 4 of wood, 125 of marsh, 3½ of pasture, 28s and 3d rent, with one pound of Cumin, several Capons, etc., per annum, in this town (Ashby), Claxton, Helgeton, Holveston, Rockland, Thurton and Carleton, with the advowsons of Ashby and Helgeton; so that the Kerdestons were lords of this Manor (Ashby) and the others mentioned; and after them the De La Poles, Gaugys, *Breretons* and ———— Crow of Caistor. Vol. X., p. 94.

Carleton, Charles Brandon, Duke of Suffolk, had a grant of it (the advowson) from the Crown and presented in 1523; from him it came to Edward Lord North; (then) to Gawdy, *Brereton,* and Crow. This lordship Manor came afterwards to William de Cheney, so to the Cressys, and the Kerdestons, and from that family to the De La Poles, Gawdy, *Brereton,* and Crow, who was lord in 1740. Vol. X., p. 120.

In this family (the Kerdestons) it (the manor and advowson of Helgeton) remained as in Claxton; and after that the *Breretons.* Vol. X., p. 135.

EXTRACTS FROM NORFOLK ARCHAEOLOGY.

Anne Brereton William Buybon, of Thursford, ob. 29 Oct. 1751, aet. 33; married Anne, dau. of Will. Brereton of Briningham (Brinton?), Co. Norfolk, Attorney-at-Law. Vol. I., p. 183.

EXTRACTS FROM FARRER'S CHURCH HERALDRY, NORFOLK.

Bixley Church. On the pulpit. (Tinctured by lines) Argent, two barrs sable, Brereton. Vol. I., p. 144.

Blakeney Church. Slab in the church yard: Two barrs with mullet for difference (Brereton, argent, two barrs sable); Crest, a bear's head muzzled (Brereton out of a ducal coronet on a bear's head sable, muzzled gules, studded OR); Motto: "Opitulante Deo," for "Elizabeth Brereton, daughter of Thomas Hudson, of Tottenham, Co. Middlesex, wife of Robert Brereton, born Oct. 1, 1756, died Nov. 27, 1821. Robert Brereton, who died June 11, 1831, age 71. Robert John Brereton, of Blakeney, who died Nov. 2, 1858, aged 62. Sarah Pearson, wife of Robert John Brereton, daughter of Pearson Walton, Esq., of Walton, who died Dec. 18, 1875, aged 80. Walton, their son, who died June 13, 1826, aged 2."

In Briningham church yard. A monument, two barrs (Brereton, argent, two barrs sable) a bear's head, Brereton. The monument in shape like a sugar loaf, and the crest on the summit for "Brereton-Seppings." Vol. II., pp. 377-8.

Brinton Church. Tablets at the east end of the north aisle, with colored shields.

(1) Argent, two barrs sable; Brereton; impaling sable, a spear-head embrued between three scaling ladders, two and one, argent, on a chief gules a castle triple-towered proper: (Lloyd, this coat of arms was granted to Cadifer, ap. Dyffnwal, ninth in descent from Roderick the Great, Prince of all Wales, by his cousin the great Lord Rhys, for taking the castle of Cardigan by escalade from the Earl of Clare and the Flemings in 1164) Crest, a bear's head couped proper (Brereton, out of a ducal coronet OR, a bear's head sable, muzzled, studded OR) motto, "Opitulante Deo" for "John Brereton, Gent., late of this Parish, who died Jan. 30, 1823, aged 70."

(2) In lozenge, Brereton impaling Lloyd; "M. S. Annae Margarettae Brereton, Dau. Lloyd, Cardigan; A. M. filiae natu maximae, Johannis Brereton hujus parochiae uxoris, quae 21 die Mart. decessit A. D. 1819, aet. 63."

Altar tombs and slabs in the churchyard, many of them much worn away.

(3) Brereton crest: The bear is here muzzled; see No. 1 for "Anne, wife of William Brereton, Gent., who died Oct. 2, 1734, aged 37." (She was the daughter of Thomas Shorting, of Cley).

"William, son of John and Cicely Brereton, who died Jan. 3, 1777, aged 89; and Margaret, second wife and relict of William Brereton, who died Jan. 13, 1784, aged 66." (She is not mentioned in the family pedigree).

(4) Lloyd: Crest, a wolf rampant holding a spear head embrued between his paws and piercing the dexter paw, underneath three drops of blood, for "Charles Herbert Lloyd, M. D., born June 1, 1766; died Sept. 16, 1821."

(5) For John, son of John and Bridget Brereton, who died Jan. 20, 1823, aged 70. Anna Margaretta, daughter of David Lloyd, who died March 21, 1819, aged 63. John Brereton, born Sept. 11, 1813; died Jan. 18, 1861.

Elizabeth, wife of William John Brereton, died Dec. 24, 1826, aged 42. William John Brereton, J. P. D. L., born Jan. 3, 1787; died May 4, 1851. Anne, wife of Abel Brereton, died Jan. 27, 1795, aged 31. Abel Brereton, died Sept. 21, 1819, aged 66. Elizabeth, second wife and relict of Abel Brereton, died July 30, 1830, aged 72. John Brereton, son of Abel and Anne Brereton, died Oct. 10, 1807, aged 16. Thornage (in list of rectors, 1734, [Rev.] Nathaniel Shorting succeeded, presented by William Brereton, Gent., of Brinton (who married Anne, daughter of Thomas Shorting). Vol. II., p. 377-8.

Felthorpe Church. "In memory of William Brereton, Gent., who died Dec. 31, 1697, and these arms, argent, two barrs sable." In White's History of Norfolk, under Felthorpe Parish, is the following: "William Brereton, in 1697, left two tenements and two acres of land (let for £2 a year) for the residence and sole benefit of two poor aged widows; and he bequeathed his other land and house in Felthorpe, and £100 to be invested for charitable purposes in the parish." This charity is still in operation. This William Brereton may have been the younger son of Rev.

HERALDIC DESIGNS

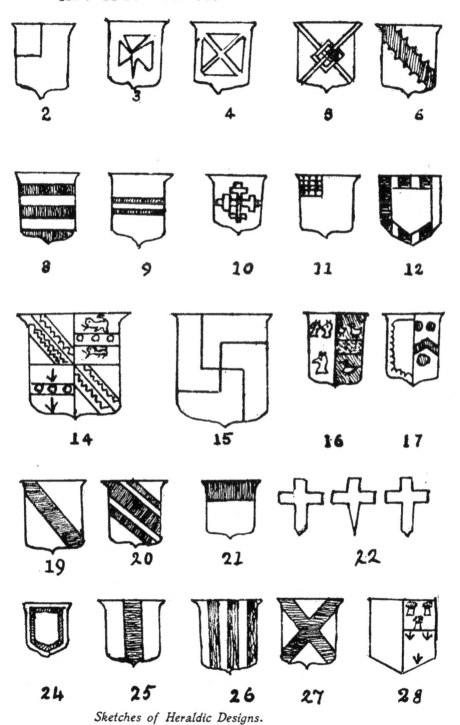

Sketches of Heraldic Designs.

John Brereton, of St. Peter Mancroft, Norwich, and younger brother of John Brereton, of Shottisham, who died 1684, and uncle to John Brereton I., of Brinton. Vol. X., p. 416.

Lidia Maria Brereton. St. Michael's-at-Plea Church, Norwich. "Near this place resteth the body of Lidia Maria Brereton, who died 16th Oct., 1743, aged 24." Vol. III., p. 95.

ILLUSTRATIONS OF HERALDIC DESIGNS.

1. A Cross, quartered.
2. A Quarter on a Shield.
3. A Cross patte fitche
4. Cross patte or forme.
5. Fret or Frette.
6. Engrailed Bend.
7. Cross.
8. Border.
9. Barrulet.
10. Cross Crosslet.
11. Canton.
12. Border Paley.
13. Chevron.
14. Inescutcheon and Impalement.
15. Quarterly in equerre.
16. Impalement.
17. Impalement with Chevron and Besants and Border engrailed.
18. Fesse.
19. Bend.
20. Bend between two Bentlets.
21. Chief.
22. Crosses with points down.
23. Mascle.
24. Orle.
25. Pale.

26.   Paley of six Argents and Gules.
27.   Saltier or Saltyre.
28.   Escutcheon or Shield with Garbs and Pheons.

GLOSSARY OF HERALDIC TERMS.

ACHIEVEMENT.—Properly, achievement of arms is an escutcheon
   or armorial shield, and signifies a complete heraldic
   composition, whether the shield alone or the shield with
   the crest, motto and supporters, if any.

ARMS.—The heraldic armorial bearings of an individual, con
   sisting of some device in heraldic tinctures (see tincture) borne on a shield, generally with the addition of
   a crest; and sometimes with supporters.   The right to
   bear the arms of the father is inherited by the sons; in
   strictness each of the younger sons should add to the
   paternal shield a label (which see) as a mark of cadency,
   or filial difference; the same right descends to a daughter only if she is her father's heiress.

BAR, BARR OR BARRY.—Is a horizontal stripe crossing the field
   or plane of the escutcheon (fig. 8); it is narrower than
   the fesse (fig. 18) and occupies about one-fifth of the
   field.   It is one of the eight ordinaries in heraldry.
   Barrs may be borne in any number, and the blazon, or
   shield, or coat of arms, always names the number.   The
   number of the divisions is always even, and is always
   mentioned as "barry of four pieces," etc.

BEARING.—Signifies any single charge of a coat of arms, any one
   of the eight ordinaries, or any heraldic bird, beast or
   other figure.

BLAZONING.—Is a description in heraldic terms of shield, crest, etc.

BORDER.—Is the outer edge of the field of the escutcheon or shield
   when of different tincture from the central portion.   Its
   width is uniform and should be one-fifth of the field.
   It is sometimes used as a mark of difference.   The border always covers the end of any ordinary, such as the

chevron, fess, etc. The border, when charged with an ordinary, shows only so much of the ordinary as comes naturally upon that part of the field occupied by the border; thus a border paley of six pieces shows in separate colors (fig. 12).

CANTON.—Is a part of the chief field of the shield or escutcheon cut off either the right or left hand upper corner (fig. 11). It is always bounded by straight, horizontal and vertical lines, and is generally considered as one of the sub-ordinaries.

CHAPEAU.—Signifies a cap of maintenance or dignity.

CHARGE.—Is a bearing or any figure borne or represented on an escutcheon, whether on the field or on an ordinary.

CHEVRON.—Is one of the honorable ordinaries; it is supposed to represent two rafters, as of a roof (fig. 13), leaning against each other at the top, but is more generally described as the lower half of a saltier or saltire (see saltier), an ordinary in the form of a St. Andrew's cross, formed by two bends, dexter (right) and sinister (left) crossing each other, completed to a point at the top. The two arms of the chevron rest upon the dexter and sinister bases of the field and are joined in the center; it occupies one-fifth of the field.

CHIEF.—Signifies the head or upper part of the escutcheon from side to side, cut off horizontally by a straight line and containing properly a third part of the dimensions of the escutcheon. It is one of the eight honorable ordinaries, and is commonly considered as divided into dexter, sinister and middle, the charge upon it being thus blazoned (fig. 21).

CREST.—Is a part of an achievement, or escutcheon, borne outside of and above the escutcheon. A crest is not properly borne by a woman, or by a city, or by a corporate body, as it is always assumed to be the ornament worn upon the helmet. When the crest is not especially mentioned as emerging from a coronet, chapeau or the like, it is assumed to be upon a wreath; thus the erazed bear's head of the Brereton family of Malpas is shown as rising from a wreath, and that of the elder line of Brereton from a ducal coronet, indicating royal descent.

CROSS.—This is one of the eight ordinaries consisting, when charged, of a fess and a pale; or, when having no charges upon it, of a barr and a pale meeting, in either case, about the fesse point (fig. 7).

CROSSLET.—Is a small cross; a cross crosslet is a cross having the ends crossed.·

DRAGON.—Is a gryphon or griffin with wings elevated, such as the additional crest borne by the Brereton family of Handford.

ENGRAILED.—Means a bearing cut into concave semi-circular indents (fig. 6).

ERAZED.—Signifies the head of the animal, representing the crest, as having been torn off by violence and not couped or cut off straight.

ESCUTCHEON.—Is the surface upon which are charged the armorial bearings other than the crest, motto, supporters, etc., which are borne separately; it is usually shield shaped.

FESSE.—Is a bearing always considered as one of the honorable ordinaries, bounded by two horizontal lines drawn across the field, and which regularly contain between them one-third of the escutcheon (fig. 18).

FLEURY, FLORY.—Signifies being decorated with a fleur de lis (flower of the lily), or with the upper part of the flower only; that is, with the cross bar and the three large leaves that rise above it, with or without the seed stems.

FRET.—Is a charge consisting of two bentlets placed in saltier, and interlaced with a mascle (a lozenge form of bearing, perforated or voided so that the field appears through the opening); also, called the lover's knot.

FRETTE.—Signifies covered with a grating composed of narrow pieces, as bentlets, fillets, etc., crossing one another and interlacing.

ittle Massingham Rectory.

GARB.—Is a sheaf of any kind of grain, but specifically a sheaf of wheat; when other than wheat the kind must be expressed.

GULE, GULES.—See tincture.

IMPALEMENT.—Is the marshaling or placing side by side of two escutcheons combined into one, such as the arms of a husband and wife (fig. 16).

INESCUTCHEON.—Is a small escutcheon, or the representation of a shield, used either as a bearing, or charged upon the escutcheon for a special purpose, as an escutcheon of pretence.

LABEL.—Is a fillet resembling a barulet (a small bar) with three or more pendant drops or points. It is used as a bearing but especially as a difference, as in cadency, to indicate the eldest son, and also the younger sons.

ORDINARIES.—There are eight of these called honorable; these are the oldest escutcheons or heraldic bearings, and in general the oldest escutcheons are those which are charged with only the ordinaries, or with these primarily, other charges having been added at a later period. The bearings most generally admitted as ordinaries are the eight following: Bar, bend, chevron, chief, cross, fesse, pale, saltier. There are others added which are termed sub-ordinaries; these are: Band-sinister, inescutcheon, quarter or franc-quartier, pile, border, canton, orle, point.

ORLE.—Is a bearing like a border but not reaching the outer edge of the escutcheon, so that the field is seen outside of it as well as within. It is usually half the width of the border, and may be considered as an inescutcheon voided of the field (fig. 24)

PALE.—Is a broad, perpendicular stripe in an escutcheon, equally distant from the two edges and usually occupying one-third of the field. It is the first and simplest kind of ordinary. When not charged it is often represented as containing only one-fifth of the field.

PALEWISE, PALEY.—Represents the escutcheon as divided into four or more equal parts by perpendicular lines, as paly of six argent and gules. There should always be an even number of parts (fig. 26).

PATTEE.—Signifies a spreading of the paw, or of the cross toward the extremity, each of its arms spreading, or dove-tailed shape (fig. 4).

PATENSE, CROSS-PATENSE.—Is an escutcheon charged with five bezants, that is, a small circle, tincture OR (gold), a gold roundel or solidus, assumed as a bearing by some of the crusaders (fig. 17).

PASSANT.—Represents an animal, such as lion or bear in the coat of arms and crest, standing and looking forward.

PHEON.—Is a barbed head, as of an arrow, differing from a broad arrow in being engrailed on the inner side of the barbs; the point is always directed downwards.

PROPER.—Signifies an animal or bird or any object used in the bearing as having its proper shape and color shown.

RAMPANT.—Signifies an animal used in the coat of arms or crest as standing up on its hind feet with paws extended.

SALTIER, SALTIRE.—Is one of the ordinaries in the form of a St. Andrew's cross, formed by two bends, dexter and sinister, crossing each other (fig. 27).

SHIELD.—Is the shield shaped form of the escutcheon, used for all displays of coat of arms.

SHIELD OF PRETENSE.—Is an inescutcheon to assert its owner's pretension to an estate. It is especially used to denote the marriage of the bearer to an heiress whose arms it bears. It is a small escutcheon charged upon the main escutcheon, and indicates claims or pretensions to some distinction, or to some estate, armorial bearings, etc., which are not his by strict right of blood descent.

SUPPORTERS—Is the representation of some living creature accompanying the escutcheon and either holding it up or standing beside it as if to keep guard over it.

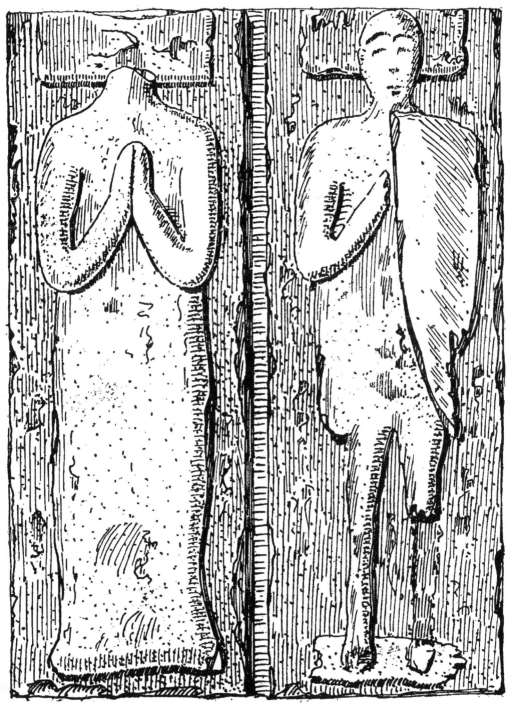

Figures Inside of Tomb.

TINCTURE.—There are only two metal colors used in heraldry:
1, OR (gold) ; 2, argent (silver or white). The colors
mainly used are: Azure (blue) ; sable (black), and
vert (green). The fur most commonly used is ermine.
A law in heraldry provides that the tincture of a bearing must be of one of the two metal colors mentioned,
if the field is a color, and vice versa. OR (gold) is
often represented as such (yellow), and in engravings,
conventionally, by dots upon a white ground. Argent
(silver) is indicated by a plain or white surface. Gule,
or gules, indicates a red color and is common.

EAST CHESHIRE

BY

J. P. EARWAKER

1877

———

HANDFORD-CUM-BOSDEN.

———

William Brereton, who was born in 1604, came of age in
1625, shortly after which, on March 10, 1626-7, he was created
a Baronet by Charles I. He was twice married, first to Susanna,
daughter of Sir George Booth, of Dunham Massey, Cheshire,
Baronet, who died in 1637, and secondly to Cicely, daughter of
Sir William Skeffington, of Fisherwick, Co. Leicester, Bart.,
by both of whom he had issue. Of Sir William Brereton's
early years little is known. In 1634-5 he traveled through a
large portion of Great Britain and crossed over into Holland
and the United Provinces. He kept a diary of the places he
visited, etc., which was published by the Chetham Society in
1844, from the original now in the possession of Sir Philip de
Malpas Grey Egerton, Bart. From it he appears to have been
of a very sober and religious turn of mind, fond of field sports,
and much attached to his native county, which he frequently
advantageously compared with the various places he passed
through in the course of his travels. There are no indications

in the diary of any love for military affairs, or that he should so soon be able to raise himself to the position of one of the most distinguished military commanders Cheshire has produced. Living at Handforth Hall, he was the friend and associate of Henry Bradshaw, of Marple, the brother of Lord President Brad shaw, of Colonel Dukinfield, of Dukinfield Hall, and by his first marriage he became intimate with Sir George Booth, who was at that time the leader of the Presbyterian party in Cheshire. These friendships no doubt helped to shape the part he subsequently took in his country's affairs. In the third Charles I. [1627-8] he was elected one of the members of Parliament for Cheshire, and in the Parliaments which assembled in 1639 and 1640 he was again elected one of the members for his native county. On the first symptoms of the Civil War he was in Chester, and there sought to assemble the disaffected of that city by causing a drum to be publicly beaten in the streets whilst he endeavored to enlist volunteers for the Parliament. The firm attitude of the Mayor subdued the disturbance at once, and Sir William was at one time in danger of his life.

Sir William Brereton warmly espoused the cause of the Parliament, and so early as January, 1642-3, the House of Commons drew up a long series of "Instructions" and addressed them to him as one of the Deputy Lieutenants of the county. These "Instructions" were printed at the time, but are unfortunately too long to repeat here; but they show the determination of the Parliament to resist the king at all hazards and to take up arms in defense of their rights and privileges. Sir William was given a high command in the forces raised in Cheshire, and was subsequently created Commander-in-Chief of the Parliamentary forces in Cheshire, Staffordshire, Shropshire, etc. The victories he gained were very numerous and important, and there can be no doubt that much of the ultimate success of the Parliament in this part of England was due to his ability as a general. The following is a contemporary account of his victories, drawn up by Josiah Rycroft in his "Survey of England's Champions and Truth's Faithfull Patriots," and published in 1647. The paragraphs in square brackets and in the notes are taken from John Vicars' "England's Worthies Under Whom All the Civill and Bloudy Warres Since Anno 1642 to Anno 1647 Are Related," also published in 1647. Each of these now rare books contains "lively pourtraitures of the severall Commanders," from the one of which given by Vicars, the accompanying woodcut portrait of Sir William Brereton is copied.

"*Upon the religious and magnanimous knight Sir William Brereton:* Constancy and stability, with much perseverance, is brave Brereton's badge of honour; and since the time of his taking up armes for the defence of King, Parliament, and kingdome, he was never found to betray his trust, or decline his proceedings, as Cheshire, Sallopshire, Lancashire, and Staffordshire can well witness. Of his prosperous proceedings I shall [here] insert the particulars.

"At his first coming into Cheshire many well-affected to the Parliament appeared, some had armes, some he armed, to the number of 2000, and hearing of the King's brigade under the command of Sir Thomas Ashton drawing up, he did prepare to give him battell near the *Nantwich.* The which the enemy hearing of prepared all the power possibly they could and ingaged their army with Sir William Brereton, who in an houres fight routed the enemy, took 100 foot and 100 horse prisoners, Jan. 28, 1643 [1642-3], and afterward marched into the country and relieved many oppressed people by taking off the heavy taxations that lay upon them. ["He beat him again most soundly at *Middlewich* [March 13, 1642-3], where he took prisoners Sir Edward Mosely, Colonel Ellis, divers Lieutenant Colonells and Majors, 11 Captaines, most of all his field officers, about 600 souldiers, 2 peeces of ordnance, many arms, all his bag and baggage, his army wholly routed and Middlewich firmely possessed by this noble and victorious commander."—Vicars.

"Hearing of the Earle of Northampton marching that way [he] gave him the meeting neare *Stafford,* and by the assistance of noble Sir John Gell gave him battell and routed him, killing upon the place the said Earle of Northampton, March 26, 1643. ["He also bravely beat the *Earl of Darby* at *Stockton Heath,* and

Sir Vincent Corbet also a second time at *Draighton* in *Shropshire* and took from him many prisoners, horses and armes."—Vicars. He presently afterwards took the strong towne of *Stafford* by a stratagem, and from thence went to *Wolverhampton* and tooke it with all the ammunition, and then retreated towards his owne countrey of Cheshire, and by the way tooke *Whitechurch,* and afterwards marched up to *Eckelsall [Eccleshall] Castle,* and tooke it with all the ammunition, June 26, 1643, and coming into Cheshire was there received with much joy. [Rycroft's dates here are exactly a year wrong and have been corrected throughout. J. P. E.]

"Many volunteers listed themselves under him, with whom he marched to *Houghton [?Halton] Castle,* Cheshire, and tooke it with much ammunition July 22, 1643, and afterward marched toward the Lord Capell near the *Nantwich* and gave him battell, routed his whole army, tooke many hundreds prisoners; and presently marched up to *Holt Castle* and besieged it, and by composition took it with much ammunition, Novemb. 21, 1644, and thence marched to *Harden [Hawarden] Castle* and tooke it with the ammunition with the towne of *Rippon,* Decemb. 3, 1643. The Lord Byron having a strong and potent army marched up to the *Nantwich* and besieged it, the which the noble Sir William Brereton understanding the greatnesse of his strength, sent to Sir Thomas Fairfax for help to raise the siege, which noble Sir Thomas did no sooner heare of, but did hasten up to Sir William Brereton, who when they were joyned, marched up to the Lord Byron and suddenly fell upon him, and after a hot fight raised his siege and routed him, tooke 152 knights and gentlemen, 126 commanders, 160 common soldiers, 120 Irish women, with long skeanes, Feb. 14, 1644 [1643-4].

"Having relieved the Wich, Sir William parted with Sir Thomas and marched up towards *Chester,* and beat up the enemies quarters and straightened the towne, the which Prince Rupert hearing, drew all his forces upon Sir William and gave him battell near Tarum [Tarvin], who quickly made the Prince retreat with the losse of 450 men, August 18, 1644. Presently having notice of a great party [who] were going to relieve the

Prince, he sent out a brigade that fell upon them and disperst them, and tooke 175 common soldiers and 15 commanders, August 27, 1644.

["This most renowned commander obtained a most glorious victory over his enemies at *Montgomery Castle* at the relieving of noble Sir Thomas Middleton's forces besieged therein, where he put the enemy, being very strong, to a totall rout and flight, took prisoners Major Gen. Sir Thomas Tildesley, Major Gen. Broughton, Lieutenant Col. Broughton, Major Williams, 19 Captaines, 23 knights and gentlemen, 33 cornets and ensignes, 57 serjeants, 61 corporals, 11 drums, 5 trumpets, 1480 common souldiers; slew 2 Lieutenant Colonels, 7 Captaines, with many other officers, 500 common souldiers, and took their armes and ammunition, bag and baggage. Hee also took the town and castle of *Leverpoole,* with all the ordnance, armes and ammunition therein; and had singular good successe in preventing a dangerous designe of Prince Rupert and Prince Maurice, to have passed their forces through Cheshire into Lancashire against our brethren of Scotland in the north. Hee also took the brave and strong town and castle of *Shrewsbury,* with all the ordnance, armes and ammunition therein, with very many riches, prisoners and prizes. He also routed the King's forces at Denbigh, in Anno 1645, and tooke 400 of the enemies prisoners, about 600 horse and many of the enemies [were] slain in the fight."—Vicars.

"After he had performed this gallant piece of service he marched towards Chester, and meeting with a great party of horse he fell suddenly upon them, routed and desperst them all, tooke 35 commanders, 420 prisoners, and 450 armes, Septem. 24, 1645, and presently after closely besieged *Beeston Castle,* [he] tooke it with all the ammunition, Octob. 15, 1645. The King's forces, under the command of Sir William Vaughan, joyned with all the Welch forces being 6000 strong, drew up towards Sir William Brereton and gave him battell, and after a long and fierce battell were routed and 400 foot taken prisoners, with 600 horse and 250 killed upon the place, Novemb. 28, 1645. Having cleared the field he went againe before *Chester* and closely besieged it, and took it with much armes and ammunition, Jan. 29, 1645 [1645-6], and afterwards marched with his army to *Lichfield* and tooke it with all the ammunition, March 5, 1645 [1645-6] ; and from thence to *Dudley Castle,* Worcestershire, and tooke it May 12, 1646.

["He also took the town of *Leitchfield.* And obtained a most glorious victory over Lord Ashley, the last and greatest prop of the King's party at *Stow in the Would,* Gloucestershire, where he·routed, the said Sir Jacob Ashley's whole army, took Lord Ashley himself prisoner, with divers other eminent. commanders, about 1800 common souldiers, with all their armes, ammunition, bag and baggage. After this hee took *Tilbury Castle* with all the ordnance, armes and ammunition therein ; together with *Dudley Castle* also, a most strong and almost impregnable castle, in the yeare 1646, with all the ordnance, armes and ammunition therein also. And at last after a long siege his valiant and victorious forces took Leichfield's strong close, where hee took prisoners 7 Colonels, 6 Commissioners of Array, 2 Lieutenant Colonels, 8 Majors, 32 Captains, 15 Lieutenants, 8 Cornets, 9 Ensigns, 21 Esquires and Gentlemen of Quality, 700 common souldiers, and all the armes and ammunition therein. And thus was a speciall instrument of ending victoriously these our un-happy and unholy civill wars."—Vicars.]

"These with many more victories hath this valiant knight performed which will to after ages stand a monument of his due praise."

The above account is only a very superficial one, showing the active part Sir William Brereton played during the Civil War. To have enlarged it would have necessitated the writing of the history of the Civil War in this part of the kingdom, and the verifying of many varying dates and names. In the British Museum (Additional Mss. 11, 331-2-3) are three volumes consisting of transcripts of letters to and from Sir William Brereton relating to Civil War matters, chiefly dated 1645, but some in 1642. These, if carefully examined, would probably add much to our present knowledge of the history of the Civil War in Cheshire, Lancashire, Staffordshire, and Shropshire. For his services to the Parliament Sir William Brereton was well re

City of Chester.

warded, the Chief Forestership of Macclesfield Forest, Cheshire, was conferred upon him, together with the Seneschalship of the Hundred of Macclesfield; he had also grants of money and land from estates sequestered by the Parliament, and had a grant of the Archepiscopal Palace of Croydon, near London, where he occasionally resided. During the Protectorate he was often in Cheshire, residing at Handforth Hall, but he died at Croydon, April 7, 1661. His will, dated April 6, 1661, is as follows:

Will of Sir William Brereton of Handforth, Co. Chester, Bart., dated 6 April, 1661. "Whereas by deed heretofore made to trustees for securing the portion of *my daughter Susanna,* now wife of Edmund Lenthall, Esq., I have engaged my manor of Ashton-super-Mersey, Co. Chester, etc., I now confirm the said settlement." "Whereas also I have secured the payment of £1000 to each of *my two younger daughters, Mary Brereton* and *Cicely Brereton,* for their portions out of my manor of Eaton, alias Yaiton, near Congleton, Co. Chester, and a further sum out of my manor of Handforth, in the said county, I now confirm the same " "To my friends, Sir Thomas Wilbraham of Woodhey, Co. Chester, Bart., the said Edmund Lenthall, Esq., Thomas Cose, of London, clerk, Robert Blayney, of London, gent., and my servant, Thomas Edwards, gent., I leave all my lands and tenements in the Forest of Macclesfield, Co. Chester, and in or near Nantwich, in the parishes of Acton, Baddiley, and Bunbury, in trust for the purposes of my will." "To *my daughter, Mrs. Frances Ward,* wife of Edward [Ward], Esq., all my ready money in gold; to *my said daughter Lenthall,* the wrought bed, etc., that was her mother's; to *my said daughter Mary,* my best bed; to *my said daughter Cicely,* all my plate in a chest with *my cousin Elizabeth Lenthall,* widow." "To *my brother Richard Brereton,* £15 per annum for his life." "To *Mr. John Brereton,* minister of the gospel, certain divinity books out of my study at Handforth."

Sir William Brereton's body was brought from London to be interred in the Handforth Chapel in Cheadle Church. There was a tradition in the parish in the last century that in crossing a river the coffin was swept away by a flood and could not be recovered. There is no entry of any burial in the Cheadle registers; the date of death is only given.

He was succeeded by his only son and heir, Sir Thomas Brereton, Bart., then twenty-nine years of age, who married Theodosia, youngest daughter of Humble, first *Baron Ward of Birmingham*. He died January 7, 1673-4, without issue, and was buried in the Handforth Chapel, where the monument shown in the woodcut on page 145 was placed to his memory. With him ended the direct male line of the Breretons of Handforth, who had been seated here as lords of the manors of Handforth, Ashton-super-Mersey. etc.. for about 150 years.

A
Briefe and true Relation of the Discoverie of the North Part of *Virginia*; being a most pleasant, fruitfull and commodious soile

Made this present yeere 1602, by
Captaine BARTHOLOMEW GOSNOLD, Captaine
BARTHOLOMEW GILBERT, and divers
other gentlemen their associats, by the
permission of the honorable knight
SIR WALTER RELEIGH, *etc*
Written by M. JOHN BRERETON
one of the voyage.

Wherein is annexed a Treatise, of M. EDWARD HAYES,
containing important inducements for the planting in those parts
and finding a passage that way to the South sea and China ;
With divers instructions of special moment newly added in this
second impression.

Londini.
Impensis Geor. Bishop.
1602.

To the honourable, Sir Walter Ralegh, Knight, Captaine of her Maiesties Guards, Lord Warden of the Stanneries, Lieutenant of Cornwall, and Governor of the Isle of Jersey.

Honourable sir, being earnestly requested by a deere friend, to put downe in writing, some true relation of our late performed voyage to the North parts of Virginia; at length I resolved to satisfie his request, who also emboldened me to direct the same to your honourable consideration; to whom indeed of duetie it per teineth. May it please your Lordship therefore to understand, that upon the sixe and twentieth of March, 1602, being Friday, we went from Falmouth, being in all, two and thirtie persons, in a small barke of Dartmouth, called The *Concord,* holding a course for the North part of Virginia, and although by chance the winde favoured us not at first as we wished, but inforced us so farre to the Southward, as we fell with S. Marie, one of the Islands of the Azores (which was not much out of our way) but holding our course directly from thence, we made our journey shorter (than hitherto accustomed) by the better part of a thousand leagues; yet were wee longer in our passage than we expected, which happened, for that our barke being weake, we were loth to presse her with much saile; also, our sailers being few, and they none of the best, we bare (except in faire weather) but low saile; besides, our going upon an unknowen coast, made us not over-bolde to stand in with the shore, but in open weather, which caused us to be certeine daies in sounding, before we discovered the coast, the weather being by chance, somewhat foggie. But on Friday the fourteenth of May, early in the morning, wee made the land, being full of faire trees, the land somewhat low,

They fell with S. Marie, one of the Azores.

They discovered land the 14. of May.

149

certeine hummocks or hilles lying into the land, the
shore full of white sand, but very stony or rocky. And
standing faire alongst by the shore, about twelve of the

Eight Indians
come aboord
of them. clocke the same day, we came to an anker, where eight
Indians, in a Baskeshallop with mast and saile, an iron
grapple and a kettle of copper, came boldly aboord us,
one of them apparelled with a wastcoat and breeches
of black serdge, made after our sea-fashion, hose and
shoes on his feet; all the rest (saving one that had a

The descrip-
of them. paire of breeches of blue cloth) were naked. These
people are of tall stature, broad and grim visage, of a
black swart complexion, their eie-browes painted white;
their weapons are bowes and arrowes. It seemed by
some words and signs they made that some Barks
of S. John de Luz, have fished or traded in this place,
being in the latitude of 43 degrees. But riding heere,
in no very good harbour, and withall, doubting the
weather, about three of the clocke the same day in the
afternoon we weighed, and standing Southerly off into
sea the rest of that day and the night following, with a
fresh gale of winde, in the morning we found our selves

"Cape Cod." embaied by a mightie headland; but comming to an
anker about nine of the clocke the same day, within a
league of the shore, we hoised out the one halfe of our
shallop, and captaine Bartholmew Goswold, my selfe,

Their first
landing. and three others, went ashore, being a white sandie
and very bolde shore; and marching all that afternoone
with our muskets on our necks, on the highest hilles
which we saw (the weather very hot) at length we
perceived this headland to be parcell of the maine, and
sundrie Islands lying almost round about it; so returning, (towards evening) to our shallop (for by that
time, the other part was brought ashore and set to-

Another
Indian. gether) we espied an Indian, a young man, of proper
stature, and of a pleasing countenance; and after some
familiaritie with him, we left him at the sea-side, and
returned to our ship; where, in five or sixe houres

absence, we had pestered our ship so with Cod fish, that we threw numbers of them over-boord again; and surely, I am persuaded that in the months of March, April, and May, there is upon this coast, better fishing, and in as great plentie, as in Newfound-land; for the sculles of Mackerell, herrings, Cod, and other fish, that we daily saw as we went and came from the shore, were wonderfull; and besides, the places where we tooke these Cods (and might in a few daies have laden our ship) were but in seven fadom water, and within less than a league of the shore; where, in Newfound-land they fish in fortie or fiftie fadom water, and farre off. From this place, we sailed round about this head A great head-land, almost all the points of the compasse, the shore land, "Cape Cod." very bolde: but as no coast is free from dangers, so I am persuaded, this is as free as any. The land some-what lowe, full of goodly woods, but in some places plaine. At length we were come amongst many faire Many faire Islands, which we had partly discerned at our first Islands. landing; all lying within a league or two one of an-other, and the outermost not above sixe or seven leagues from the maine, captaine Gosnold, my selfe, The first and some others, went ashore, and going round about Island called Marthaes it, we found it to be foure English miles in compasse, Vineyard. without house or inhabitant, saving a little old house made of boughes, covered with barke, an olde piece of a weare of the Indians, to catch fish, and one or two places, where they had made fires. The chiefest trees of this Island, are Beeches and Cedars, the outward Beeches. parts all overgrowen with lowe bushie trees, three or Cedars. foure foot in height, which beare some kinde of fruits, as appeared by their blossomes; Strawberries, red and white, as sweet and much bigger than ours in Eng-land, Rasberies, Gooseberies, Hurtleberries, and such an incredible store of Vines, as well in the wooddie Vines in abundance. part of the Island, where they run upon every tree, as on the outward parts, that we could not goe for tread-

151

ing upon them; also, many springs of excellent sweet water and a great standing lake of fresh water, neere the sea-side, an English mile in compasse, which is mainteined with the springs running exceeding pleasantly thorow the wooddie grounds which are very rockie. Here are also in this Island, great store of Deere, which we saw, and other beasts, as appeared by their tracks; as also divers fowles, as Cranes, Hernshawes, Bitters, Geese, Mallards, Teales, and other fowles, in great plenty, also, great store of Pease, which grow in certeine plots all the Island over. On the North side of this Island we found many huge bones and ribs of Whales. This Island, as also all the rest of these Islands, are full of all sorts of stones fit for building, the sea sides all covered with stones, many of them glittring and shining like minerall stones, and very rockie, also, the rest of these Islands are replenished with these commodities, and upon some of them, inhabitants, as upon an Island to the Northward, and within two leagues of this; yet we found no townes, nor many of their houses, although we saw manie Indians, which are tall big boned men, all naked, saving they cover their privy parts with a blacke tewed skin, much like a Black smith's apron, tied about their middle and betweene their legs behinde: they gave us of their fish readie boiled (which they carried in a basket made of twiggs, not unlike our osier) whereof we did eat, and judged them to be fresh water fish: they gaev us also of their Tobacco, which they drinke greene, but dried into powder, very strong and pleasant, and much better than any I have tasted in England; the necks of their pipes are made of clay hard dried (whereof in that Island is a great store both red and white) the other part is a piece of hollow copper, very finely closed and cemented together. Wee gave unto them certeine trifles, as knives, points, and such like, which they much esteemed. From hence we went to another

152

Island, to the Northwest of this, and within a league or two of the maine, which wee found to bee greater than before we imagined, being 16 English miles at the least in compasse; for it conteineth many pieces or necks of land, which differ nothing fro' severall Islands, saving that certeine banks of small bredth, do, like bridges, joine them to this Island. On the outsides of this Island are many plaine places of grasse, abundance of Strawberies and other berries before mentioned. In mid May we did sowe in this Island (for a triall) in sundry places, Wheat, Barley, Oats, and Pease, which in fourteen daies were sprung up nine inches and more. The soil is fat and lustie, the upper crust of gray colour; but a foot or lesse in depth, of the colour of our hempe lands in England; and being thus apt for these and the like graines; the sowing or setting, (after the ground is clensed) is no greater labour, than if you should set or sow in one of our best prepared gardens in England. This Island is full of high timbred Oakes, their leaves so broad as ours; Ceders, straight and tall; Beech, elm, hollie, Walnut trees in aboundance, the fruit as bigge as ours, as appeared by those we found under the trees, which had lien all the yeere ungathered; Hazlenut trees, Cherry trees, the leafe, barke and bignesse not differing from ours in England; but the stalk beareth the blossoms or fruit at the end thereof, like a cluster of Grapes, forty or fifty in a bunch; Sassafras trees great plentie all the Island over, a tree of high price and profit; also divers other fruit trees, some of them with strange barkes, of an Orange colour; in feeling soft and smooth like Velvet: in the thickest parts of these woods, you may see a furlong or more round about. On the Northwest side of this Island, neere to the sea side, is a standing Lake of fresh water, almost three English miles in compasse, in the middest whereof stands a plot of woody ground, an acre in quantitie or not above: this Lake is full of

Marginal notes:
Wheat, Barley, and Oats sowed came up nine inches in fourteen daies.

Oakes, Cedars, Beech, Elme, Hollie, Walnut trees, Cherry trees.

Sassafras trees. Divers other trees.

A Lake three miles about.

Small
Tortoises.

small Tortoises, and exceedingly frequented with all
sorts of fowles before rehearsed, which breed, some

Abundance
of fowles

low on the banks, and others on low trees about this
Lake in great aboundance, whose young ones of all

much bigger
than ours in
England.

sorts we tooke and eat at our pleasure: but all these
fowles are much bigger than ours in England. Also, in
every Island, and almost in every part of every Island,

Ground nuts.

are great store of Ground Nuts, fortie together on a
stringe, some of them as bigge as hennes egges; they
grow not two inches under ground: the which nuts we
found to be as good as Potatoes. Also, divers sorts of

Shell fish.

shell fish, as Scallops, Muscles, Cockles, Lobsters,
Crabs, Disters and Wilks, exceeding good and very
great. But not to cloy you with particular rehearsall
of such things as God and Nature hath bestowed on
these places, in comparison whereof, the most fertil
part of al England is (of it selfe) but barren; we went
in our light horsman from this Island to the maine,
right against this Island some two leagues off, where
comming ashore, we stood a while like men ravished at

The exceeding
beautie of the
maine Land.
Great Lakes.
Large
medowes.

the beautie and delicacie of this sweet soile; for besides
divers cleere Lakes of fresh water (whereof we saw no
end) Medowes very large and full ot greene grasse;
even the most woody places (I speake onely of such as
I saw) doe grow so distinct and apart, one tree from
another, upon greene grassie ground, somewhat higher
than the Plaines, as if Nature would shew her selfe

Seven
Indians.

above her power, artificiall. Hard by, we espied seven
Indians, and cumming up to them, at first they expressed some feare; but being emboldned by our curte-
ous usage, and some trifles which we gave them, they
followed us to a necke of land, which we imagined had
been severed from the maine, but finding it otherwise,

A broad
river.

we perceived a broad harbour or river's mouth, which
ranne up into the maine, and because the day was farre
spent we were forced to return to the Island from
whence we came, leaving the discovery of this har-

bour for a time of better leasure. Of the goodnesse of A good harbour. which harbour as also of many others · thereabouts, there is small doubt, considering that all the Islands, as also the maine (where we were) is all rockie grounds and broken lands. Now the next day, we determined to fortifie our selves in a little plot of ground in the midst of the Lake above mentioned, where we built an The English house. house, and covered it with sedge, which grew about this lake in great aboundance, in building whereof, we spent three weeks and more; but the second day after our comming from the maine, we espied 11 canowes or Eleven canowes with fiftie Indians in them. boats, with fiftie Indians in them, comming towards us from this part of the maine, where we two daies before landed, and being loth they should discover our fortification, we went out on the sea side to meete them; and comming somewhat neere them, they all sat downe upon the stones, calling aloud to us, (as we rightly ghessed) to doe the like, a little distance from them: having sat a while in this order, captaine Gosnold willed me to goe unto them, to see what countenance they would make, but as soone as I came up unto them, one of them, to whom I had given a knife two daies before in the maine, knew me (whom I also very well remembered) and smiling upon me, spake somewhat unto their lord or captaine, which sat in the midst of Their captaine. them, who presently rose up and tooke a large Beaver skin from one that stood about him and gave it unto me, which I requited for that time the best I could: but I, pointing towards Captaine Gosnold, made signes unto him, that he was our captaine, and desirous to be his friend ,and enter league with him which (as I perceived) he understood, and made signes of joy: whereupon captaine Gosnold with the rest of his companie, being twenty in all, came up unto them; and after many signes of gratulations (captaine Gosnold presenting their Lord with certaine trifles which they wondered at, and highly esteemed) we became very great friends, and sent for meat aboord our shallop, and gave them such meats as we had then readie dressed, whereof they misliked nothing but our mustard, whereat they made many a soure face. While they were thus mery, one of them had conveied a target of ours into one of their canowes, which we suffered, onely to trie whether they were in subjection to this Lord to whom we make signes (by shewing him another of the same likenesse, and pointing to the canow) what one of his companie had done: who suddenly expressed some feare, and speaking angerly to one about him (as we perceived by his countenance) caused it presently to be brought backe againe. So the rest of the day we spent in trad-

Severall sorts of Furres.

ing with them for Furres, which are Beavers, Luzeines, Marterns, Otters, Wild-cat skinnes, very large and deepe Furre, black Foxes, Conie Skinnes, of the colour of our Hares, but somewhat less, Deere skinnes, very large, Seale skinnes and other beasts skinnes, to us

Red Copper in abundance.

unknown. They have also great store of copper, some very redde, and some of a paler colour; none of them but have chaines, earrings, or collars of this mettall: they head some of their arrows herewith much like our broad arrow-heads, very workmanly made. Their

Chaines.

chaines are many hollow pieces semented together, each piece of the bignesse of one of our reeds, a finger in length, ten or twelve of them together on a string,

Collars.

which they weare about their necks; their collars they weare about their bodies like bandelieres a handfull broad, all hollow pieces, like the other, but somewhat shorter, four hundred pieces in a collar, very fine and evenly set together. Besides these, they have large

Drinking cuppes of Copper.

drinking cups made like sculles and other thinne plates of Copper made much like our boare-speare blades, all which they so little esteem, as they offered their fairest collars or chaines, for a knife or such like trifle, but we seemed little to regard it; yet I was desirous to under-

Mines of Copper.

stand where they had such store of this mettall, and

made signes to one of them (with whom I was very
familiar) who taking a piece of Copper in his hand,
made a hole with his finger in the ground, and withall
pointed to the maine from whence they came.   They
strike fire in this manner, every one carrieth about him
in a purse of sewed leather, a Minerall stone (which I ^{Minerall}
take to be their Copper) and with a flat Emerie stone ^{Stones.}
Emeric
(wherewith Glasiers cut glasse, and Cutlers glase ^{stones.}
blades), tied fast to the end of a little sticke, gently he
striketh upon the Minerall stone, and within a stroke
or two, a sparke falleth upon the piece of touchwood
(much like our Spunge in England) and with the least
sparke he maketh a fire presently.   We had also of their
Flaxe, wherewith they make many strings and cords, ^{Flaxe.}
but it is not so bright of colour as ours in England.   I
am persuaded they have great store growing upon the
maine, as also Wines and many other rich commodities,
which we, wanting both time and meanes, could not
possibly discover.   Thus they continued with us three
daies, every night retiring them selves to the further-
most part of our Island two or three miles from our
fort, but the fourth day they returned to the maine,
pointing five or six times to the sun, and once to the
maine, which we understood, that within five or six
daies they would come from the maine to us againe:
but being in their canows a little from the shore, they
made huge cries and shouts of joy unto us; and we with
our trumpet and cornet, and casting up our coppers into
the aire, made them the the best farewell we could;
yet six or seven of them remained with us behinde, ^{Indians apt}
bearing us company every day into the woods, and ^{for service.}
helpt us to cut and carie our Sassafras, and some of ^{Sassafras.}
them lay aboord our ship.   These people, as they are
exceeding courteous, gentle of disposition, and well ^{A goodly peo-}
^{ple, & of good}
conditioned, excelling all others that we have seene: ^{conditions.}
so for shape of bodie and lovely favour, I think they
excell all the people of America, of stature much higher

than we; of complexion or colour, much like a darke Olive; their eie-browes and haire blacke, which they weare long, tied up behinde in knots, whereon they pricke feathers of fowles, in fashion of a crownet; some of them are blacke thin bearded; they make beards of the haire of beasts; and one of them offered a beard of their making to one of their sailers, for his that grew on his face, which because it was of a red colour, they judged to be none of his owne. They are quicke-eied, and stedfast in their looks, fearelesse of other's harmes, as intending none themselves; some of the meaner sort given to filching, which the very name of Salvages (not weighing their ignorance in good or evill) may easily excuse; their garments are of Deere skins and some of them weare Furres round and close about their necks. They pronounce our language with great facilitie; for one of them one day sitting by me, upon occasion I spake smiling to him these words: How now (sirrha) are you so saucie with my Tobacco? which words (without any further repetition), he suddenly spake so plaine and distinctly, as if he had beene a long scholar in the language. Many other such trials we had, which are heere needlesse to repeat. Their women (such as we saw) which were but three in all, were but lowe of stature, their eie-browes, haire, apparell, and maner of wearing like to the men, fat, and very well favoured, and much delighted in our company; the men are very dutifull towards them. And truely, the holsomnesse and temperature of this Climat, doth not onely argue this people to be answerable to this description, but also of a perfect constitution of body, active, strong, healthfull, and very wittie, as the sundry toies of theirs cunningly wrought, may easily witnes. For the agreeing of this Climat with us (I speake of my selfe, and so I may justly do for the rest of our company that we found our health and strength all the while we remained there, so to renew and in-

Their apparell.

Their women.

The goodnesse of the Climat.

crease, as notwithstanding our diet and lodging was none of the best, yet not one of our company (God be thankful) felt the least grudging or inclination to any disease or sicknesse, but were much fatter and in better health than when we went out of England. But after our barke had taken in so much Sassafras, Cedar, Furres, Skinnes, and other commodities, as were thought convenient; some of our company that had promised Captaine Gosnold to stay, having nothing but a saving voyage in their minds, made our company of inhabitants (which was small enough before) much smaller: so as captaine Gosnold seeing his whole strength to consist but of twelve men, and they but meanly provided, determined to return for England, Their leaving this Island (which he called Elizabeths Island) return. with as many sorrowfull eies, as were before desirous to see it. So the 13 of June, being Friday, we weighed and with indifferent faire winde and weather came to anker the 23 of July, being also Friday (in all, bare five weeks) before Exmouth.

Your Lordships to command
John Brereton.

THE

MOST PLEASANT SONG

OF

𝔏𝔞𝔡𝔶 𝔅𝔢𝔰𝔰𝔶;

AND HOW SHE MARRIED KING HENRY THE SEVENTH OF THE HOUSE OF LANCASTER.

Edited by

James Orchard Halliwell, Esq.

LONDON ·
Printed for the Percy Society
by T. RICHARDS, St. Martin's Lane.

MDCCCXLVII.

PREFACE.

Our materials for the period of English history to which the following ballad relates are so remarkably scanty, that no source of information possessing the least claim to credit can be willingly passed over. Were it otherwise, a poem undoubtedly containing many supposititious particulars, and which may well be considered a very unsafe historical guide, would deserve little attention apart from its poetical merits; but we unfortunately possess no other contemporary account of the proceedings of Elizabeth of York, from Christmas 1484, till the death of Richard III. On this account the "Song of Lady Bessy" possesses a considerable degree of interest.

Only two copies of this poem have been preserved, differing considerably from each other, and no doubt varying in a great degree from the author's original composition, not in facts, but in language. One copy is contained in a Ms. of the time of Charles II, in the possession of Mr. Bateman, who has obligingly collated our text in proof with the original manuscript. The other copy is preserved in Ms. Harl. 367, and appears to have been transcribed about the year 1600.

We have thought it expedient to give both of these versions, for they explain each other, and exhibit the changes which transcribers of later days made in remote originals. The first was edited in 1829, by Mr. Thomas Heywood, with an able introduction and judicious notes; but the work was privately printed, and is now very rarely to be met with.

The copy in the Harl. Ms. is not so much modernized, and is of much better authority than that printed by Mr. Heywood.

It appears from some passages, where the writer changes abruptly from the third to the first person, that the poem was composed by Bessy's "true esquire," Humphrey Brereton, who was in the service of Lord Stanley. Mr. Heywood conjectures him to have been a native of Cheshire, and informs us that "in the pedigree of the Breretons of Shochlach and Malpas, a younger branch of the house of the same name seated at Brereton, Humphrey appears to have been the third son of Bartholomew Brereton, and to have lived in the reign of Henry the Seventh. He left three daughters, the eldest of whom marrying into the neighbouring family of Dod of Edge, her descendants still exist in the representatives of that ancient house. Humphrey is described in the Dod pedigree as seated at Grafton, a township near Malpas." This conjecture is borne out by the porter's reason for his gratification at seeing Humphrey,—

> "For a Cheshire man born—am I certain,
> From the Malpas but miles three."

The antiquity of the poem is satisfactorily proved by the multiplicity of those minute traits of language and manners, which must have been forgotten by a more recent writer. The author's mistakes in the general history of the period are not of a nature to weaken his credibility; and as Sir H. Nicolas justly observes, with reference to his speaking of Lord Stanley as Earl of Derby, "though that nobleman did not possess the latter title when the events described took place, it was usual for early writers to allude to individuals by the designations borne by them at the time thev wrote." The peculiar features of the age, the costume, and the difficulty of correspondence, are too faithfully described to leave any reasonable doubt of the early period of the author.

For·all the known particulars respecting Elizabeth of York, we may refer to Sir H. Nicolas's able and excellent memoir prefixed to the "Privy Purse Expenses of Elizabeth of York," 8 vo. 1830, and Miss Strickland's "Lives of the Queens of England," vol. IV. The latter work contains an analysis of the following poem :

Feb. 22nd, 1847.

The Most Pleasant

Song of Lady Bessye,

The Eldest Daughter of King Edward The Fourth, and

How She Married King Henry The Seventh

Of The House of Lancaster.

For Jesus' sake be merry and glad,
    Be blythe of blood, of bone and blee,
And of your words be sober and sad,
    And a little while listen to me:
I shall tell you how Lady Bessy made her moan
    And down she kneeled upon her knee
Before the Earle of Darby her self alone,
    These were her words fair and free:—
Who was your beginner, who was your ground
    Good Father Stanley, will you tell me?
Who married you to the Margaret Richmond,
    A Dutchess of a high degree?
And your son the Lord George Strange
    By that good lady you had him by.
And Harden lands under your hands,
    And Moules dale also under your fee,
Your brother Sir William Stanley by parlament,
    The Holt Castle who gave him truely?
Who gave him Bromofield, that I now ment?
    Who gave him Chirk-land to his fee?·
Who made him High Chamberlain of Cheshire?
    Of that country farr and near
They were all wholly at his desire,
    When he did call they did appear;
And also the Forrest of Delameer,
    To hunt therein both day and night
As often as his pleasure were,
    And to send for baron and knight;

Who made the knight and lord of all?
  Good Father Stanley, remember thee!
It was my father, that king royall,
  He set you in that room so high.
Remember Richmond banished full bare,
  And lyeth in Brittain behind the sea,
You may recover him of his care,
  If your heart and mind to him will gree:
Let him come home and claim his right,
  And let us cry him King Henry!
And if you will maintain him with might,
  In Brittain he needeth not long to tarry.
Go away, Bessy, the Lord said then,
  I tell thee now for certainty,
That faire words make oft fooles full faine,
  When they be but found vain glory.
Oh! father Stanley, to you I call,
  For the love of God remember thee,
Since my father King Edward, that king royall,
  At Westminster on his death bed lee;
He called to him my unckle Richard,
  So he did Robert of Brackenbury,
And James Terrill he was the third;
  He sent them to Ludlow in the west country,
To fetch the Duke of York, and the Duke of Clarence,
  These two lords born of a high degree.
The Duke of York should have been prince,
  And king after my father free,
But a balle-full game was then among,
  When they doomed these two lords to dye:
They had neither justice nor right, but had great wrong,
  Alack! it was the more pitty!
Neither were they burried in St. Maries,
  In church or churchyard or holy place;
Alas! they had dolefull destinies,
  Hard was their chance, worse was their disgrace!
Therefore help, good father Stanley, while you have space
  For the love of God and mild Mary,
Or else in time to come you shall, alas!
  Remember the words of Lady Bessy:
Good Lady Bessy, be content,
  For tho' your words be never so sweet,
If King Richard knew, you must be shent,
  And perchance cast into prison deep;

Then had you cause to wail and weep,
    And wring your hands with heavy chear;
Therefore, good lady, I you beseek
    To move me no more in this matter.
Oh! good father Stanley, listen now and hear;
    Heare is no more but you and I:
King Edward that was my father dear,
    On whose estate God had mercy,
In Westminster as he did stand,
    On a certain day in a study,
A book of reason he had in his hand,
    And so sore his study he did apply,
That his tender tears fell on the ground,
    All men might see that stood him by:
There were both earls and lords of land,
    But none of them durst speak but I.
I came before my father the king,
    And kneeled down upon my knee;
I desired him lowly of his blessing,
    And full soon he gave it unto me:
And in his arms he could me thring,
    And set me in a window so high;
He spake to me full sore weeping,—
    These were the words he said to me:
Daughter, as thou wilt have my blessing,
    Do as I shall councell thee,
And to my words give good listning,
    For one day they may pleasure thee:
Here is a book of Reason, keep it well,
    As you will have the love of me;
Neither to any creature do it feel,
    Nor let no living lord it see,
Except it be to the Lord Stanley,
    The which I love full heartiley:
All the matter to him show you may,
    For he and his thy help must be;
As soon as the truth to him is shown
    Unto your words he will agree;
For their shall never son of my body be gotten
    That shall be crowned after me,
But you shall be queen and wear the crown,
    So doth expresse the prophecye!
He gave me tax and to land,
    And also diamonds to my degree,

To gett me a prince when it pleaseth Christ,
    The world is not as it will be:
Therefore, good father Stanley, grant my request
    For the love of God, I desire thee; .
All is at your commandment down in the west,
    Both knight and squire and the commentie;
You may choose then where you like best
    I have enough both of gold and fee;
I want nothing but the strength of men,
    And good captains two or three.
Go away, Bessy, the lord said then,
    To this will I never agree,
For women oft time cannot faine,
    These words they be but vain glory!
For and I should treason begin
    Against King Richard his royalty.
In every street within London
    The Eagle's foot should be pulled down,
And as yet in his great faour I am,
    But then should I loose my great renown!
I should be called traitor thro' the same
    Full soon in every markett towne!
That were great shame to me and my name,
    I had rather spend ten thousand pounde.
O father Stanley, to you I mak my moane,
    For the love of God remember thee;
It is not three days past and gone,
    Since my uncle Richard sent after me
A batchelor and a bold baron,
    A Doctor of Divinitye,
And bad that I should to his chamber gone,
    His love and his leman that I should bee;
And the queen that was his wedded feere,
    He would her poyson and putt away;
So would he his son and his heir,
    Christ knoweth he is a proper boy!
Yet I had rather burn in a tuune
    On the Tower Hill that is so high,
Or that I would to his chamber come,
    His love and his leman will I not be!
I had rather be drawn with wild horses five,
    Through every street of that citty,
Or that good woman should lose her life,
    Good father, for the love of mee.

I am his brother's daughter dear·
    He is my uncle, it is no nay;
Or ever I woud be his wedded feere,
    With sharp swords I will me slay;
At his bidding if I were then,
    And follow'd also his cruel intent
I were well worthy to suffer pain,
    And in a fire for to be brent.
Therefore, good father Stanley, some pitty take
    On the Earle Richmond and me,
And the rather for my father's sake,
    Which gave thee the Ile of Man so free;
He crowned thee with a crown of lead,
    He holpe the first to that degree;
He set thee the crown upon thy head,
    And made thee lord of that country;
That time you promised my father dear,
    To him to be both true and just,
And now you stand in a disaweare,
    Oh; Jesus Christ, who may men trust?
O good lady, I say againe
    Your fair words shall never move my mind;
King Richard is my lord and sov'reign,
    To him I will never be unkind.
I will serve him truly till I die,
    I will him take as I him find;
For he hath given to mine and me,
    His bounteous gifts do me so bind.
Yet good father Stanley, remember thee,
    As I have said so shall it prove,
If he of his gift be soe free,
    It is for fear and not for love;
For if he may to his purpose come,
    You shall not live these years three,
For these words to me he did once move
    In Sandal Castle underneath a tree:
He said there shall no branch of the eagle fly
    Within England, neither far nor nigh;
Nor none of the Talbot's to run him by,
    Nor none of their lineage to the ninth degree;
But he would them either hang or head,
    And that he swear full grievously.
Therefore help, gentle lord, with all speed;
    For when you woud fain it will not be.

Your brother dwellith in the Holt Castle,
　A noble knight forsooth is he;
All the Welsh-men love him well,
　He may make a great company.
Sir John Savage is your sister's son,
　He is well-beloved within his shire
A great company with him will come,
　He will be ready at your desire.
Gilbert Talbott is a captain pure,
　He will come with main and might;
To you he will be fast and sure,
　Against my uncle king and knight.
Let us raise an host with him to fight,
　Soon to the ground we shall him ding,
For God will stand ever with the right,
　For he hath no right to be king!
Go away, Bessy, the Lord can say;
　Of these words, Bessy, now lett be;
I know king Richard would not me betray,
　For all the gold in Christantye.
I am his subject, sworn to be true:
　If I should seek treason to begin,
I and all mine full sore should rue,
　For we were as like to lose as winne.
Beside that, it were a deadly sin
　To refuse my king, and him betray:
The child is yet unborne that might moan in time,
　And think upon that woefull day:
Wherefore, good lady, I do you pray,
　Keep all things close at your hart root;
So now farr past it is of the day,
　To move me more it is no boot.
Then from her head she cast her attire,
　Her colour changed as pale as lead,
Her faxe that shoan as the gold wire
　. She tair it of besides her head,
And in a swoon down can she swye,
　She spake not of a certain space!
The Lord had never so great pitty
　As when he saw her in that case,
And in his arms he can her embrace;
　He was full sorry then for her sake.
The tears fell from her eyes apace,
　But at the last these words she spake,

She said, to Christ my soul I betake,
    For my body in Tem'ms drown'd shall be!
For I know my sorrow will never slake,
    And my bones upon the sands shall lye!
The fishes shall feed upon me their fill;
    This is a dolefull destinye!
And you may remedy this and you will,
    Therefore the bone of my death I give to thee!
And ever she wept as she were woode,
    The Earle on her had so great pitty,
That her tender heart turned his mood.
    He said, stand up now, Lady Bessye,
As you think best I will agree.
    Now I see the matter you do not faine,
I have thought in this matter as much as yee:
    But it is hard to trust women,
For many a man is brought into great woe,
    Through telling to women his privity·
I trust you will not serve me so
    For all the gold in Christantie.
No, father, he is my mortall foe,
    On him fain wrooken woud I bee!
He hath put away my brethren two,
    And I know he would do so by me;
But my trust is in the Trinity,
    Through your help we shall bale to him bring,
And such a day on him to see
    That he and his full sore shall rue!
O Lady Bessye, the Lord can say, ·
    Betwixt us both forcast we must
How we shall letters to Richmond convey,
    No man to write I dare well trust;
For if he list to be unjust
    And us betray to King Richard
Then you and I are both lost;
    Therefore of the scribe I am afraid.
You shall not need none such to call,
    Good father Stanley, hearken to me
What my father, King Edward, that king royal,
    Did for my sister, my Lady Wells, and me:
He sent for a scrivener to lusty London,
    He was the best in that citty;
He taught us both to write and read full soon,
    If it please you, full soon you shall see:

Lauded be God, I had such speed,
    That I can write as well as he,
And also indite and full well read,
    And that (Lord) soon shall you see,
Both English and alsoe French,
    And alsoe Spanish, if you had need.
The earle said, You are a proper wench,
    Almighty Jesus be your speed,
And give us grace to proceed out,
    That we may letters soon convey
In secrett wise and out of doubt
    To Richmond, that lyeth beyond the sea.
We must depart, lady, the earl said then;
    Wherefore keep this matter secretly,
And this same night, betwixt nine and ten,
    In your chamber I think to be.
Look that you make all things ready,
    Your maids shall not our councell hear,
For I will bring no man with me
    But Humphrey Brereton, my true esquire.
He took his leave of that lady fair,
    And to her chamber she went full tight,
And for all things she did prepare,
    Both pen and ink, and paper white.
The lord unto his study went,
    Forecasting with all his might
To bring to pass all his intent;
    He took no rest till it was night.
And when the stars shone fair and bright,
    He him disguised in strange mannere,
He went unknown of any wyght,
    No more with him but his esquire.
And when he came to her chamber near,
    Full privily there can he stand,
To cause the lady to appeare
    He made a signe with his right hand;
And when the lady there him wist,
    She was as glad as she might be.
Char-coals in chimneys there were cast,
    Candles on sticks standing full high;
She opened the wickett and let him in,
    And said, welcome, lord and knight soe free!
A rich chair was set for him,
    And another for that fair lady:

They ate the spice and drank the wine,
  He had all things at his intent;
They rested thene as for a time,
  And to their study then they went.
Then that lady so fair and free,
  With rudd as red as rose ih May,
She kneeled down upon her knee,
  And to the lord thus can she say:
Good father Stanley, I you pray,
  Now here is no more but you and I;
Let me know what you will say,
  For pen and paper I have ready.
He saith commend me to my son George Strange,
  In Latham Castle there he doth lye,
When I parted with him his heart did change,
  From Latham to Manchester he road me bye.
Upon Salford Bridge I turned my horse againe,
  My son George by the hand I hent;
I held so hard forsooth certaine,
  That his formost finger out of the joint went:
I hurt him sore, he did complain,
  These words then to him I did say:
Son, on my blessing, turne home againe,
  This shall be a token another day.
Bid him come like a merchant of Farnfield,
  Of Coopland, or of K'endall, wheather that it be,
And seven with him, and no more else,
  For to bear him company.
Bid him lay away watch and ward,
  And take no heed to mynstrel's glee;
Bid him sit at the lower end of the board,
  When he is amongst his meany,
His back to the door, his face to the wall,
  That comers and goers shall not him see·
Bid him lodge in no common hall,
  But keep him unknown right secretly.
Commend me to my brother Sir William so dear,
  In the Holt Castle there dweileth hee;
Since the last time that we together were,
  In the forest of Delameere both fair and free,
And seven harts upon one hearde,
  Were brought to the buck sett to him and me;
But a forester came to me with a whoore bearde,
  And said, good sir, awhile rest ye,

I have found you a hart in Darnall Park,
  Such a one I never saw with my eye.
I did him crave, he said I should him have;
  He was brought to the broad heath truely;
At him I let my grayhound then slipp,
  And followed after while I might dree.
He left me lying in an ould moss pitt,
  A loud laughter then laughed hee;
He said, Rise up, and draw out your cousin;
  The deer is dead, come you and see.
Bid him come as a marchant of Carnarvon,
  Or else of Bew-morris whether it be;
And in his company seven Welshmen,
  And come to London and speak to me;
I have a great mind to speak with him,
  I think it long since I him see.
Commend me to Sir John Savage, that knight,
  Lady, he is my sister's sone,
Since upon a Friday at night
  Before my bedside he kneeled downe:
He desired me as I was uncle dear,
  Many a time full tenderly,
That I would lowly King Richard require
  If I might get him any fee.
I came before my soveraigne Lord,
  And kneeled down upon my knee,
So soon to me he did accord
  I thanked him full courteously,
A gatt him an hundred pounds in Kent
  To him and his heirs perpetually,
Alsoe a manor of a duchy rent,
  Two hundred pounds he may spend thereby,
And high sheriff of Worcestershire,
  And alsoe the park of Tewksbury.
He hath it all at his desire,
  Therewith dayley he may make merry.
Bid him come as a merchant man
  Of West Chester, that fair city,
And seven yeomen to wait him on,
  Bid him come to London and speak with me.
Commend me to good Gilbert Talbott,
  A gentle esquire forsooth is he;
Once on a Fryday, full well I woot
  King Richard called him a traitour high:

But Gilbert to his fawchon prest,
    A bold esquire forsooth is he;
Their durst no sarjant him arreast,
    He is called so perlous of his body.
In the Tower Street I meet him then
    Going to Westminster to take sanctuarie;
I light beside my horse I was upon,
    The purse from my belt I gave him truely;
I bad him ride down into the North-West
    Perchance a knight in England I might him see:
Wherefore pray him at my request
    To come to London to speak with me.
Then said the royall Lord so just,
    Now you have written, and sealed have I,
There is no messenger that we may trust,
    To bring these writeings into the West Country,
Because our matter it is so high,
    Least any man wou'd us descry.
Humphrey Brereton, then said Bessye,
    Hath been true to my father and me;
He shall take the writeings in hand,
    And bring them into the West Country:
I trust him best of all this land
    On this message to go for me.
Go to thy bed, Father, and sleep full soon,
    And I shall wake for you and me,
By tomorrow at the riseing of the sune,
    Humphrey Brereton shall be with thee.
She brings the Lord to his bed so trimly dight
    All that night where he shoud lye,
And Bessy waked all that night,
    There came no sleep within her eye:
In the morning when the day can spring,
    Up riseth young Bessye,
And maketh hast in her dressing;
    To Humphrey Brereton gone is she:
But when she came to Humphrey's bower bright,
    With a small voice called she,
Humphrey answered that lady bright,
    Saith, who calleth on me so early?
I am King Edward's daughter right,
    The Countesse clear, young Bessy,
In all hast with mean and might
    Thou must come speak with the Earle of Darby.

Humphrey cast upon him a gowne,
  And a pair of slippers upon his feet;
Alas! said Humphrey, I may not ride,
  My horse is tired as you may see;
Since I came from London city,
  Neither night nor day, I tell you plain,
There came no sleep within my eye;
  On my business I thought certaine.
Lay thee down, Humphrey, he said, and sleep,
  I will give space of hours three:
A fresh horse I thee beehyte.
  Shall bring thee through the West Country.
Humphrey slept not hours two,
  But on his journey well thought hee;
A fresh horse was brought him tooe
  So bring him through the West Country.
Then Humphrey Brereton with mickle might,
  Hard at Latham knocketh hee;
Who is it, said the porter, this time of the night,
  That so hastily calleth on mee?
The porter then in that state,
  That time of the night riseth hee,
And forthwith opened me the gate,
  And received both my horse and me.
Then said Humphrey Brereton, truely
  With the Lord Strange speak would I faine,
From his father the Earle of Darby.
  Then was I welcome that time certaine;
A torch burned that same tide,
  And other lights that he might see;
And brought him to the bedd side
  Where as the Lord Strange lie.
The lord mused in that tide,
  Said Humphrey Brereton, what mak'st thou here?
How fareth my father, that noble lord,
  In all England that hath no peer?
Humphrey took him a letter in hand,
  And said, Behold, my lord, and you may see.
When the Lord Strange looked the letter upon,
  The tears tricked downe from his eye:
He said, we must come under a cloud,
  We must never trusted bee:
We may sigh and make a great moane,
  The world is not as it will bee.

176

Have here, Humphrey, pounds three,
    Better rewarded may thou bee;
Commend me to my father dear,
    His daily blessing he would give me;
He said also in that tide,
    Tell him also thus from me;
If I be able to go or ride,
    This appointment keep will I.
When Humphrey received the gold, I say,
    Straight to Manchester rideth hee
The sun was light up of the day,
    He was aware of the Warden and Edward Stanley;
The one brother said to the other
    As they together their mattins did say:
Behold, he said, my own dear brother,
    Yonder comes Humphrey Brereton, it is no nay,
My father's servant at command,
    Some hasty tydings bringeth hee
He took them either a letter in hand,
    And bad them behold, read and see:
They turn'd their backs shortly tho',
    And read those letters readily.
Up they leap and laughed too,
    And also they made game and glee,—
Fair tall our father, that noble lord,
    To stir and rise now beginneth hee;
Buckingham's blood shall be wroken,
    That was beheaded in Salsbury;
Fare fall that countesse, the king's daughter,
    That fair lady, young Bessye,
We trust in Jesus in time hereafter,
    To bring thy love over the sea.
Have here, Humphrey, of either of us shillings ten,
    Better rewarded may thou bee.
He took the gold of the two gentlemen,
    To sir John Savage then rideth hee;
He took him then a letter in hand,
    And bad him behold, read and see:
When Sir John Savage looked the letter upon,
    All blackned the knight's blee;
Woman's wisdom is wondrous to hear, loe,
    My uncle is turned by young Bessye:
Whether it turn to waile or woe,
    At my uncle's bidding will I bee.

To Sheffield Castle at that same tide,
    In all the hast that might bee,
Humphrey took his horse and forth could ride
    To Gilbert Talbot fair and free.
He took him a letter in his hand,
    Behold, said Humphrey, read and see;
When he the letter looked upon,
    A loud laughter laughed hee,—
Fare fall that lord in his renowne there,
    To stir and rise beginneth hee:
Fair fall Bessye that countesse clear,
    That such councell cou'd give truely;
Commend me to my nephew nigh of blood
    The young Earle of Shrewsbury,
Bid him neither dread for death nor good;
    In the Tower of London if he bee,
I shall make London gates to tremble and quake,
    But my nephew borrowed shall bee.
Commend me to the countesse that fair make,
    King Edward's daughter young Bessy;
Tell her I trust in Jesus that hath no peer,
    To bring her love over the sea.
Commend me to that lord to me so dear,
    That lately was made the Earle of Darby;
And every hair of my head
    For a man counted might bee,
With that lord without any dread
    With him will I live and dye.
Have here, Humphrey, pounds three,
    Better rewarded may thou bee:
Look to London gates thou ride quickly,
    In all the hast that may bee;
Commend me to that countesse young Bessy,
    She was King Edward's daughter dear,
Such a one she is, I say truely,
    In all this land she hath no peer.
He took his leave at that time,
    Straight to London rideth he,
In all the hast that he could wind,
    His journey greatly he did apply.
But when he came to London, as I weene,
    It was but a little before the evening,
There was he warr, walking in a garden,
    Both the earle, and Richard the King.

When the earle did Humphrey see,
  When he came before the king,
He gave him a privy twink then with his eye,
  Then downe falls Humphrey on his knees kneeling;
Welcome, Humphrey, says the lord,
  I have missed thee weeks three.
I have been in the west, my lord,
  There born and bred was I,
For to sport and play me certaine,
  Among my friends far and nigh.
Tell me, Humphrey, said the earle then,
  How fareth all that same country?
Of all the countreys I dare well say,
  They be the flower of chivalry;
For they will bycker with their bowes,
  They will fight and never fly.
Tell me, Humphrey, I thee pray,
  How fareth King Richard's his commenty?
When King Richard heard him say so,
  In his heart he was right merry;
He with his cap that was so dear,
  He thanked that lord most courteously:
And said, father Stanley, thou art to me near,
  You are the chief of our poor commenty;
Half England shall be thine,
  It shall be equall between thee and me;
I am thine and thou art mine,
  So two fellows will we bee.
I swear by Mary, that mild maiden,
  I know no more such under the sky;
When I am king and wear the crown, then
  I will be chief of the poor commenty:
Task nor mise I will make none
  In no countrey farr nor nigh;
If their goods I should take and pluck them downe,
  For me they woud fight full faintly:
There is no riches to me so rich,
  As is the love of our poor commenty.
When they had ended all their speeches
  They take their leave full heartily;
And to his bower King Richard is gone.
  The earle and Humphrey Brereton
To Bessy's bower anon were gone;
  When Bessy Humphrey did see anon,

She took him in her arms and kissed him times three.
  Welcome, she said, Humphrey Brereton,
How hast thou spedd in the West Country
  I .pray thee tell me quickly and anon.
Into a parlor they went from thence,
  There were no more but he and she:
Humphrey, said Bessy, tell me e're we go hence
  Some tidings out of the West Country;
If I shall send for yonder prince
  To come over the sea for the love of me,
And if King Richard shoud him convince,
  Alas! it were great ruthe to see,
Or Murthered among the Stanley's blood to be,
  Indeed that were great pitty;
That sight on that prince I woud not see,
  For all the gold in Christantie!
Tell me, Humphrey, I thee pray,
  How hast thou spedd in the West Country?
What answer of them thou had now say,
  And what reward they gave to thee.
By the third day of May, it shall be seen,
  In London all that they will bee;
Thou shalt in England be a queen,
  Or else doubtless that they will dye.
Thus they proceed forth the winter then,
  Their councell they kept close all three,
The earle he wrought by prophecy certaine,
  In London he would not abide or bee,
But in the subburbs without the city
  An ould inn chosen hath hee.
A drew an Eagle foot on the door truely,
  That the western men might know where he did lye.
Humphrey stood on a high tower then,
  He looked into the West Country;
Sir William Stanley and seven in green,
  He was aware of the Eagle drawne;
He drew himselfe so wonderous nigh,
  And bad his men go into the towne,
And drink the wine and make merry;
  Into the same inn he went full prest,
Whereas the earle his brother lay.
  Humphrey full soon into the west
Looks over a long lee;
  He was aware of the Lord Strange and seven in green,

Come rideing into the city.
    When he was aware of the Eagle drawn,
He drew himself so wonderously nigh,
    He bad his men go into the towne certain,
And drink the wine and make merry;
    And he himself drew then,
Where as his father in the inne lay.
    Humphrey looked in the west, I say,
Sixteen in green then did he see;
    He was aware of the Warden and Edward Stanley,
Come rideing both in one company.
    When they were aware of the Eagle drawne,
The gentlemen they drew it nee;
    And bad their men go into the towne,
And drink the wine and make merry.
    And did go themselves into the same inn full prest,
Where the earle their father lay.
    Yet Humphrey beholdeth into the west,
And looketh towards the north country;
    He was aware of Sir John Savage and Sir Gilbert Talbot,
Come riding both in one company.
    When they were aware of the Eagle drawne,
Themselves grew it full nigh,
    And bad their men go into the towne,
To drink the wine and make merry
    They did go themselves into the same inn
Where as the earle and Bessy lye.
    When all the lords together were,
Amongst them all Bessy was full buissy;
    With goodly words Bessy then said there,
Fair lords, what will you do for me?
    Will you relieve yonder prince,
That is exiled beyond the sea?
    I woud not have King Richard him to convince,
For all the gold in Christentye.
    The Earle of Darby came forth then,
These words he said to young Bessye,
    Ten thousand pounds will I send,
Bessy, for the love of thee,
    And twenty thousand Eagle feet,
The queen of England for to make thee;
    Then Bessy most lowly the Earle did greet,
And thankt his honor most heartiley.
    Sir William Stanley came forth then,

These words he said to fair Bessy:
  Remember, Bessy, another time,
Who doth the most, Bessy, for thee;
  Ten thousand coats, that shall be red certaine,
In an hour's warning ready shall bee;
  In England thou shalt be our queen,
Or doubtlesse I will dye.
  Sir John Savage come forth then,
These words he said to young Bessye,
  A thousand marks for thy sake certaine,
Will I send thy love beyond the sea.
  Sir Gilbert Talbott came forth then,
These were the words he said to Bessy:
  Ten thousand marks for thy sake certaine,
I will send to beyond the sea.
  The Lord Strange came forth then,
These were the words he said to Bessy:
  A little money and few men,
Will bring thy love over the sea;
  Let us keep our gold at home, said he,
For to wage our company;
  For if we should send it over the sea,
We should put our gold in jeopartie.
  Edward Stanley came forth then,
These were the words he said to Bessye:
  Remember, Bessye, another time,
Who that now doth the best for thee,
  For there is no power that I have,
Nor no gold for to give thee;
  I will be under my father's banner, if God me save,
There either to live or dye.
  Bessye came forth before the lords all,
And downe she falleth upon her knee;
  Nineteen thousand pound of gold, I shall
Send my love behind the sea,
  A love letter, and a gold ring,
From my heart root rite will I.
  Who shall be the Messenger the same to bring,
Both the gold and the writeing over the sea?
  Humphrey Brereton, said Bessy,
I know him trusty and true certaine,
  Therefore the writeing and the gold truly
By him shall be carried to Little Brittaine.
  Alas, said Humphrey, I dare not take in hand,

To carry the gold over the sea;
    These galley shipps they be so strange,
They will me night so wonderously;
    They will me robb, they will me drowne,
They will take the gold from me.
    Hold thy peace, Humphrey, said Bessye then,
Thou shalt it carry without jepordye;
    Thou shalt not have any caskett nor any male,
Nor budgett, nor cloak sack, shall go with thee;
    Three mules that must be stiff and strong withall,
Sore loaded with gold shall they bee,
    With saddle-side shirted I do tell thee
Wherein the gold sowe will I:
    If any man faine whose is the shipp truely
That saileth forth upon the sea,
    Say it is the Lord Lislay,
In England and France well beloved is he.
    Then came forth the Earle of Darby,
    These words he said to young Bessy·
He said, Bessye, thou art to blame
    To appoint any shipp upon the sea;
I have a good shipp of my owne,
    Shall carry Humphrey with the mules three;
An eagle shall be drawne upon the mast top,
    That the Italians may it see;
There is no freak in all France
    The eagle that dare come nee
If any one ask whose shipp it is, then
    Say it is the Earles of Darby. ·
Humphrey took the three mules then,
    Into the west wind wou'd hee,
Without all doubt at Liverpoole
    He took shipping upon the sea:
With a swift wind and a liart,
    He so sailed upon the sea,
To Beggrames Abbey in Little Brittaine,
    Whereas the English Prince lie;
The porter was a Cheshire man,
    Well he knew Humphrey when he him see;
Humphrey knockt at the gate truely,
    Whereas the porter stood it by,
And welcomed me full heartiley,
    And received then my mules three;
I shall thee give in this breed

To thy reward pounds three;
I will none of thy gold, the porter said,
    Nor Humphrey none of the fee,
I will open thee the gates certaine
    To receive thee and the mules three;
For a Cheshire man born am I certain,
    From the Malpas but miles three.
The porter opened the gates that time
    And received him and the mules three.
The wine that was in the hall that time
    He gave to Humphrey Brereton truely.
Alas! said Humphrey, how shoud I doe,
    I am strayed in a strange countrey,
The Prince of England I do not know,
    Before I never did him see.
I shall thee tell, said the porter then,
    The Prince of England know shall ye.
Low where he siteth at the butts certaine
    With other lords two or three;
He weareth a gown of velvet black
    And it is cutted above the knee,
With a long visage and pale and black
    Thereby know that prince may ye;
A wart he hath, the porter said,
    A little alsoe above the chinn,
His face is white, his wart is red,
    No more than the head of a small pinn;
You may know the prince certaine,
    As soon as you look upon him truely.—
He received the wine of the porter, then
    With him he took the mules three.
When Humphrey came before that prince
    He falleth downe upon his knee,
He delivereth the letters which Bessy sent,
    And so did he the mules three,
A rich ring with a stone,
    Thereof the prince glad was hee;
He took the ring of Humphrey then,
    And kissed the ring times three.
Humphrey kneeled still as any stone,
    As sure as I do tell to thee;
Humphrey of the prince answer gott none
    Therefore in heart was he heavy;
Humphrey stood up then full of skill,

184

And then to the prince said he:
Why standest thou so still at thy will,
    And no answer dost give to me?
I am come from the Stanley's blood so dear,
    King of England for to make thee,
A fairer lady then than shalt have to thy fair,
    There is not one in all Christantye;
She is a countesse, a king's daughter, Humphrey said,
    The name of her it is Bessye,
She can write, and she can read,
    Well can she work by prophecy;
I may be called a lewd messenger,
    For answer of thee I can get none,
I may sail home with heavy cleare,
    What shall I say when I come home?
The prince he took the Lord Lee,
    And the Earle of Oxford was him nee,
The Lord Ferris wou'd not him beguile truely,
    To councell they are gone all three;
When they had their councell taken,
    To Humphrey then turned he;
Answer, Humphrey, I can give none truely
    Within the space of weeks three;
The mules into a stable were taken anon
    The saddle skirts unopened were,
Therein he found gold great plenty
    For to wage a company.
He caused the abbott to make him chear;
    In my stead now let him be,
If I be king and wear the crown
    Well acquited Abbott shalt thou be.
Early in the morning they made them knowne,
    As soon as the light they cou'd see;
With him he talketh his lords three,
    And straight to Paris he took his way.
An herriott of arms they made ready,
    Of men and money they cou'd him pray,
And shipps to bring him over the sea,
    The Stanley's blood for me hath sent,
The King of England for to make me,
    And I thank them for their intent,
For if ever in England I wear the crowne,
    Well acquited the King of France shall be:
Then answered the King of France anon,

Men nor money he getteth ·none of me,
 Nor no shipps to bring him over the sea;
  In England if he wear the crowne,
 Then will he claim them for his own truely:
  With this answer departed the prince anon,
 And so departed the same tide,
  And the English lords three
 To Beggrames Abbey soon coud the ride,
  There as Humphrey Brereton then be;
 Have Humphrey a thousand mark here,
  Better rewarded may thou be;
 Commend me to Bessy that Countesse clear,
  Before her never did I see:
 I trust in God she shall be my feer,
  For her I will travell over the sea;
 Commend me to my father Stanley, to me so dear,
  My owne mother married hath he,
 Bring him here a love letter full right
  And another to young Bessye,
 Tell her, I trust in Jesus full of might
  That my queen that she shall bee;
 Commend me to Sir William Stanley,
  That noble knight in the west country,
 Tell him that about Michaelmas certaine
  In England I do hope to be;
 Att Millford haven I will come inn
  With all the power that make may I,
 The first towne I will come inn
  Shall be the towne of Shrewsbury;
 Pray Sir William Stanley, that noble knight,
  That night that he will look on me:
 Commend me to Sir Gilbert Talbot, that royall knight,
  He much in the north country,
 And Sir John Savage, that man of might,
  Pray them all to look on me,
 For I trust in Jesus Christ so full of might,
  In England for to abide and be.
 I will none of thy gold, sir prince, said Humphrey then
  For none sure will I have of thy fee,
 Therefore keep thy gold thee within,
  For to wage thy company;
 If every hair were a man,
  With thee, sir prince, will I be:
 Thus Humphrey Brereton his leave hath tane,

And saileth forth upon the sea,
Straight to London he rideth then,
There as the earle and Bessy lay;
And bad them behold, read and see.
The earle took leave of Richard the King,
And into the west wind wou'd he;
He left Bessye in Leicester then
And bad her lye in privitye,
For if King Richard knew thee here anon,
In a fire burned thou must be.
Straight to Latham the earl is gone,
There as the Lord Strange then lee;
He sent the Lord Strange to London,
To keep King Richard company.
Sir William Stanley made anone
Ten thousand coats readily,
Which were as redd as any blood,
Thereon the hart's head was set full high,
Which after were tryed both trusty and good
As any cou'd be in Christantye.
Sir Gilbert Talbot ten thousand doggs
In one hour's warning for to be,
And Sir John Savage fifteen white hoods,
Which wou'd fight and never flee;
Edward Stanley had three hundred men,
There were no better in Christantye:
Sir Rees ap Thomas, a knight of Wales certain,
Eight thousand spears brought he,
Sir William Stanley sat in the Holt Castle,
And looked over his head so high;
Which way standeth the wind, can any tell?
I pray you, my men, look and see.
The wind it standeth south-east,
So said a knight that stood him by.
This night yonder prince, truly
Into England entereth hee.
He called a gentleman that stood him nigh,
His name was Rowland of Warburton,
He bad him go to Shrewsbury that night,.
And bid yonder prince come inn:
But when Rowland came to Shrewsbury,
The port culles was let downe;
They called him Henry Tydder, in scorn truely,
And said, in England he shou'd wear no crowne;

Rowland bethought him of a wyle then,
And tied a writeing to a stone,
    And threw the writeing over the wall certain,
And bad the baliffs to look it upon:
    They opened the gates on every side,
And met the prince with procession;
    And wou'd not in Shrewsbury there abide
But straight he drest him to Stafford towne.
    King Richard heard then of his coming,
He called his lords of great renown;
    The Lord Tearey he came to the king
And upon his knees he falleth downe,
    I have thirty thousand fighting men
For to keep the crown with thee.
    The Duke of Northfolk came to the king anone,
And downe he falleth upon his knee;
    The Earle of Surrey, that was his heir,
Were both in one company;
    We have either twenty thousand men here,
For to keep the crown with thee.
    The Lord Latimer, and the Lord Lovell,
    And the Earle of Kent he stood him by,
    The Lord Ross, and the Lord Scrope, I you tell,
They were all in one company;
    The Bishop of Durham, he was not away,
Sir William Bonner he stood him by,
    The good Sir William of Harrington, as I say,
Said, he wou'd fight and never fly.
    King Richard made a messenger,
And sent him into the west country,
    And bid the Earle of Darby make him bowne,
And bring twenty thousand men unto me,
    Or else the Lord Strange his head I will him send,
And doubtless his son shall dye;
    For hitherto his father I took for my friend,
And now he hath deceived me.
    Another herald appeared then
To Sir William Stanley that doughty knight
    Bid him bring to me two thousand men.
Or else to death he shall be dight.
    Then answered that doughty knight,
And spake to the herald without letting;
    Say, upon Bosseworth Field I meen to fight,
Upon Monday early in the morning;

Such a breakfast I him behight,
As nev'er did knight to any king.
The messenger home can him gett,
To tell King Richard this tideing.

Fast together his hands then cou'd he ding,
And said, the Lord Strange shou'd surely dye;
And putt him into the Tower of London,
For at liberty he shou'd not bee.

Lett us leave Richard and his lords full of pride,
And talk we more of the Stanley's blood,
That brought Richmond over the sea with wind and tyde,
From Little Brittain into England over the flood.

Now is Earle Richmond into Stafford come,
And Sir William Stanley to Little Stoone;
The prince had rather then all the gold in Christantye,
To have Sir William Stanley to look upon;

A messenger was made ready anone,
That night to go to Little Stoon;
Sir William Stanley he rideth to Stafford towne,
With a solemn company ready bowne.

When the knight to Stafford was comin,'
That Earle Richmond might him see,
He took him in his arms then,
And there he kissed him times three;

The welfare of thy body doth comfort me more
Than all the gold in Christantye.
Then answered that royall knight there,
And to the prince these words spake he,—

Remember, man, both night and day,
Who doth now the most for thee;
In England thou shalt wear a crown, I say,
Or else doubtless I will dye;

A fairer lady then thou shalt have for thy feer,
Was there never in Christianty;
She is a countesse, a king's daughter,
And there to both wise and witty;

I must this night to Stone, my soveraigne,
For to comfort my company.
The prince he took him by the hand,
And said, farewell, Sir William, fair and free.

Now is word come to Sir William Stanley there,
Early in the Monday, in the morning,
That the Earle of Darby, his brother dear,
Had given battle to Richard the king.

That wou'd I not, said Sir William anone,
For all the gold in Christaintye,
That the battle shou'd be done;
Straight to Lichfield cou'd he ride,
In all the hast that might bee,
And when he came to Lichfield that tyde,
All they cryed King Henry:
Straight to Bolesworth can they go
In all the hast that might be,
But when he came Bolesworth Field unto,
There met a royall company;
The Earle of Darby thither was come,
And twenty thousand stood him by;
Sir John Savage, his sister's son,
He was his nephew of his blood so nigh,
He had fifteen hundred fighting men,
That wou'd fight and never flye;
Sir William Stanley, that royall knight, then
Ten thousand red coats had he,
They wou'd bicker with their bows there,
They wou'd fight and never flye;
The Red Rosse, and the Blew Boar,
They were both a solemn company;
Sir Rees ap Thomas he was thereby,
With ten thousand spars of mighty tree;
The Earle of Richmond went to the Earle of Darby,
And downe he falleth upon his knee,
Said, father Stanley full of might,
The vaward I pray you give to me,
For I am come to claime my right,
And fain revenged wou'd I bee.
Stand up, he said, my son quickly,
Thou hast thy mother's blessing truely,
The vaward, son, I will give to thee,
So that thou wilt be ordered by me:
Sir William Stanley, my brother dear,
In the battle he shall be;
Sir John Savage, he hath no peer,
He shall be a wing then to thee;
Sir Rees ap Thomas shall break the array,
For he will fight and never flee;
I myselfe will hove on the hill, I say,
The fair battle I will see.
King Richard he hoveth upon the mountaine;

He was aware of the banner of the bould Stanley,
And saith, Fetch hither the Lord Strange certain,
  For he shall dye this same day;
To the death, Lord, thee ready make,
  For I tell thee certainly
That thou shalt dye for thy uncle's sake,
  Wild William of Stanley.
If I shall dye said the Lord Strange, then,
  As God forbid it shou'd so bee,
Alas! for my lady that is at home,
  It should be long or shee see me,
But we shall meet at doomsday,
  When the great doom shall be.
He called for a gent in good fay,
  Of Lancashire, both fair and free,
The name of him it was Latham;
  A ring of gould he took from his finger,
And threw it to the gent then,
  And bad him bring it to Lancashire,
To his lady that was at home;
  At her table she may sit right,
Or she see her lord it may be long,
  I have no foot to fligh nor fight,
I must be murdered with the king:
  If fortune my uncle Sir William Stanley loose the field,
As God forbid it shou'd so bee,
  Pray her to take my eldest son and child,
And exile him over behind the sea;
  He may come in another time
By field or fleet, by tower or towne,
  Wreak so he may his father's death in fyne,
Upon Richard of England that weareth the crown.
  A knight to King Richard then did appeare,
The Good Sir William of Harrington.
  Let that lord have his life, my dear
Sir king, I pray you grant me this boone,
  We shall have upon this field anon,
The father, the son, and the uncle all three;
  Then shall you deem, lord, with your own month then,
What shall be the death of them all three.
  Then a block was cast upon the ground,
Thereon the lord's head was laid,
  A slave over his head can stand,
And thus that time to him thus said:

In faith there is no other booty tho',
But need that thou must be dead.
　　Harrington in hart was full woe,
When he saw that the lord must needs be dead.
　　He said, our ray breaketh on ev'ry side
We put our feyld in jepordie.
　　He took up the lord that tyde,
King Richard after did him never see.
　　Then they blew up their bewgles of brass,
　　That made many a wife to cry alas!
　　And many a wive's child father lesse;
They shott of guns then very fast,
　　Over their heads they could them throw;
Arrows flew then, between,
　　As thick as any hayle or snowe,
As then that time might plaine be seene;
　　Then Rees ap Thomas with the black raven,
Shortly he brake their array;
　　Then with thirty thousand fighting men
The Lord Pearcy went his way;
　　The Duke of Northefolke wou'd have fledd with a good will,
With twenty thousand of his company,
　　They went up to a wind millne uppon a hill,
That stood soe fayre and wonderousse hye;
　　There he met Sir John Savage, a royall knight,
And with him a worthy company;
　　To the death was he then dight,
And his sonne prisoner taken was he;
　　Then the Lord Abroes began for to flee,
And so did many other moe;
　　When King Richard that sight did see,
In his heart hee was never soe woe:
　　I pray you, my merry men, be not away,
For upon this field will I like a man dye,
　　For I had rather dye this day,
Than with the Stanley prisoner to be.
　　A knight to King Richard can say there,
Good Sir William of Harrington;
　　He said, sir king, it hath no peer,
Upon this feyld to death to be done,
　　For there may no man these dints abide;
Low, your horse is ready at your hand:
　　Sett the crown upon my head that tyde,
Give me my battle axe in my hand;

I make a vow to myld Mary that is so bright,
I will dye the king of merry England.
    Besides his head they hewed the crown down right,
That after he was not able to stand;
    They dinge him downe as they were woode,
They beat his bassuet to his heade,   ,
    Until the braynes came out with the bloode;
They never left him till he was dead.
    Then carryed they him to Leicester,
And pulled his head from under his feet.
    Bessye mett him with a merry cheare,
And with these words she did him greete;
    How like you the killing of my brethren dear?
Welcome, gentle uncle, home!
    Great solace ytt was to see and hear,
When the battell yt was all done;
    I tell you, masters, without lett,
When the Red Rosse soe fair of hew,
    And young Bessye together mett,
It was great joy I say to you.
    A bishop them marryed with a ringe
The two bloods of great renowne.
    Bessy said, now may we singe,
Wee two bloods are made all one.
    The Earle of Darby hee was there,
And Sir William Stanley, that noble knight,
    Upon their heads he set the crown so fair,
That was made of gould so bright.
    And there he came under a cloud,
That sometime in England looked full high;
    But then the hart he lost his head,
That after no man cou'd him see.
    But Jesus, that is both bright and shine,
And born was of mylde Mary,
    Save and keepe our noble kinge,
And also the poore commentie. Amen.

RECORD OF R. M. BRERETON'S PROFESSIONAL CAREER DURING THE PAST FIFTY-TWO YEARS FOR THE INFORMATION OF HIS CHILDREN.

1852-56.

Pupilage in Isambard Kingdom Brunel's office, London; employed as Assistant Engineer on the new passenger and locomotive stations of the Great Western Railway at Paddington; on the construction of the Saltash bridge over the Tamar river, connecting Devon and Cornwall; on the laying out and construction of the Cornwall Railway between Saltash and Truro; on the Parliamentary Surveys of the Devises and Salisbury branches of the Great Western Railway.

1857 70.

On the Great Indian Peninsula Railway, connecting Bombay with Calcutta and Madras. (1) As Assistant and Resident Engineer in the laying out and construction of the line between Munmar and Bosawell in Khandeish; between Bosawell and Nagpur, through the Berars and portion of the Central Provinces; between Gulbargur and the Krishna river in the Deccan and the Nizam's dominion. (2) As Chief Engineer of the Bombay and Jubbulpoor line connecting Bombay with Calcutta, and of the Nagpur branch, to the period of their completion; making connection with Calcutta in March, 1870. Eighteen hundred and fifty-seven and fifty-eight embraced the mutiny period in India; during that period the survey and construction work was a trying and dangerous one through Khandeish and the Berars and

Nagpur districts, owing to the Bheels, or hill, tribes being on the war path. In January, 1858, the Bheels attacked and looted my camp near Nagpur. I had a providential escape from them. I was with the Hydrabad troops and the Khandeish police in an all-day fight with these Bheels who had looted my camp, in which one officer was killed and two severely wounded. For my continued service in the field during this period I received the thanks of the Bombay government. The opening of the Bombay & Calcutta Railway in March, 1870, was attended by the Viceroy (the Earl of Mayo), the Duke of Edinburgh (Prince Alfred, Queen Victoria's second son), the Governor of Bombay (Sir Seymour Fitzgerald), the Governor of the Northwest Provinces, the Chief Commissioner of the Central Provinces, and by several of the chief princes and nobles of India, among whom was Sir Salar Jung, the Prime Minister of the Nizam. I received the following resolution passed by the government:

"No. 1272 of 1870. Resolution.—His Excellency the Governor in Council, desires, on the retirement of Mr. Brereton, to record his sense of the valuable services rendered by that gentleman, more especially in furthering the through opening of the Great Indian Peninsula Railway line to Jubbulpoor in March last.

"2. The establishment of an unbroken communication be tween Calcutta and Bombay is one of the most important events connected with the progress of railways in India, and Govern ment considers that to the energy, activity and skill displayed by Mr. Brereton the avoidance of further delay in the completion of the line is mainly due. His Excellency in Council learns with regret that Mr. Brereton's connexion with the Great Indian Peninsula Railway Company is about to terminate."

Captain Brooks, the private secretary to Lord Mayo, wrote as follows:

"September 8, 1870.—The Viceroy desires me to inform you that he is very greatly pleased with all you have done in con nexion with the Great Indian Peninsula Railway, and that he will not forget you when a chance arises."

Lord Lawrence, ex-Viceroy of India, wrote:

"I quite concur in the general view which has been taken in India of your labors and merits in regard to the Jubbulpoor Railway, and I shall be very glad if the authorities reward them in a suitable manner."

Mr. George Turnbull, Chief Engineer of the East Indian Railway, wrote:

"I most sincerely congratulate you on this very successful opening through to Jubbulpoor. It is a very great achievement, and one you may well be proud of. Such a concurrence of Prince and Viceroy does not happen every day."

Sir Neville Chamberlain, A. D. C. to H. R. H. the Duke of Edinburgh, wrote:

"I am desired by H. R. H. to say he will be much obliged if you will send him a good photograph of the 'Alfred' Viaduct. (The Duke opened this.) His Royal Highness has been greatly pleased and interested in having been allowed to take part in this great opening of the through line between Bombay and Calcutta, and he congratulates you on your success. I enclose seven photographs of H. R. H with his autographs, and the Duke requests that you will distribute them, as may seem best to you, among the most deserving of those gentlemen who have struggled so hard with you to complete the line in time."

Colonel Daly, the Resident at India, wrote:

"The Maharajah (Holkar) wishes me to thank you for all kindness and assistance, and for your hospitality to him during his recent trip to Jubbulpoor to meet the Viceroy and the Duke of Edinburgh. Your success is wonderful, and you certainly deserve all the credit of the achievement."

Sir Salar Jung wrote·

"I write a few lines to congratulate you on your very successful achievement. I am delighted with all I have seen.· ·These railways are really wonderful inventions, and I hope we may soon have one to Hyderabad."

Sir Henry Durand, member of the Council at Simla (the father of the present Ambassador at Washington), wrote:

"You will, of course, call on Sir William Baker at the India Office to give him all information as to your labors on the Great Indian Peninsula Railway, and please mention my name to him. I hope to send him a line about yourself. Keep your name before the Secretary of India at the India Office, and the Government of India out here, for sometimes men are wanted suddenly."

At the request of Lord Mayo, the Secretary of State for India (the late Duke of Argyll) presented me at the Levee held at St. James Palace in March, 1871, and he, also, informed me that my name had been entered for future consideration on the list for the Star of India. Owing to my not returning to India, and to my absence in the United States whilst engaged in the irrigation work in California, I did not get the Star, although I had been recommended for it by Lord Mayo, Lord Lawrence, Sir Bartle Frere, Sir George Yule and Sir Richard Temple.

In 1864, at the request of the Chief Commissioner (Sir Richard Temple) of the Central Provinces, I examined and reported on a water supply for the City of Nagpur from the Telinkery Tank, and received copy of the government resolution recording thanks for the same, dated March 29, 1864.

I was appointed by the Governor General of India in Council as one of a committee of two, the other being Colonel Anderson, R. E., to investigate, and report to the government, a serious accident to the new Barracks at Allahabad, and on the general condition of the other buildings. This order was No. 691 B-M, dated Simla, July 7, 1870.

During my service in the Deccan I was consulted by Sir Salar Jung on many points connected with the public works in the Nizam's dominion. Upon my leg being broken in several places in a trip to Hyderabad, Sir Salar Jung wrote to Sir George Yule, the Resident at Hyderabad, as follows:

"I heard with much concern yesterday that Mr. Brereton had met with a severe accident. I am anxious to know about him, and trust the accident does not entail very much suffering. Pray kindly assure him of my sympathy, and my earnest hope that he will be all right again very soon, and be able to give me his opinion about the steam carriage. I am sure neither his friends nor the

public can spare for any lengthened time the counsels and assistance of a man of his talents."

1871.

I was engaged in examining the railway system of the
United States, and especially the rapid methods of building the
transcontinental lines. I had been furnished with the necessary
introductions from the India Office, from the Foreign Office,
and from the Secretary of the Institution of Civil Engineers.
I furnished information thereon to the India Office, and to the
Railway Department in India.

1872 76.

Employed as Consulting Engineer for irrigation enterprise in
California. Prepared a large scheme for the irrigation of the
great San Joaquin Valley, a portion of which only was carried
out, owing to the death of Mr. Ralston, the financial backbone
of the enterprise, and to the serious financial collapse which
followed in California at his death in 1875. I was sent by the
leading men of California to Washington, D. C., in 1873-4, to
interest congress and the government in furthering irrigation
enterprise on the Pacific coast, and succeeded in obtaining the
appointment by congress of a commission to examine and report
to congress as to the best way to further irrigation enterprises in
California. This was the seed of the present U. S. enterprise in
extended irrigation on the Pacific coast.

1877-78.

Engaged as Consulting Engineer for mines in California and
Nevada. Consulting Engineer and General Manager for a time
of the Richmond mine, at Eureka, Nevada. Consulting Engineer
in London for the supply of water to Kimberley, S. A., by means
of long distance wrought iron pipe lines, similar to those in
use on the Pacific coast Examining the American locomotives,

and comparing the duty performed with those of the English standard. Reported thereon for the information of the India Office, and of the Railway Department of the Public Works in India. Supplied the India Office and the Irrigation Department in India with information about the machinery in use in California for the cheap and rapid construction of canals and levees.

1879-85.

County Surveyor of Roads and Bridges in Norfolk, under the new act of Parliament which provided for the creation of main roads and the maintenance thereof by the county with contributions from the government. Also, in 1884-5, in charge of the county buildings, jails and lunatic asylum. Received on retiring from the county service the following testimonial signed by the High Sheriff, the Lord Lieutenant of the County, the Prince of Wales (the present King Edward VII), the Bishop of Norwich, the Earl of Kimberley, the Earl of Rosebery, and the county magistrates and owners of lands and the large tenants:

"We, the principal land owners and ratepayers of Norfolk, desire to record our hearty appreciation of the useful manner in which, during the past six years, our County Surveyor of Roads and Bridges, etc., Mr. Robert Maitland Brereton, C. E., has performed his county duties. We consider that by the energy, ability, patience and tact he has displayed during this period, he has fairly earned this testimonial. We are sorry that the county is about to lose his services, and we trust that this testimonial may assist him to obtain an appointment wherever he may go."

The following resolution was passed by the Norfolk County Quarter Sessions, January, 1885:

"We, the Magistrates assembled in Quarter Sessions, upon receiving the resignation of Mr. Brereton, desire to record our entire satisfaction with the energy, ability, and tact he has dis played in the performance of his county duties during the past six years."

In passing the foregoing resolution the Earl of Kimberley spoke as follows·

"As a member of the Highways Act Committee, I desire to express my own feeling as to the loss which the court sustains by the resignation of Mr. Brereton. In having to inaugurate, as they have done, a new system, it certainly has been extraordinarily fortunate for this county to have had an officer of such singularly striking experience, knowledge and energy. He thought he was not wrong in saying that there was no magistrate in the county who thoroughly understood the condition of the roads, and the system on which they were worked, until they had read the admirable reports which Mr. Brereton had laid before them, and every magistrate would feel regret at losing his services.'"

Mr. Harvey Mason, the chairman of the Highways Act Committee and High Sheriff for the County, said:

"The county would lose the most active, intelligent, and capable officer that had ever served the county. The amount of good work which Mr. Brereton had done, and the savings which he had effected for the county in various ways, had become very apparent to the committee. During his term of office Mr. Brereton had submitted some very excellent reports to the court, including the last, as to the breakdown of the audit system of the county. It afforded them most valuable information, because, without such information, setting forth the defects of the present system, they would not be able to effect a reform."

Mr. R. T. Gurdon, M. P., senior chairman of the court, said:

"I must be permitted to say how thoroughly I agree with all that has been said as to the loss to the county by the resignation of Mr. Brereton. Wherever Mr. Brereton went he would carry with him not only the good wishes of this court, but of all sorts and conditions of men."

1885-6.

General Manager for the Montana Mining Company, at Marysville, Montana.

1886-9.

As Commissioner to the late Duke of Sutherland, having sole charge of his and the late Duchess' estates in Sutherlandshire and Rossshire. As one of the Directors of the Highland Railway. As chairman of the Committee of Roads in Sutherlandshire. During the early part of this period the Crofters were in a very discontented state of mind, and considerable lawlessness and destruction of property had prevailed. This was gradually overcome, and a considerable number of Crofter families were enabled to settle in the Northwest Territories of Canada. In this matter I had the active co-operation of Sir Donald Smith (now Lord Strathcona), Mr. Joseph Chamberlain, M. P., Mr. Jessie Collins, M. P., and others, in quieting the Crofters, and I personally never had any trouble with them or received any insult from any one of them. On resigning the Commissionership, the Sheriff for Sutherland and Rosshire, Mr. John Cheyne, the Deputy Sheriff, Mr. Thomas Mackenzie, several of the Free Kirk ministers, representing the Crofters, the leading tenants on the estates, the late Duke of Westminster, and the late Duke of Argyll, and members of the Sutherland family, wrote expressing their deep regret at my departure. The net revenue from the Sutherland estates when I assumed charge amounted to ten per cent of the gross; when I gave up the management it amounted to thirty-seven per cent.

1889-1904.

Engaged as Consulting Engineer for mining, irrigation, and real estate investments in California, Nevada, Oregon, Idaho, Washington, British Columbia, Southeastern Alaska, and North west Territories of Canada.

Elected member of the Institution of Civil Engineers, January 10, 1865.

Elected member of the Bombay branch of the Royal Asiatic Society, April 14, 1870.

Elected life member of the California Academy of Sciences, January 6, 1873.

Lightning Source UK Ltd.
Milton Keynes UK
UKOW05f2327190916

283389UK00017B/234/P